# THE EUCHARISTIC HYMNS OF JOHN AND CHARLES WESLEY

BY THE SAME AUTHOR

*The Conversion of the Wesleys*
*The Evangelical Doctrine of
  Charles Wesley's Hymns*
*Wesley's Legacy to the World*
*Vital Elements of Public Worship*
  etc. etc.

# THE EUCHARISTIC HYMNS
## OF
## JOHN AND CHARLES WESLEY

to which is appended
Wesley's Preface extracted from Brevint's
*Christian Sacrament and Sacrifice*
together with
*Hymns on the Lord's Supper*

By
J. ERNEST RATTENBURY

WIPF & STOCK · Eugene, Oregon

Wipf and Stock Publishers
199 W 8th Ave, Suite 3
Eugene, OR 97401

The Eucharistic Hymns of John and Charles Wesley
To Which is Appended Wesley's Preface Extracted from
Brevint's *Christian Sacraments and Sacrifice* together with
*Hymns on the Lord's Supper*
By Rattenbury, J. Ernest
Copyright©1948 Methodist Publishing - Epworth Press
ISBN 13: 978-1-4982-0505-4
Publication date 9/12/2014
Previously published by Epworth Press, 1948


Every effort has been made to trace the current copyright owner
of this publication but without success. If you have any information
or interest in the copyright, please contact the publishers.

DEDICATED
TO THE MEMBERS
OF THE
METHODIST SACRAMENTAL
FELLOWSHIP

All hymns in Parts One and Two, and citations from Dr. Brevint's *Christian Sacrament and Sacrifice*, are reproduced from the first edition (1745) of *Hymns on the Lord's Supper*.

In Part Three, the complete extract from Dr. Brevint is reproduced. The hymns are from the modernized edition of Dr. Osborn's *Poetical Works of John and Charles Wesley* (1869).

*M.H.B.: The Methodist Hymn-book* (1933).
*H.A.M.: Hymns Ancient and Modern.*

# PREFACE

IN THE PREFACE of my Fernley-Hartley Lecture, *The Evangelical Doctrines of Charles Wesley's Hymns*, I expressed the hope that one day I might publish a companion volume on the Eucharistic Hymns and Doctrines of the Wesleys. The following pages are the fulfilment of that hope.

I am very pleased that it has been possible to add to the book a new issue of *Hymns on the Lord's Supper*, first published in 1745, with its original Preface extracted by John Wesley from Dean Brevint's *Christian Sacrament and Sacrifice*. For a long time this volume has been out of print. No adequate understanding of the Eucharistic teaching of the Wesleys is possible without it. It will, I think, be a great boon to readers of my book to have at hand these writings to which reference is essential for confirmation of my arguments.

The topics I deal with are often of a controversial character. I have tried to the best of my ability to write objectively and without that denominational bias which has too often characterized Methodist writers on this and kindred subjects. Such bias is never justified, even when rejoinders to the biased statements of our critics are not unnatural. How far I have succeeded I must leave my readers to judge. I have tried to state the views of the Wesleys frankly and fairly, even when I do not personally hold their opinions, as for instance on 'Succession' (whether Episcopal with Charles or, as one deduces from his actions, Presbyteral with John) of the Priesthood.

While I hope the exposition of the hymns may be of value to Wesley students and to such as are interested in Eucharistic writing, my purpose in these pages is not merely expository and less still antiquarian. I believe these hymns have a great present-day value. While some readers may find Chapters 2 and 3 purely expositional, if they persevere they will discover that the second part of the book, on which my principal stress lies, deals with very live questions. In the past, Methodists have given little or no attention to the sacrificial aspects of the Eucharist which are so emphasized by Dean Brevint and the Wesleys. I have tried to demonstrate that the hymns, instead of showing a tendency toward Roman doctrine, of which they have sometimes been accused and often suspected, in reality express, develop, and enrich the Reformation doctrine of the Priesthood of all Believers.

The obvious abuses of priesthood, and sacramental oblations, in the Middle Ages caused a natural and desirable reaction at the Protestant Reformation, which however went so far that it is necessary now to affirm that Priesthood and Sacrifice are abiding features, in spite of abuses, of Christianity. When we affirm the corporate character of the Church; that the Ministry is the instrument of a sacred priestly body and not a substitute for it; that the propitiatory oblations of individual priests are meaningless if not abhorrent—then the importance of priesthood and oblation become intelligible. The Christian Church itself as a corporation is the Priest, not any member of it. Ministers are the instrument of the priesthood.

I believe that the Wesleys' Eucharistic hymns do actually express, and even more indicate, the way in which the corporate priesthood of the Church is to be exercised both in ritual and ethical oblation. They express and interpret, not only the inspiration of the Early Methodists, but the facts, practice, and worship of primitive Christians; they contain the true reply to the opinions of a group of modern Anglo-Catholics recently expressed in their manifesto, *The Apostolic Ministry*.

If the main contention of Dom Gregory Dix in *The Shape of the Liturgy* is that the Holy Sacrifice in the Early Church was the oblation of the whole Church and not of selected individuals be admitted, a common ground of united witness may well be found amongst Christians of very diverse opinions, since that is also clearly the teaching of the Wesleys' Eucharistic hymns. May we not find once more in the Lord's Supper a Sacrament of Unity—*Sacramentum unitatis*—instead of the source of strife and division which it has so disastrously become? May these pages tend toward the restoration of the united witness of Christian men in our torn and divided world!

### SOME WORDS OF THANKS

I am very grateful to friends who have helped me to produce this book, and particularly to my nephew, the Rev. H. Morley Rattenbury, for his painstaking reading of the proofs and his illuminating suggestions and comments; to Miss Marjorie Harry for her most generous help with the Index and typing; to the Rev. Dr. Leslie F. Church for valuable suggestions and much encouragement; for the courtesy, care, and skilful reading of the Editorial Staff of the Epworth Press; and not least to the members of the Methodist Sacramental Fellowship, who have listened with patience on more than one occasion to the contents of these pages, and have encouraged me by their sympathy with my work.

J. E. R.

# CONTENTS

PREFACE . . . . . . . . vii

## PART ONE—THE CHRISTIAN SACRAMENT

1. BACKGROUND . . . . . . . .
2. A PROTESTANT CRUCIFIX . . . . . . 20
3. SYMBOL AND INSTRUMENT . . . . . 31
4. REALIZED ESCHATOLOGY . . . . . . 61

## PART TWO—THE CHRISTIAN SACRIFICE

5. PRIESTHOOD AND SACRIFICE . . . . . 81
6. SACRIFICE AND THE ALTAR . . . . . 101
7. SACRIFICE OF THE CHURCH . . . . . 125
8. THE EUCHARIST AND MODERN METHODISM . . . 148
   ADDENDUM I—THE AMERICAN ORDERS . . . 159
   ADDENDUM II—APOSTOLIC MINISTRY AND VALIDITY . 164
   ADDENDUM III—CONSTANT COMMUNION . . . 171
   'ARISE, MY SOUL, ARISE' . . . . . . 173

## PART THREE

'THE CHRISTIAN SACRAMENT AND SACRIFICE' (*Extracted from Dr. Brevint*) . . . . . . . 176
'HYMNS ON THE LORD'S SUPPER,' (*By John and Charles Wesley*) . . . . . . . . 195

PART ONE

# THE CHRISTIAN SACRAMENT

## CORRIGENDUM

Pages 153-4.

The words 'The Apostolic Ministry' in italics at the top of page 154 are not intended as a subheading, but should read on with the last line of page 153, thus:

Catholic manifesto that the priesthood is a separate body—*The Apostolic Ministry*.

CHAPTER I

# BACKGROUND

THE EUCHARISTIC hymns of the Wesleys, to be properly understood, must be read in their eighteenth-century context and not in that of the twentieth. The Oxford Movement, with its resultant Anglo-Catholic cult, gave new values to the liturgical and ecclesiastical terminology and valuations of the earlier period. When, for instance, John Wesley wrote that he was a 'High-Churchman and the son of a High-Churchman', he did not mean that in the modern sense of the term he was a 'High-Churchman'—an Anglo-Catholic of our own times. His use of the term 'high' was political rather than ecclesiastical. Similarly, such words as 'sacrifice', 'priest', 'oblation', and others, even when their definitions do not differ in the dictionaries of the two centuries, have an accent, emphasis, and application so different as to make careful watchfulness, if misleading conclusions are to be avoided, essential. It is therefore important if the value and meaning of these hymns is rightly to be estimated that they should be examined in their relation to the thought and practice of the period in which they were written, and not in that of ours.

The claim has sometimes been made that the religious revival of the eighteenth century might as truly be called Sacramental as Evangelical. But the Sacramental Revival must nevertheless be seen in its true relation to the mission of the Wesleys so that exaggeration of its relative importance may be avoided. While it is true that the Churchmanship of the Wesleys was more Catholic than that of their followers, their great work was the proclamation of the Gospel to heathen England, and John subordinated everything to that object. If Charles thought sometimes of the work—especially in his later life—primarily as a Revival of the Church of England, he was, notwithstanding, a great Evangelist. These men must always be remembered as Apostles to England. The words of Jane Stoddart are true:

Come where the Abbey's great lantern burns full o'er the wave:
Once this lamp of St. Peter was low and dim;
*Then Christ to His English another Apostle gave.*
Souls of the righteous, bless ye the Lord for him.

A conception of Wesley's Churchmanship can be distorted either by visualizing it in the light of nineteenth-century Anglo-Catholicism or by an emphasis which disregards the overwhelming Evangelical appeal to the English people, the centrality of which was expressed by Charles Wesley's conversion hymn:

Outcasts of men, to you I call,
Harlots, and publicans, and thieves![1]

and by the renunciation by John Wesley of his family and University traditions, when, like David dancing in the sight of the aristocratic Michal, 'he made himself more vile' by preaching in the open-air to illiterate mobs. But the Sacramental Revival is, notwithstanding, a fact to be noted. Abbey and Overton are witnesses of the increase of Sacramental observance in the Church of England during the century. The early Methodists flocked to the celebration of Holy Communion in such numbers that the clergy were really embarrassed with the multitude of communicants with which they had to deal. The later decline of Sacramental observance of many of the children of the Revival will be considered later. But here I will set down a summary of what I have written in former works[2] concerning the Sacramental beliefs, practices, and teaching of the Wesleys and their followers, with some considerable additions, especially in a later chapter, on their sacerdotal beliefs and teachings.

The general neglect of Eucharistic worship in the eighteenth century in the Church of England is noted by all Anglican authorities. Archbishop Secker, when Bishop of Oxford, in a charge to his clergy actually found it necessary to recommend that there should be at least one celebration in the long interval between Whitsuntide and Christmas. In many parish churches there were only three celebrations in the year. Generally speaking, the Sacrament seems to have been little observed,

[1] *M.H.B.*, No. 361.
[2] *Wesley's Legacy to the World; The Conversion of the Wesleys; The Evangelical Doctrines of Charles Wesley's Hymns.*

but toward the end of the century, in consequence no doubt of the general revival of religion, there was a marked improvement. Abbey[3] notes that crowds came to communicate as a result of Wesley's preaching. And what crowds they were! They are almost incredible.[4] Here is a summary of attendances made by an Anglo-Catholic writer from Wesley's *Journal* of the years 1780–90:

Here are a few illustrations, taken from the fifth volume of Mr. Wesley's *Journal*, extending over the last ten years of his life (1780–90):
LEAKE—'Easter Day. I preached in the church morning and evening, when we had about 800 communicants'; 'at the Communion was such a sight as I am persuaded was never seen at Manchester before, 11 or 12,00 communicants at once'; LEEDS—'We were ten clergymen and 7 or 8,00 communicants'; 'I found it work enough to read prayers and preach, and administer the Sacrament to several hundred people'; MACCLESFIELD—'We administered the Sacrament to about 13,00 persons'; MANCHESTER again—'Mr. Baily came very opportunely to assist me, it was supposed there were 13 or 14,00 communicants'; Easter Day, near 1000 communicants'; LEEDS—'Having five clergymen to assist me, we administered the Lord's Supper to 16 or 17,00 persons'; BRISTOL—'It was supposed we had 1000 communicants, and I believe none went empty away'; MANCHESTER—'We had 12,00 communicants'; KINGSWOOD—'I read prayers and preached and administered the Sacrament to above 500 communicants'; OLD CHURCH, LEEDS—'We had eighteen clergymen and about 11,00 communicants'; SHEFFIELD—'I read prayers preached and administered the Sacrament to 6 or 7,00'; BIRMINGHAM—'Mr. Heath read prayers and assisted me in delivering the Sacrament to 7 or 8,00 communicants'; BOLTON—'We had five clergymen and 12 or 13,00 communicants. The Master of the Feast was with us, as many found to their unspeakable comfort'; LONDON—'The number of communicants was so great that I was obliged to consecrate thrice'; 'I preached, and with Dr. Coke's assistance administered the Sacrament to 11 or 12,00 communicants'; BIRSTALL—'With the assistance of three other clergymen I administered the Sacrament to 15 or 16,00 persons'; BATH—'I know not that ever I had so large a number of communicants before'; MANCHESTER—'Easter Day, I think we had about 16,00 communicants'; PLYMOUTH—'In the morning I believe we had not less than 600 communicants: they were all admirably behaved, as if they indeed *discerned* the Lord's Body'; DUBLIN—'I

[3] *The English Church in the Eighteenth Century*, Abbey and Overton.
[4] These numbers so surprised me when I first read them in Mr. Holden's book, *Wesley among High Churchmen*, that I carefully verified them all by an examination of the *Journal*.

preached in the new room at 7, at 11 I went to the Cathedral. I desired those of our Society, who did not go to their parish Churches, would go with me to S. Patrick's. Many of them did so. It was said the number of communicants was about 500; more than went there in the whole year before Methodists were known in Ireland.'

This enthusiasm for Holy Communion was the result of the zeal kindled in the hearts of the people by the flaming message of the love of God which they received from the Methodist preachers. Evidently Sacramental observance was urged upon them as a primary privilege. The early Methodist 'Bands' were little associations for a mutual confession and fellowship of groups consisting of four persons of one sex. Their first rule was: Be at church and the Lord's Table every week—an extraordinary rule for such companies of often very crude people.

A letter to John Wesley from John Fletcher in 1756 suggests the embarrassments to which the clergy were subjected by these multitudes of communicants. Indeed, the crowds made some reorganization of the conduct of the service necessary. So Fletcher makes suggestions, and incidentally gives us a hint of a novelty—the singing of hymns—which the Wesleys had already introduced. Having expressed his admiration for the decency and order of the services conducted by them, he writes:

As the number of communicants is generally very great, the time spent in receiving is long enough for many to feel their devotion languish for want of outward fuel. In order to prevent this, you interrupt, from time to time, the service of the Table, to put up a short prayer, or to sing a verse or two of a hymn; and I do not doubt but many have found the benefit of that method. But as you can spare very little time, you are obliged to be satisfied with scattering these few drops, instead of a continual rain. Sir, would not this want be easily supplied, if you were to appoint the preachers, who may be present, to do what you cannot possibly do yourself, to pray and sing without interruption, as at a watch-night?[5]

It is very improbable that Wesley took Fletcher's advice. The letter, however, is interesting not only because it indicates the difficulties created by the crowds, but because it suggests one of the causes of the writing of the Eucharistic hymns.

There can be no doubt that Holy Communion was the central devotion of the Evangelical Revival. It was not only the special devotion of the Wesleys, whose early church training

[5] From *The Life and Times of John Wesley*, Tyerman, Vol. II, p. 264.

would largely account for that, but quite a conspicuous feature of the devotional life of the early Methodist preachers. Over and over again they refer to blessings received at the Lord's Table. Fervid Evangelists as they were, they knew where to seek the power of their Evangelism. A few instances may be given, taken from the *Lives of the Early Methodist Preachers*: Thomas Oliver speaks of a time of blessing before his conversion when he was uplifted for weeks; John Roberts received the Sacrament at church almost every Lord's Day—'divine light', he says, 'broke in upon my soul'; Rankin witnesses to the blessing he received at a Presbyterian Communion service; Thomas Tennant was converted at Sacrament; George Shadford speaks of three months' deep benefit after his confirmation; John Pritchard not only himself experienced 'the deep things of God' at Holy Communion, but testified to one who was 'justified' at such a service. Such men as Nelson, Walsh, Pawson, and Taylor refer repeatedly to the benefits they received at Holy Communion, and Taylor speaks of the degeneracy of the Leeds Methodists toward the end of the century on account of their neglect of the divine ordinance; so one might continue. These remarkable life stories of flaming Evangelists contradict the foolish antithesis of some modern Methodists—Sacrament or Evangelism: as if one were exclusive of the other!

Some of the early Methodist preachers were able and educated men, but many were as illiterate as the Apostles of whom they were the true eighteenth-century successors. Much trouble was caused to the Wesleys through the desire of these unordained preachers to administer the Sacrament. They felt that Wesley was very severe in his refusal of permission to them to do so. But, however mixed their motives were, we may be assured that their own deep Sacramentalism and their sense of the necessity of Holy Communion to the spiritual life of their people, was what made them so urgent, since the spiritual condition, both of church and parson, sometimes alienated Methodists from the parish churches.

The practice of John Wesley himself has become well known of recent years through the analyses of some of his hitherto unread shorthand diaries. In a most illuminating article in *The London Quarterly Review* of July 1923, the Rev. T. H. Barratt proved from one diary that Wesley communicated at least once every four days in one year, and rather more than one in five in another. His sermon on 'Constant Communion',[6] written for his students when at Oxford in 1732 and re-published in 1788, is remarkable in its claim that Communion should be constant, nor merely frequent; and also for the note with which he prefaced it, asserting that he had seen no reason to change his views on any of the statements in this sermon.

The practice of Charles Wesley was similar. Whitfield emphasized continually the importance of Holy Communion. In the next century, Simeon, the great Evangelical leader in the Church of England, was strong in his rebuke of those who neglected Communion. Nothing is more clear than the tremendous emphasis of the leading Evangelicals on the necessity of Eucharistic worship. Neglect, alas, followed all too soon, so that when the Oxford Catholic Revival re-emphasized this devotion, its leaders were justified in their criticism of neglect of it by their contemporary Evangelicals. The difference between the Evangelicals of the nineteenth century and John Wesley is outstanding. Holy Communion to him was not only a duty but a joy. With what pleasure, for instance, he recalls 'an octave' in which he celebrated every day. It seems to have been his custom when in London, in the twelve days between Christmas and Epiphany, to have celebrated every day at City Road. The great Evangelical Revivalists knew that Evangelism could only be grounded on worship, and that the central act of Christian worship is at the Table of the Lord, keeping His command: 'Do this in remembrance of Me.'

Curiously enough we have little definite account of John Wesley's actual teaching on the subject. We have to deduce it from such writings as the criticism he made on Roman Catholicism in *Popery calmly Considered*. A longer treatise, entitled *A Roman Catechism with a Reply thereto*, had been published by him earlier. I have to acknowledge that when I wrote on this subject in my *Wesley's Legacy to the World* I thought, perhaps not unnaturally, that this was Wesley's own work, and quoted it as such; but Richard Green has shown that Wesley did not write a word of it. It has been traced to an anonymous author of the reign of James the First. However, it is not a matter of material importance, because I find by a comparison

[6] See Addendum Three, p. 171 *infra*.

of *Popery calmly Considered* with the *Roman Catechism and Reply* that Wesley's own book is really an abridgement of the earlier work. It is very anti-Roman in relation to transubstantiation, the refusal of the Cup to the laity, and the worship of the Elements; but it is an interesting fact that he omits altogether the section in *A Roman Catechism and Reply* on the Roman Catholic use of Eucharistic Sacrifice and Ceremonies. Sound deductions, I am sure, cannot often be made from Wesley's abridgements, because abbreviation was almost an obsession with him. But I do suspect that while he would repudiate Roman sacrificial practices and some of their ceremonies, he would not wish to be taken to repudiate entirely the idea of sacrifice; and his feeling about ceremonies—that they were more of the superficials than the essentials of religion—is one that he put with considerable emphasis. Along with this negative treatment of the subject must be set his brief and quite unsatisfactory notes on the Gospel narratives of the Lord's Supper and that of the Epistle to the Corinthians, which consist largely of strong objections to the Roman theory of transubstantiation, but give little or no positive doctrine except that on 1 Corinthians $10^{16}$, he does teach a real Sacramental communication in the bread and the cup. His most explicit teaching is to be found in two of his standard sermons: the first on 'The Means of Grace' where he writes:

Is not the eating of that bread, and the drinking of that cup, the outward, visible means whereby God conveys into our souls all that spiritual grace, that righteousness, and peace, and joy in the Holy Ghost which were purchased by the body of Christ once broken, and the blood of Christ once shed for us? Let all, therefore, who truly desire the grace of God, eat of that bread, and drink of that cup.[7]

Commenting on 'our daily bread' in another standard sermon, he writes that many ancient fathers regarded 'daily bread' as sacramental and refers with approval to the fact that it was

daily received in the beginning by the whole Church of Christ, and highly esteemed till the love of many waxed cold, as *the grand channel* whereby the grace of His Spirit was conveyed to all the souls of the children of God.[8]

[7] *The Standard Sermons of John Wesley*, Vol. I, p. 253.
[8] ibid., p. 440. (Italics mine.)

The *grand channel*—that was always Wesley's teaching and experience.

What he meant by God's grace is illustrated by an interesting comment in his *Journal* of 10th November 1739. He was greatly influenced by a woman's testimony, probably his mother's, on whose tombstone were afterwards inscribed these words:

> The Father then revealed His Son
> Him in the broken bread made known;

—words descriptive of her evangelical conversion at Holy Communion. But whether or no this woman was his mother, she experienced—she said—the forgiveness of her sins at the Table of the Lord. Wesley believed that the Lord's Supper was actually a converting ordinance. On 27th June 1740 he called his people to witness to the fact that

Ye are the witnesses. For many now present know, the very beginning of your conversion to God (perhaps, in some, the first deep conviction) was wrought at the Lord's Supper.[9]

On Saturday 28th June he writes:

I showed at large: That the Lord's Supper was ordained by God to be a means of conveying to men either preventing, or justifying, or sanctifying grace, according to their several necessities.[10]

Generally speaking, all that can be deduced from these few and slight references to the subject is that Wesley deeply reverenced the Eucharist and practised it as a central devotion of his spiritual life; that he regarded the Sacramental Elements as a material but real means of the communication of divine grace; that he repudiated vigorously the Roman Mass and its doctrine of transubstantiation. Moreover, it seems from an early correspondence between him and his mother that though they both believed in the 'real Presence', they rejected not only the Roman, but the Lutheran interpretation of it. Curiously, Tyerman regards this correspondence as an instance of Wesley's High-Churchmanship, of which he always spoke with rather savage criticism. Tyerman, in any case, makes no claim to be a theologian, and his comments on the ritualism of

[9] *Journal of John Wesley* (Standard Edition), Vol. II, p. 361.
[10] ibid., loc. cit.

Wesley in this connexion is rather unreasonable, because the passage shows that Wesley's conception of the real Presence was much more Calvinistic than Lutheran or Roman. It must be remembered that at this time Wesley was formulating his views; although there is no reason to think that he changed them, they undoubtedly were juvenile expressions. One other thing should perhaps be noted: in his sermon on 'The Means of Grace', from which I have already quoted, Wesley carefully guarded his people from making any means of grace—even Bible reading and Holy Communion—ends in themselves. Their benefits depended on the faith of the men who used the means, as well as upon the means they used.

Where then can we find a satisfactory account of the early Methodist teaching on the Eucharist? The answer is plain: in the hymns of John and Charles Wesley on the Lord's Supper, and in the extract from Dr. Brevint,[11] which Tyerman rightly says: 'by publishing Wesley made his own.' The truth is that the extract from Brevint and the hymns on the Lord's Supper by the Wesleys do contain the true Methodist doctrines on the Eucharist. By this is not meant that they were standard doctrines to which subscription was demanded of preachers, as it was to the substance of the *Notes on the New Testament* and the first four volumes of *Wesley's Sermons*. But it does mean that the *Hymn-book* contained the avowed doctrine of the Wesleys, continually preached to and sung by the Methodist people in the eighteenth century and even after.

The importance of hymns published before 1749 as a medium of Wesley's doctrine must never be overlooked. All the early hymn-books had on their title page the imprimatur of John Wesley. The ninth edition of the *Hymns on the Lord's Supper* was published in Wesley's life-time, and one soon afterwards. The book was the most widely circulated and continually used of all the hymn-books, except the General Collections. No objections to the doctrines were made as far as I know by any early Methodist, except Edward Perronet, who was a violent anti-Anglican. His objections will be considered later.[12] That these hymns expressed the common teaching of the early

---

[11] The extract from Dr. Brevint's *Christian Sacrament and Sacrifice* will be found on pp. 176-93, *infra*.

[12] pp. 97ff., *infra*.

Methodists cannot be contradicted. No doubt it is possible to challenge the doctrinal value of verses on account of the extravagances of metaphor, but Wesley's claim that they 'speak common sense both in prose and verse' must never be forgotten. A reference to his book on *Christian Perfection,* and to his careful corrections in order to avoid false doctrinal inferences of some of the earlier hymns, clearly shows that he definitely regarded as authoritative doctrinal statements the hymns which he had published under his and his brother's signatures. When the date of this book (1745) is considered and its general use throughout his life-time as well as before the Collections of 1779, we may conclude that its doctrines remained his teaching.[13] It would be altogether discordant with the honesty and outspoken character of John Wesley to believe that if he had altered his opinion, especially in teaching of the Holy Sacrifice, he would not have said so.

There is no conclusive evidence that these hymns were all written by Charles Wesley. His biographer, Thomas Jackson, always speaks of the hymns as 'theirs', not 'his'. It is unlikely that more than a few, in any case, were from the pen of John, and perhaps none were; but if they can be attributed to him by use of the prosodic rules formulated by Dr. Bett, then a good case can, in some instances, be made out for John's authorship. However, in my opinion, no more than a possibility can be established on such rules, and I shall assume the probability of the authorship of Charles. The editorial pen of John of course is likely to have been used, but the arrangement of the hymns shows little evidence of his careful and orderly mind. The extract from Brevint undoubtedly was his, and almost certainly the bowdlerization of George Herbert. How much more we cannot say, but we can say that he deliberately took the responsibility of joint authorization of their doctrine.

If objection may be made to the doctrines of Charles Wesley's hymns on the ground of their non-technical doctrinal character, the objection cannot be sustained in the case of the Eucharistic hymns, because, printed along with them, is the theological argument of Dr. Brevint, the substance of which is expressed in the succeeding hymns. Between Brevint's prose and Wesley's

---

[13] See J. E. Rattenbury, *The Evangelical Doctrines of Charles Wesley's Hymns.* Chapter III.

verse there is no theological clash whatever. There are material additions in the hymns, though few to the actual material of the prose. Charles Wesley gives Brevint wings, and adds very significantly the confirmation of Methodist experience to Brevint's doctrine. In some of his verses he turns the devotional theology of a High-Church Caroline divine into the flaming Methodist Evangel without losing Anglican values. He accentuates certain of the words of Brevint so that the stress differs in some degree, but the doctrinal agreement of the verse and prose show, so far as I can find, no divergence anywhere.

Although Wesley depended on Brevint for his material and symbolism, his hymns are rarely, although they have often been called so, a mere paraphrase. Many of them are quite original and could have been written had Wesley never read Brevint at all. What is remarkable throughout the book is the Methodist accent which he gives to High Anglican teaching. In one section, as I shall show, this is quite conspicuous, but throughout the book, the evangelical experience of the Methodist gives colour and life and distinctiveness to many of these verses. Wesley often falls back on Methodist experience as the supreme verification of his Sacramental theories.

How, then, are we to account for the dislike of these hymns and of Brevint's tractate so often displayed in the writings of certain influential Methodist authorities on Wesley? As this problem is considered later in relation to the views of the Wesleys on Eucharistic sacrifice and priesthood, I will only point out now that the sort of criticism which we read, for example, in Rigg and Stephenson, and find to some extent in Tyerman, is not to be found in the earlier biographers, Moore, Whitehead, and Jackson. The probability is that writers like Dr. Rigg thought of sacramental terminology in the light of nineteenth-century controversy, arising from the Oxford Movement and the Anglo-Catholic Revival. They were the victims of what Wesley once called 'an overgrown fear of Popery'. But it is fair to say in their defence that the Oxford Movement criticism of the Protestant Reformation raised, not unnaturally, the Anti-Roman antipathies which lurk in the hearts of most English people. Wesley himself was really as anti-Roman as any of them, but far more far-visioned in his outlook, and of much wider knowledge. While a true son of the Reformation, he was unwilling to throw away great Christian values because of medieval misinterpretations and abuses. It is true that words and expressions can be found both in Charles Wesley and Brevint capable of Roman interpretations which were actually given to them by Anglo-Catholic controversialists of the later nineteenth century. The Catholicism of the Wesleys, however, was never medieval, but always ante-Nicene. They honoured and so far as possible observed and restored the customs of the Christianity of the first three centuries. John regarded the works of the Apostolic Fathers as first-rate authorities only subordinate to the New Testament itself—at one time he says he even regarded them as co-ordinate. Both the Anglo-Catholic and their contemporary Methodist controversialists tended to judge the hymns in relation to a contemporary controversy, which unfortunately led to extravagant expressions on both sides.

Who, then, was Dr. Daniel Brevint? He was a Caroline divine, born in Jersey, who had been educated amongst the Protestants at Saumur, but afterwards went to Oxford where he became a Fellow of Jesus College. He was ejected from his Fellowship during the Civil War for refusing to sign the Covenant and escaped to France, where he became the Pastor of a Protestant congregation in Normandy until he was appointed by the Vicomte de Turenne (afterwards Marshal of France), whose wife was distinguished for her piety, as one of her chaplains. When in Paris he met Charles the Second, who after the Restoration gave him preferment in England. In 1681 he became Dean of Lincoln.

Brevint, while anti-Puritan, was also anti-Roman, as his polemical writings clearly show. The first of his two tractates on the Sacrament was entitled: '*Missale Romanum*', or *The Depth and Mystery of the Roman Mass*. In it he utterly rejected transubstantiation and exposed the practices of priests who claimed to offer again and again the flesh and blood sacrifice on the Cross. He criticized the Roman use of the word 'altar'. Dean Waterland highly commended his book and its teaching, and claimed that no one had better understood the meaning of Eucharistic sacrifice than Brevint. Of the second tractate, *On the Christian Sacrament and Sacrifice*, from which Wesley made the extract which prefaces the *Hymns on the Lord's Supper*, and which both Tyerman and Simon agree must be accepted as the sacramental doctrine of the Wesleys, Dean Waterland said:

> I could heartily join my wishes with a late learned writer that that excellent little book, entitled *The Christian Sacrament and Sacrifice*, might be reprinted for the honour of God and the benefit of the Church.[14]

But it was John Wesley who fulfilled that aspiration and it is with this and not the earlier tractate with which we are concerned.

Dean Brevint seems to have written his essay for the edification of his old pupils, the Princesses of Turenne, who were wearied with the sacramental controversies with which they were too well acquainted, so that they might 'contemplate and embrace the Christian religion in all its beauty'.[15]

> Dr. Brevint took no more notice of either Papists or Sectaries [against both of whom he was in typical Anglican opposition], no, nor Protestants neither, than as if the former had never appeared in the world to trouble and spoil the Church of God, nor the latter to assert and redress it.[16]

He produced this beautiful devotional booklet, positive in its sacramental and evangelical teaching, which has become the one satisfactory account, together with the *Hymns*, of the Eucharistic teachings of the Wesleys.

Dr. J. S. Simon,[17] of whose excellent and impartial account I make the foregoing brief summary, does seem to me slightly to under-estimate the positive sacrificial teaching of Brevint; and does he not over-estimate the importance of the too-much bowdlerized poems[18] of George Herbert which the Wesleys inserted? Simon might seem to some people to suggest that the doctrines to which certain Protestants object are only to be found in these two hymns. I am bound to confess that I think this suggestion is misleading. They are poor hymns as they now stand, and were omitted from Dr. George Osborn's edition of 1869 because they had been published in an earlier Methodist hymn-book. Moreover, the objections of Left-Wing Protestants can be more forcibly made against some

---

[14] From J. S. Simon, *John Wesley and the Methodist Societies*, p. 305.
[15] ibid., p. 305.   [16] ibid., pp. 305–6.
[17] ibid., pp. 303–4.   [18] 'The Invitation' and 'The Banquet'.

of the original sacrificial hymns of the Wesleys. Perhaps it should be said that George Osborn, who had a unique insight into the mind of Charles Wesley and a greater knowledge of his verse than any other Methodist authority, was sufficiently unaffected by the controversies of his day to write without hesitation unqualified praise of Daniel Brevint's book, of which he says in his short introduction in his great edition of the Wesley *Poetical Works*: 'This small volume, read with care, will prove a most valuable preparation for the Lord's Table.'[19] Dr. Simon has done great service by defending the Protestantism of Brevint and by not allowing prejudices, begotten of Anglo-Catholic controversy, to deflect his judgement.

The Wesley doctrine, while anti-Zwinglian, is undoubtedly anti-Roman. Often the accusation of Romanism arises from people who hold a mere memorialist theory of the Eucharist, which Wesley would have considered as defective in sacramental doctrine as he would have considered the Roman excessive.

Brevint's book is divided into two parts, following the title: the first concerning the Eucharist as a Sacrament, and the second, as a Sacrifice. The titles of the chapters are as follows:[20]

1. The importance of well understanding the Nature of this Sacrament.
2. Concerning the Sacrament, as it is a Memorial of the Sufferings and Death of Christ.
3. Concerning the Sacrament, as it is a Sign of Present Graces.
4. Concerning the Sacrament, as it is a Means of Grace.
5. Concerning the Sacrament, as it is a Pledge of Future Glory.

The sacrificial section contains three further chapters:

6. Concerning the Sacrament, as it is a Sacrifice. And first, of the Commemorative Sacrifice.
7. Concerning the Sacrifice of Ourselves.
8. Concerning the Sacrifice of our Goods.

The sacred poems and hymns of John and Charles Wesley follow this classification closely, with one or two slight differentiations. The eight sections are made by the Wesleys into six. The Nature of the Sacrament is illustrated by general hymns scattered throughout the book, and the section entitled 'After the Sacrament' of Wesley's hymns is substituted for

[19] Vol. III, p. 184.  [20] See pp. 176ff., *infra*.

Section I of Brevint. Wesley's Sections I–V follow exactly Brevint's II–VII, with the exception that Brevint's two sections (III and IV) are combined into Section II of Wesley. Section V of Brevint is III of Wesley; and VI and VII of Brevint, are IV and V of Wesley. In Section IV of Wesley important paragraphs of Brevint's Section II are used instead of in Wesley's Section II, where they might have been expected. The following is Wesley's arrangement:[21]

1. As it is a Memorial of the Sufferings and Death of Christ.
2. As it is a Sign and a Means of Grace.
3. The Sacrament a Pledge of Heaven.
4. The Holy Eucharist as it implies a Sacrifice.
5. Concerning the Sacrifice of our Persons.
6. After the Sacrament.

By way of introduction to a more detailed study of the hymns it might be noted with what general fidelity the Wesleys follow the arrangements and arguments of Brevint. While the order is the same in both cases, there is some overlapping, and an occasional hymn seems to have strayed from its proper section. There are, for instance, two or three hymns in the memorial section, as will be seen later, more suitably placed under the Eucharist as a Sacrifice. In the second section, which deals with sacramental symbols, and the Sacrament as a Means of Grace, there are two hymns that would be better classified amongst the memorial hymns of Section I. The emphasis on the offering of our goods, to which Brevint gives a section, is hardly more than alluded to in Wesley's last section. Section III can properly be called the Methodist Section, because it has an accent on experimental religion unusual in Eucharistic hymns.

One of the things to be noted about the hymns is the number of devotional verses, very often of two-versed hymns, that have little particular relation to the section in which they are placed and are general hymns of consecration. Reference to the letter, already quoted, of John Fletcher to John Wesley will show how suitable for singing these short hymns would be in the intervals in a big Communion Service in which they were used. Their general character seems to be determined by these facts. These devotional meditations are exhortations suitable for any part

[21] See pp. 195ff., *infra*.

of the service. Some of the most noble of the hymns are general in character, though placed in particular sections, and can really be better considered along with the post-Communion hymns than in any other place.

Perhaps it is appropriate to notice one significant fact about this book—its origin. It was one of a series of hymn-books published in 1744–5, of which the purpose was to illustrate the historic facts of Christianity; the others were for Easter, Ascension, and Whitsuntide, with a few hymns for Trinity Sunday. It must be noted that these little books were published at the very height of the Methodist Revival, at the time when Charles was carrying on his flaming itinerant missions to England. Why? The Revival was a time of great emotion, not unaccompanied by spurts of fanaticism. There was need of restraint as well as expression. The objective historic facts of Christianity needed forceful teaching. Emotional extravagance needed the curb of institutional Christianity. The controversies with the Moravian Quietists, as is indicated by more than one of the hymns on the Lord's Supper, makes this very clear. John Wesley's sermon on 'The Means of Grace' was a powerful corrective to the subjective extravagance of revivalistic emotionalism. Consequently, the Eucharistic hymns and the emphasis of the Lord's Supper were a particularly valuable product of the times: they expressed deep evangelical emotion, but repressed some of the by-products of a Revival which endangered not only decency and order, but even morality. The hymn-book was a product of the two outstanding facts of the Revival: its experimental religion, and the orderliness of the Wesleyan-Anglican tradition. And both were necessary for that permanent work of God of which the Wesleys were His instruments. It should never be forgotten that these hymns were Revival hymns, and that Sacramental worship was not only not contrary to Evangelical, but in the eighteenth century, in its intensified form, one of its chief results. While these hymns were corrective of extravagance, they were the fruit of the Revival. They come from the first period of Charles Wesley's career when his itinerary missionary work was as ardent as John's. Many modern Methodists make an antithesis between the words 'Sacramental' and 'Evangelical', partly because they can find no harmony between the formality of the Sacrament and the freedom of evangelistic worship. The antithesis is seen to be ridiculous when one remembers the fervent freedom of Charles Wesley's evangelism at the very time he was writing these hymns and practising and insisting so strongly on sacramental observance. One thing is really notable about them, as we shall see. They contribute a distinct note of Evangelism to Eucharistic worship. Here they differ most from the Brevint traditional Anglo-Catholicism. No more rapturous evangelical hymns are to be found than some of those which the early Methodists sang at the Eucharist. In this sense Dr. H. Bett was well justified in his dictum that the Wesleys 'evangelized' the Sacrament.

CHAPTER II

# A PROTESTANT CRUCIFIX

THE SECOND section of Brevint's Treatise and the first of Wesley's—'Concerning the Sacrament, as it is a Memorial of the Sufferings and Death of Christ'—suffers from the fact that neither Brevint nor Wesley was a pure memorialist. Brevint's writing is everywhere saturated with his sacrificial conception of Holy Communion. Even in Section II, which is applied to the memory of the historical event of Calvary, he seems chiefly interested to assert that the Sacrament is more than a memorial of a past event; that it represents the sacrifice still pleaded in heaven of our present and risen Saviour—the topic of the later sections of his treatise. In his first section Wesley wrote several hymns to illustrate the sacrificial views of Brevint which were his own as well, but when Brevint in his third section on the Sacrament 'as it is a sign of present graces' inserted another sacrificial passage, Wesley did not follow him. He boldly classified his illustrative hymns on these paragraphs in his later sacrificial section,[1] where logically they belong. For our better understanding of the general underlying argument of this book, it seems preferable to consider the sacrificial hymns of Section I[2] under Wesley's Section V, and also to add certain memorial hymns which appear to have strayed into Wesley's Section II, to this chapter. For the sake of clarity it seems also wise to classify the symbolic hymn[3] with those which may be called 'Hymns of the Mixed Chalice', of which there are several in Wesley's Section II.

Now, what do the words 'in memory of Me', or better, 'as a memorial of Me' (*eis anamnesis*) mean? The word *anamnesis* primarily signifies 'calling to mind'. To call to mind a past event is obviously to exercise memory; and a custom, a monument, or practice which calls such a past event to mind is

---

[1] Section IV: 'The Holy Eucharist as it implies a Sacrifice' (p. 231, *infra*).
[2] Hymns Nos. 2, 3, 4, and 8.    [3] Hymn No. 28.

fittingly named a 'memorial'. But while 'memorial' fittingly describes a past event when it is called to mind, it seems inadequate to describe a present event. Undoubtedly the word as applied to the Sacrament always recalls the historical fact of Calvary. But Jesus did not tell His disciples to remember Calvary, but to remember Him; to remember, of course, 'Christ crucified', but not merely the crucifixion of Christ, but the Christ who was crucified. The difficulty of Brevint and Wesley was that He who had died was to them alive for evermore, and while they valued immeasurably the fact of his historic death, that was by no means all that they valued. The Sacrament could never mean to them a bare memorial of the dead Christ, for the simple reason that He was living—still bearing upon His hands and feet glorious scars, but ascended to heaven, where He pleaded His cause with His Father for them. Hence, however much they commemorated the past event when they called Jesus to mind, they also re-presented more than that event. The memory of Calvary was only a part of the *anamnesis* made by Holy Communion. The pure memorialist excludes, when he is quite consistent with his own sacramental theory—as fortunately he rarely is—the living present Christ. In extreme cases what he teaches is 'the real absence of Christ'. Mr. G. W. E. Russell records in one of his books a story of an Anglican clergyman of his youth: 'I perfectly remember a sermon preached on Sacrament Sunday', which ended with such words as these: 'I go to yonder Table today; not expecting to meet the Lord because I know He will not be there.' His past death was presumably to be called to mind by a reverent act of devotional imagination, but He was not there—He was risen!

The truth, as Brevint and Wesley saw it, was that because He was risen He was present, ascended, and yet so near, just behind the veil—the Sacramental veil to those who approached in penitence and faith and love—'He, Himself, with His human air'. The memorialist undoubtedly is right in his assertion of the centrality of Christ's death, but that is not excluded by Christians who believe in His presence. Quite the contrary. This is not to say that memorialism cannot be an uplifting and powerful creed, but only that a severely restricted memorialism was impossible to the Wesley type of Christian, who says:

> Thou Shepherd of Israel, and mine,
> The joy and desire of my heart,
> For closer Communion I pine.[4]

It is not, therefore, surprising that the purely memorial hymns are not the most effective of the Eucharistic poems of the Wesleys.

A genuine memorialist, though influenced by his deep faith in a living Saviour, wrote a Communion Hymn, purely memorial, which is one of the richest treasures of Christian devotion. None of Charles Wesley's memorial hymns, though perhaps some of the verses in one of them may be excepted, can compare with the great Communion hymn of Dr. Watts: 'When I survey the wondrous Cross.'[5] The memorialist theory of the Sacrament is really the Protestant equivalent of the Catholic crucifix. What, for instance, is this hymn but a crucifix? Is it not a verbal crucifix, built up of carven words?

> See, from His head, His hands, His feet,
> Sorrow and love flow mingled down:
> Did e'er such love and sorrow meet,
> Or thorns compose so rich a crown.

Whether such a picture, created by a devout imagination, is carven of wood or stone, or depicted in colour or words, makes little difference. But the question remains, why the Sacrament should be a necessity of Christianity if it only does what a crucifix can do—call to mind the death of a dead hero, the greatest of all martyrs. Both sorts of crucifix evoke grateful response, awaken sacred emotions, have helped numerous people; but in what way a merely memorial Eucharist is different from a crucifix to a penitent, believing man it is difficult to say. Perhaps one can find the reason here why bare memorialists tend to give less regard to the Eucharist than men of Catholic sympathies.

There are hymns of Wesley's which were written from the memorialist's point of view, as, for instance, his great hymn, or rather Sacred Poem: 'God of unexampled grace.'[6] In some of its verses he rises to the heights of Watts's more famous hymn. His rich devotional imagination pictures the scene, though more subjectively than Watts, in memorable words:

[4] *M.H.B.*, No. 457.   [5] ibid., No. 182.   [6] *Hymns on the Lord's Supper*, No. 21.

> Jesus, Lord, what hast Thou done!
>   Publish we the Death Divine,
> Stop, and gaze, and fall, and own
>   Was never Love like Thine!
>
> Never Love nor Sorrow was
>   Like that my Jesus show'd;
> See Him stretch'd on yonder Cross
>   And crush'd beneath our Load!
> Now discern the Deity,
>   Now His heavenly Birth declare!
> Faith cries out 'Tis He, 'tis He,
>   My God that suffers there!

While these verses, no doubt, are interfused with Catholic theology and Methodist experience, as those of Watts are not, they are the product of the imagination of a devout Christian man who called Calvary with its significance to mind, in moving and beautiful words. The whole hymn is as memorialist as Wesley could ever be. The events of the tragedy of Calvary are viewed by a Classical Scholar who is at the same time a fervent Christian, but most of the verses are quite unsingable. The picture of Watts is simpler and clearer, it is objective like a crucifix, where Wesley's is more like a medieval picture of the crucifixion, or perhaps one should say a Renaissance picture where even the heathen comes straying in. Botticelli could have written it had he been a poet. Wesley calls Mythology to service in this hymn—the event is cosmic:

> Dies the glorious Cause of All,
>   The true Eternal *Pan*.
>
> . . . . .
>
> Lo! the Powers of Heaven He shakes;
>   Nature in Convulsions lies,
> Earth's profoundest Centre quakes,
>   The great *Jehovah* dies!

When Jesus

> Tears the Graves and Mountains up
>   By His expiring Groan,

can we wonder that

> . . . *Sol* withdraw his light

and that

> Heaven be cloath'd with black
>   And solemn Sackcloth wear.

The solemn tragedy of Calvary is vividly depicted in the words:

> Silence saddens all the Skies,
> Kindler of Seraphick Love
> The God of Angels dies.

But not only Mythology but Methodism comes to help—here is her authentic voice:

> See Him hanging on the Tree—
> A Sight that breaks my Heart!
> O that all to Thee might turn!
> Sinners, ye may love Him too,
> Look on Him ye pierc'd, and mourn
> For One who bled for You.

And then all the memorialism is swallowed up in praise:

> Weep o'er your Desire and Hope
> With Tears of humblest Love;
> Sing, for Jesus is gone up,
> And reigns enthron'd above!

Another hymn of this section (No. 26) echoes these verses, but rather feebly. In all these memorial verses of Wesley there is nothing really notable except the two verses of the hymn which I have quoted (No. 21). In point of fact the greatest memorial hymns of Charles Wesley are not to be found in this but in other of his books as, for instance:

> Would Jesus have the sinner die?
> Why hangs He then on yonder tree?[7]

with its fine paraphrase of the Litany in its second verse.

Now to return to Brevint. What, in brief summary, does he say in his first two sections? A short introduction simply expresses the necessity of a true understanding of the Eucharist, the consideration of which the pamphlet divides into two parts: (1) the Sacrament; and (2) the Sacrifice. In his second section, though entitled 'As it is a Memorial', he says little about its memorial character, but makes it a general introduction to his book. The Sacrament, he claims, is:

1. To represent the sufferings of Christ which are past, whereof it is a memorial.

[7] M.H.B., No. 173.

2. To convey the first-fruits of these sufferings, in present graces, whereof it is a means.
3. To assure us of glory to come, whereof it is an infallible pledge.[8]

The three following paragraphs, which deal with these truths, are closely followed by Wesley in his hymns. Brevint then makes a few brief comments on monuments as memorials of the past, with Old Testament illustrations, but quickly passes on to the assertion already commented upon that the Eucharist is not a *bare* memorial of the past.

> The main intention of Christ herein, was not the bare *remembrance* of His passion, but over and above, to invite us to His sacrifice, not as done and gone many years since, but, as to grace and mercy, still lasting, still new, still the same as when it was first offered for us.[9]

After this digression he returns to the proper topic of the section, and in the form of a private prayer calls to mind what the Passion means, using symbols, one of which is used by Wesley in a hymn in Section I, and the others in hymns of later sections. He calls to mind that the bread on the altar was made of corn which was cut down, beaten, ground, and bruised by men, as typifying the suffering body of our Lord. And again by a second symbol, as the Rock of Israel was stricken, so Christ was stricken and the two streams of blood and water that flowed from His side were for the pardon of men's sins and their sanctification, that the Christian (now using a New Testament symbol) may so touch the hem of His garment as to be healed.

Wesley follows Brevint in his hymns in this section less closely than usual. But though like Brevint, always limited when he tries to write as if he were a memorialist, does keep much more to the central topic of the section. He stands as it were, or kneels, before the Cross, like Mary Magdalene in Perugino's picture of the crucifixion, or like Fra Angelico in his. He pictures, as we have seen, the day of terror and mercy, and examines at the Cross its meaning, but even more, he tearfully contemplates its love. These hymns may be roughly classified, especially when we join to them memorial hymns from his second section, first as memorial hymns; second, as hymns of

---
[8] Sect. II, par. 1 (p. 176, *infra*).
[9] Sect. II, par. 7 (p. 178, *infra*).

theological reflection; and thirdly, as hymns of devotional reflection. But the classification must not be regarded as rigid, because there is a mingling of devotion and theology in most of these verses. One at least has a general significance to be considered later,[10] others are sacrificial; and two are prayers to the Holy Spirit.[11] Others, though placed in this section, are of quite general significance. Some of the earlier verses really should be called Sacred Poems rather than Hymns, but the general devotional verses are genuine hymns which might well be placed in any section of the book. Indeed, one almost wishes that their author had collected the general hymns and made a separate section of them. It may be that the overlapping is an evidence that John Wesley, whose arrangement and classification of sections was so excellent in his collections, had little to do with the arrangement of this book.

Thus we are to gather at the Lord's Table by first of all calling to mind the historical event of the crucifixion, as we saw in the great hymn: 'God of unexampled grace.'[12] The first poem[13] of the section is a brief account of the Last Supper, a remarkably fine description of the 'death-recording rite':

> He took, and bless'd, and brake the Bread,
> And gave His Own their last Bequest,
>
> . . . . .
>
> Do this, My dying Love to shew,
> Accept your precious Legacy,
> And thus, My Friends, remember Me.

The only purely memorial hymns to be added to No. 21 are Nos. 12 and 18, along with No. 26, to which reference has already been made. While Nos. 22 and 25 stress the memorial character of the Eucharist, they are perhaps most significant because of their sense of the difficulty of calling to mind the crucifixion.

> Give us now the dreadful Power.
> Now bring back Thy Dying Hour.[14]

And thus, by an effort of divinely assisted imagination,

> Place us near th'accursed Wood[15]

[10] No. 4. (See pp. 44, 103, *infra*.)   [11] Nos. 7 and 16.   [12] No. 21.
[13] No. 1.   [14] No. 22.   [15] ibid.

In Hymn No. 25 we read:

> Thou bidst us call Thy Death to mind.
> But Thou must give the Solemn Power.

So much does Wesley feel the need of a supernatural quickening of the imagination that he actually addresses two hymns[16] as prayers to the Holy Spirit and says:

> Come, Holy Ghost, set to Thy Seal,
> Thine inward Witness give,
> To all our waiting Souls reveal
> The Death by which we live.
>
> Spectators of the Pangs Divine
> O that we Now may be,
> Discerning in the Sacred Sign
> His Passion on the Tree.[17]

and again:

> Come, Thou everlasting Spirit,
> Bring to every thankful Mind
> All the Saviour's dying Merit
> All His Suffering for Mankind.[18]

These prayers to the Spirit for power to realize the Passion and Death of Christ must not be confused with the *epiclesis*, that is to say, the prayer to the Spirit to quicken the bread and wine into means of grace, of which we find examples in later parts of the book.

The attitude of Wesley in the memorialist hymns is generally one of theological reflection and devotion, rather than of visualization. The hymns of theological contemplation of Calvary have considerable doctrinal importance, because with the exception of several in his anti-Calvinistic volume, *The Everlasting Love*, they are the principal sources for an understanding of his doctrine of the Atonement. I will not repeat here what I have written in another book[19] on this subject, but a reference to the hymn-book appended to this volume will illustrate my meaning.[20] While it must be admitted that there is a crudity in his theological statements which makes them unacceptable to modern Christians, the more objectionable aspects of certain antiquated doctrines of the Atonement,

---

[16] Nos. 7 and 16.   [17] No. 7.   [18] No. 16.
[19] *Evangelical Doctrine of Charles Wesley's Hymns*, Chapter 6.
[20] Nos. 2, 11, 17, 23, 32, 45, 88, and 89.

though not entirely absent, are quite rare in his verses, which are valuable for their emphasis of God's love in Christ. Really, the best thing that Wesley ever said about the Atonement is in one of his earliest and greatest hymns:[21]

> 'Tis mystery all! The Immortal dies:
>   Who can explore His strange design?
> In vain the first-born seraph tries
>   To sound the depths of love divine.
> 'Tis mercy all! let earth adore,
> Let angel minds inquire no more.

The interesting instance of his use of a figure of Brevint is to be found in Hymn No. 2—a memorialist poem in which occurs the line:

> 'Tis done, the Martyr dies!

The figure is then developed in a form which hardly commends itself to us today:

> The Bread dried up and burnt with Fire
> Presents the Father's vengeful Ire
>   Which my Redeemer bore,

on which our best comment may be Wesley's words just quoted:

> 'Tis mercy all! let earth adore,
> Let angel minds inquire no more.

Charles Wesley knew by experience the mercy of God, but was unable to solve a mystery, which baffles the minds of angels. The fact, not the theory, is the important feature of his witness to:

> 'Tis mercy all, immense and free;
> For, O my God, it found out me![22]

If we do not find Wesley's examination of the meaning of the Atonement altogether satisfactory, what of his devotional contemplation, when, as a penitent man, having called to his memory the crucifixion of the Christ, he wept his way into the love of God and made the great discovery that St. John made at Calvary—'Herein is love, not that we loved God, but that he loved us.[23] The hymns that express his penitent and devotional meditations are to be found in all sections of the book, but in this section they are generally of a special memorial

[21] *M.H.B.*, No. 371.   [22] ibid., No. 371.   [23] 1 John 4$^{10}$.

character.[24] Whilst several of them will repay careful devotional study, only No. 20 is of outstanding value:

'Lamb of God, whose Bleeding Love.'

This is one of the most perfect of Wesley's hymns. It has been detached, like so many others in the book, from its original context and devoted to the general purposes of worship. The slight changes that have been made in our current version of the hymn perhaps rather weaken it. We read, for instance,

> Lamb of God, whose dying love
> We *now* recall to mind.[25]

But the change from 'thus' to 'now' weakens the hymn on account of its primary direct reference to the Holy Table and to the fact that it must have been a meditation on the *Agnus Dei*.

It is not difficult to realize how Wesley in some mood of penitence at Holy Communion, when the death of Christ was vividly called to his mind, possibly when he was drinking from the Chalice, suddenly thought of the dying thief's piteous cry, 'Lord, remember me', and so reverently called to the Saviour to make this His own memorial feast as well as His disciples'.

> O remember Calvary,

he sings,

> And bid us go in Peace.[26]

This two-line refrain to each verse has a haunting cadence—'a dying fall' which no one can rid himself of who has felt its tender power and plea. The hymn is very simple, but the plaintive rhythm and perfect structure of the verses reveal the true poet, just as its deeply moving prayer brings, as it were, to the surface the thoughts and feelings of a sincere penitent whose passionate love of his Lord to him is called to mind as he beseeches Him never to leave or forsake the soul that trusts in Him:

> Think on us, who think on Thee
> And every struggling Soul release:
> O remember *Calvary*,
> And bid us go in Peace.

[24] Nos. 6, 8, 11, 14, 15, 19, 20, 22, and 23.
[25] *M.H.B.*, No. 181.    [26] No. 20.

In a word, this beautiful hymn is a call to the Saviour Himself to make his *anamnesis* of Calvary as we make ours. Our Eucharist calls to mind his infinite love. Will not He who eats and drinks in the heavenly feast remember Calvary and that dying thief whom He forgave and cheered with a new hope? So we sing:

> O remember *Calvary*,
> And bid us go in Peace.

The influence of Brevint on Wesley in this section is slight. The truth is that Anglo-Catholic controversialists and some Methodists have very much exaggerated when they have spoken of Wesley as only a paraphraser of Brevint's prose. The Caroline divine supplied Wesley with an outline and a number of figures, some of which were not very rich and belonged to a common stock of Eucharistic commonplaces, which Wesley uses and often transforms. A comparison of these hymns with those he wrote on the Trinity, which are often mere paraphrases of the prose of Jones of Nayland, will show the difference between a mere paraphrase and the use of metaphors in the construction of original verses. But many of his hymns have no relation whatever to Brevint, and in the few cases in which Wesley paraphrases Brevint slavishly the result is often unsatisfactory. Many of the memorial hymns are not specifically Eucharistic, and very often, though devout and helpful, are mediocre verses. This, I think, is accounted for by the fact that Wesley was not really a memorialist; other aspects of Eucharistic worship inspired him much more powerfully.

CHAPTER III

## SYMBOL AND INSTRUMENT

THE NOTION that Roman Catholic sympathies are to be found either in Brevint or Charles Wesley is entirely erroneous, as both of them were definitely anti-Medieval. Both Brevint's anti-Roman writings and Wesley's repudiation of 'local Deity' in one of his hymns clearly show they were stalwart sons of the Reformation, but undoubtedly of the Anglican rather than of the Continental type. They were anti-Zwinglian, although in some degree influenced both by Luther and Calvin. Their Lutherism, for instance, is definitely marked by their frequent use of the word 'legacy' in reference to the benefits of the Eucharist. Their insistence on Communion places them on the side of Luther against Zwingli, whose emphasis is rather upon the memorialist character of the Sacrament. While they held a doctrine of the real Presence of Christ, John Wesley in his Oxford days seems to have repudiated not only transubstantiation but consubstantiation.[1] It is possible that Charles may have held a doctrine more akin to Luther's, but John's doctrine of the Presence, and I think that of Charles too, seems rather to have approximated to Calvin's. The evidence is by no means conclusive. What is clear is, that both Brevint and the Wesleys, when they communicated, did not only remember Calvary, but expected as they declare as we shall see, in specific language, to meet the Lord at His Table.

Section II of *Hymns on the Lord's Supper* deals with the Eucharist as a symbol and a means of grace. But the symbol gives significance to the means of grace. While the Wesleys and Brevint realized the fundamental character of the historic fact of Calvary as acutely as any memorialist does, they knew that Christ was alive, and believed that He was really present working, in the Eucharist, in a specific manner in the hearts of men through the instrumentality of the divinely appointed ordinance which was a means of present graces.

[1] See p. 10 *supra* and *The Letters of John Wesley* (Standard Edition), Vol. I, p. 118.

The two sections of Brevint's treatise on the Eucharist as a 'Sign' and as a 'Means of Grace' are combined together and treated as one by Charles Wesley. What is most valuable in the Sacramental part of Brevint's Eucharistic pamphlet are the prayers and meditations, with which each section concludes, which are often rich and moving. But in Section I Brevint is so much dominated by the thought of sacrifice that he often anticipates his treatment of that aspect of Holy Communion in a manner hardly logically relevant to its purely symbolical aspect. He seems to have had no firmer purpose, while repudiating strongly the Roman abuses of meritorious Masses, than to preserve the great underlying truth of sacrifice which Protestant indignation was in danger of banishing, and often, unfortunately, has banished from its Eucharistic worship. Brevint and Wesley both show us, as we shall see later, that the Lord's Supper, while rejecting Roman abuses, can preserve Catholic truth. The substance of this section Brevint summed up in his first paragraph:

As to the Present Graces that attend the Due Use of this Sacrament, it is first a *Figure* whereby God *represents*; 2, An *Instrument* whereby He *conveys* them.[2]

Ordinarily, God accompanies His blessings by figure or sign: as the burning bush was a sign to Moses, so *water* and *bread* and *wine* assure men of cleansing and sustenance. Bread does not sustain our bodies, he continues to argue, till wheat is cut down, milled and baked; and so does the Son of God succour us by being Himself 'bruised'. Not only does the Sacrament bring to mind the Passion of Christ, but since His is a saving passion these symbols of the maintenance of physical life support our spiritual life.

The first breath of spiritual life in our nostrils, is the first purchase of Christ's Blood. But . . . how soon would this first life vanish away, were it not followed and supported by a second?[3]

So 'the sacrifice of Christ procures also grace, to renew and preserve the life He hath given'.[4] So 'the Sacrament alone represents at once both what Our Lord suffered and what He still doth for us'.[5]

---

[2] Sect. III, par. 1 (p. 179, *infra*).
[4] ibid.
[3] ibid., par. 4 (p. 180, *infra*).
[5] ibid., par. 6 (p. 180, *infra*).

The Sacrament, however, does more than *re-present* what Christ did and does. It effects what it re-presents.

Much more is contained therein than a mere Memorial or Representation.[6]

(1) *The end of Holy Communion is to make us partakers of Christ in another manner, than only when we hear His word.*[7]

(2) It meets the wants and desires of those who receive it; who seek not a bare *re-presentation* or *remembrance*, but more. I want and seek my Saviour Himself, and I haste to this Sacrament for the same purpose, that Sts. Peter and John hasted to His Sepulchre; because I hope to find Him there.

(3) Other passages of Scripture show how much more there is in Holy Communion than representation. '*Is it not the communion of the blood of Christ?* A means of communicating the blood there represented and remembered, to every believing soul!' ... 'I come ... to God's altar with a full persuasion, that these words, *This is my body*, promise me more than a *figure*; that this holy banquet is not a *bare memorial* only, but may actually *convey* ... blessings ...'[8]

'I know that this bread hath nothing in itself', but it is God's method to work by using instruments, such as a rod to divide a sea; the blast of trumpets to break down walls; a dip in the Jordan to heal leprosy; even common woollen and linen garments can become instruments of healing. But it is not the instrument which saves, but the hand of God which wields it. What bread and wine cannot of themselves do, Christ can with His instruments, bread and wine, which are a Sacramental and mystical body and blood. Behind all is Christ's sacrifice,

offered up ... in the midst of the world, which is Christ's great Temple, and having been thence carried up to Heaven, which is His sanctuary; from thence spreads salvation all around, as the burnt-offering did its smoke.[9]

This sacrificial idea, it must be repeated, is fundamental to all Brevint's teaching. Wesley, however, evidently regarded the words I have quoted as irrelevant to this section, and quite logically places his paraphrases of them amongst the sacerdotal hymns of Section V. Brevint goes on to claim that while God blesses us sometimes more and sometimes less by other means of grace,

[6] Sect. IV, par. 1 (p. 181, *infra*).
[7] ibid. *Italics mine.*
[8] ibid., pars. 1, 3 (pp. 181–2, *infra*).
[9] ibid., par. 5 (p. 183, *infra*).

The Holy Communion, when well used, exceeds as much in blessing as it exceeds in danger of a curse, when wickedly and irreverently taken.[10]

It is the star which outshines all other stars in glory.

This great and holy Mystery communicates to us, the death of our blessed Lord, both as offering Himself to God, and as giving Himself to man. . . . It sets me on the very shoulders of that eternal Priest, while He offers up Himself and intercedes for His spiritual Israel. And by this means it conveys to me the *communion of His sufferings*. . . . *He offers Himself to man* [saying], *Take and eat, this is My Body which was broken for you. And this is the Blood which was shed for you.*[11]

Wesley, in the hymns of Section II, though the meaning and spirit are the same, does not follow Brevint in detail, though most of his figures are woven into the hymns of this and other sections of the book. For instance: the Israelites in the Wilderness; the Rock stricken by Moses; the world as the great temple of Christ; the true sacrifice of peace offerings; works done through instruments, as the washing in Jordan, the fall of Jericho at the trumpets' blast, and the healing shadow and garments. All of them are regarded as arbitrary instruments in which there is no inherent power; the virtue is that of Christ. The figures sometimes elaborately, sometimes allusively, are used by Charles Wesley.

The sixty-five hymns in this, the longest section of the book, are difficult to classify though there are some signs of attempted grouping. Wesley's one section illustrates two of Brevint's— 'The Sacrament as it is a Sign of Present Graces', and 'The Sacrament as it is a Means of Grace', are combined in Wesley under the title: '(The Sacrament) as it is a Sign and a Means of Grace.' But it is clear that the earlier hymns of the section do rather deal with the *symbolic* character of Eucharistic worship than the later hymns, which all stress the *instrumental* character. The inference may be made, I think, that Wesley's original purpose was to follow Brevint and classify these hymns in two sections. But when he read those that he had written, he discovered that his symbolical hymns were really instrumental. Evidently he found it difficult to treat a symbol, as Brevint did in his earlier section, as pure figure. The Sacramental symbol to him was always operative, and hence he

[10] Sect. IV, par. 6 (p. 183, *infra*).    [11] ibid., par. 7 (p. 183, *infra*).

made no general distinction, though the earlier are more symbolical than the later hymns. Even in those earlier hymns the sense of the rite as operative in value is never absent from his thought. For instance, we read:[12]

> Jesu, dear, redeeming Lord,
>
> . . . . .
>
> In the *rite* Thou hast enjoyn'd,
> Let us now our Saviour find.

Another of them[13] is reminiscent of John's Sermon on the Means of Grace, and stresses as emphatically as any of the later hymns the central value of the Eucharist—indeed, it would be more appropriately placed in later groups.

> Fasting He doth and Hearing bless,
> And Prayer can much avail,
> Good Vessels all to draw the Grace
> Out of Salvation's Well.
>
> But none like this Mysterious Rite
> Which dying Mercy gave
> Can draw forth all His promis'd Might,
> And all His Will to save.
>
> This is the richest Legacy
> Thou hast on Man bestow'd,
> Here chiefly, Lord, we feed on Thee,
> And drink thy precious Blood.

Confirmation of the truth of my inference is to be found in the group[14] of rather indistinctive though beautiful hymn-prayers. In the other sections of the book similar groups always appear to terminate a section. Hence I suggest the best way of treating these hymns is to regard Nos. 29–52 as one sub-section—the Symbolic Hymns; and Nos. 53–92 as the second sub-section—the Instrumental hymns (but a subdivision of this section is perhaps necessary, as Nos. 70–92 are a rather miscellaneous assortment). Another distinction may be useful in the examination of the hymns. Some are better called Poems, as they tend to be doctrinal or controversial arguments, not very good for singing; and the others, often brief sets of verses, Hymns. Moreover, in relation to the section as a whole, there are a few compositions which would have been better placed in other

[12] No. 33.  [13] No. 42.  [14] Nos. 46–52.

sections. Some of them have already been treated as memorial hymns in the former chapter.[15] Several also have sacrificial allusions, but on account of their instrumental character, are considered in this section. A special note is made on the quaint hymn[16] about the Aaronic and Melchizedekian priesthood on page 210. There remain, therefore, fifty-nine hymns to consider, including the last hymn of the previous section which is added to the Mixed Chalice Group. The standpoint from which Wesley views the Eucharist in this section is different from that of the former, where he contemplates Calvary, the historical foundation of all Eucharistic worship. In this, the object of his thought is not so much Calvary but the Sacramental method itself, whereby the blessings of Calvary are communicated to believing people.

(A.) HYMNS NOS. 28–47, WITH THEIR DEVOTIONAL APPENDIX—
HYMNS NOS. 48–53

Three hymns[17] give a general account of this great mystery, treating both the meaning of the figures and their instrumental value for achieving what they symbolize as the following verses show:

> The sacred true effectual Sign
>  Thy Body and thy Blood it shews,
> The glorious Instrument Divine
>  Thy Mercy and Thy Strength bestows.[18]

The great hymn, 'Jesu, at whose supreme command'[19] declares as comprehensively as any the Wesleyan valuation of the Sacrament as the means of divine revelation:

> Now, Saviour, now Thyself reveal,
>  And make thy Nature known,
> Affix the Sacramental Seal,
>  And stamp us for thine own.
>
> The Tokens of thy Dying Love,
>  O let us All receive,
> And feel the Quick'ning Spirit move,
>  And *sensibly* believe.

[15] Nos. 32, 36, 48, 78, and 79.   [16] No. 46.   [17] Nos. 28–30.
[18] No. 28.   [19] No. 30.

> The Cup of Blessing blest by Thee,
>     Let it thy Blood impart;
> The Bread thy Mystic Body be,
>     And chear each languid Heart.

A belief in the instrumental value of the Sacrament becomes clear by an analysis of these three hymns. Wesley knows what it is *sensibly*—that is to say, through his senses, eating and drinking—to believe.

There are some interesting instances of versification of figurative episodes in the Liturgy, for instance, of the words 'Lord, I am not worthy that thou shouldest come into my house'.[20]

> I am not worthy, Lord,
> So foul, so self-abhor'd,
> Thee, my God, to entertain
>     In this poor polluted Heart;
> I am a frail Sinful Man,
>     All my Nature cries, depart!

The symbolical use which Brevint makes of such Gospel incidents as the touching of the garments of Jesus, is well expressed in the words:

> In his Ordinances still,
>     Touch his Sacramental Cloaths,
> Present in his Power to heal,
>     Virtue from his Body flows.[21]

This figure of the 'woman with the issue of blood' was a favourite Sacramental symbol of Wesley's which he used in a long hymn not included in the *Hymns on the Lord's Supper*, as an answer to the Moravian Quietists who criticized Eucharistic devotions. In other hymns he records how before his conversion he *trusted* in the outward Sacrament, and how since, he writes: 'I *use* but trust in means no more.' So in his anti-Moravian hymn we read:

> Salvation is in Jesu's Name,
> Could I but touch his Garment's Hem,
>     Even I should be made whole.

[20] No. 43.   [21] No. 39.

> His Body doth the Cure dispense,
> His Garment is the Ordinance,
>     In which He deigns t' appear;
> The Word, the Prayer, the broken Bread,
> Virtue from Him doth here proceed,
>     And I shall find Him here.[22]

Two hymns also are inspired by the Paschal Feast.[23]

Perhaps the most interesting of the symbolical poems are those to be found in the first two sections which I have ventured to name Hymns of the Mixed Chalice.[24] While I know of no instance in which the Wesleys made a devotional use of this expression, in a letter John wrote to Dr. Middleton in 1749 he defends the Mixed Chalice and argues that on account of Jewish custom Jesus must have used it at the Last Supper. It may therefore be legitimately inferred that John Wesley did not cease from his earlier known custom in his later ministry. 'Hymns of the Mixed Chalice' seems to be quite a happy description of these interesting verses. While I have rather arbitrarily collected them from their different contexts, their common teaching justifies the grouping. The main idea in these hymns is really expressed more forcibly in Toplady's famous hymn, 'Rock of Ages'.

> Let the water and the blood,
> From Thy riven side that flowed,
> Be of sin the double cure,
> Cleanse me from its guilt and power.[25]

Anyone who reads together Hymns Nos. 27 and 31 may wonder whether 'Rock of Ages' was quite as original as it was thought to have been. No doubt it is a greater hymn than either of those I have referred to, but would it ever have been written if Toplady had no knowledge of Wesley's verses, which are echoed and sometimes verbally repeated in his hymn? The essential teaching of the Hymns of the Mixed Chalice is expressed by Toplady's words: 'Cleanse me from its guilt and power.' The argument seems to be that the blood of Jesus saves from guilt but does not cleanse. Water is a necessity as well as blood. Some allusion to baptism is probably to be

---

[22] Wesley's *Journal*, 1st. edn., and *Hymns and Sacred Poems, Poetical Works*, Vol. IV, p. 452.
[23] Nos. 35 and 44.    [24] Nos. 27, 31, 37, 74, and 75.    [25] *M.H.B.*, No. 498.

found in the use of the word 'water'. Charles Wesley's conception of the New Birth is in some ways different from that of John's, and is difficult to expound.[26] What seems plain here is that the blood and water were means both of justifying and sanctifying grace, as John Wesley claimed this sacrament to be —not only a symbol, but a means of grace.

> Rock of *Israel*, cleft for me,
>
> . . .
>
> Now, e'en now we all plunge in
>     And drink the purple Wave,
> This the Antidote of Sin,
>     'Tis This our Souls shall save:
> With the Life of Jesus fed,
>     Lo! from Strength to Strength we rise,
> Follow'd by our Rock, and led
>     To meet Him in the Skies.[27]
>
> The Sin-atoning Blood apply,
> And let the Water sanctify,
> Pardon and Holiness impart,
> Sprinkle and purify our Heart.[28]

The figure of the rock struck by Moses in the wilderness, which is worked out in these two hymns, does not recur in the others, but the double healing does: 'The Pard'ning and the Hallowing Grace.'[29] Hymns Nos. 74 and 75 are perhaps the best, because the simplest expressions of the meaning of the Mixed Chalice.

> Jesus is our atoning Lamb,
>     Our sanctifying God.[30]

In Hymn No. 75, the double grace is claimed—pardon and sanctification—the two outstanding doctrines of the Evangelical Revival are symbolized by the Mixed Chalice, which is more than a symbol—it is a means of converting and sanctifying grace. It would be idle to try to harmonize the figures of the blood and water, founded as it obviously is on St. John's record of the spear-piercing of our Lord's side after the crucifixion, with the words of the Epistle, 'the blood of Jesus Christ, God's Son, cleanses us from all sin'.[31] The words in Brevint, on which Wesley's hymns are a verse comment, are:

[26] See *Evangelical Doctrine of Charles Wesley's Hymns*, pp. 260, 299.
[27] No. 27.    [28] No. 31.    [29] No. 38.    [30, 31] See Nos. 74 and 75.

As the blood which He shed, satisfied the Divine Justice, and removed our Punishment, so the Water washes and cleanses the Pardon'd Soul; and both these Blessings are inseparable; even as the Blood and Water were, which flowed together out of His Side.[32]

Nothing is more futile than the attempt so often made to harmonize logically different uses of symbol, but it may be that Charles Wesley had in his mind the clash of symbols when he wrote:

> The Water cannot cleanse
> Before the Blood we feel.[33]

The Sacred Poems which deal with the symbolic meaning of the Sacrament are followed by a group of short hymns of devotional meditation.[34] They are indistinctive, and for the most part equally suitable to other sections of the book. They are brief sung prayers of individual devotion, expressing in different ways the aspirations of devout and penitent souls.

> Jesu, thy weakest Servants bless,
>   Give what these Hallow'd Signs express,
> And what Thou giv'st secure.[35]

The other hymns of this group are exquisitely phrased prayers for blessings which might well be collected and published in a manual for Eucharistic devotion.

### (B.) INSTRUMENTAL

The instrumental character of the Eucharist is the one fact which generally characterizes the loosely arranged sacred poems and hymns[36] which are to be regarded as sub-section 2. When the Wesleys called the Lord's Supper a 'Means of Grace', that term expressed not the vague sense in which we often use it today, but rather a definite and particular channel for the conveyance of the grace of God—as John says: 'both justifying and sanctifying grace to the souls of believers.' For notwithstanding the inherent value of the Sacramental Elements to convey the grace of God, that grace can only be received by faith. It is important to note that the hymns of this section (and later, as will be seen), carefully guard the Sacramental doctrine from the Roman theory and its pernicious perversions. Their Sacramentalism is definitely anti-Roman:

[32] Sect. III, par. 4 (p. 180, *infra*).    [33] No. 74.
[34] Nos. 47–52.    [35] No. 47.    [36] Nos. 54–92.

> No Local Deity
> We worship, Lord, in Thee:
> Free thy Grace and unconfin'd,
> Yet it here doth freest move;
> In the Means thy Love enjoin'd
> Look we for thy richest Love.[37]

The Protestant character of these hymns is distinctly emphasized by their clear expression that faith is the only means by which Sacramental benefit can be received, but in no way must this be taken to imply that the instruments themselves are useless. We read:

> The Sign transmits the Signified,
> The Grace is by the Means applied.[38]

But while 'we feel the Virtue from above' and 'the Mystic Flesh of Jesus eat', we must beware of any Roman misconception:

> Thro' Faith we on his Body feed,
> Faith only doth the Spi'rit convey.[39]

Hence,
> Gross Misconceit be far away![40]

and so,
> The Prayer, the Fast, the Word conveys,
> *When mixt with Faith*, thy Life to me,
> In all the Channels of thy Grace
> I still have Fellowship with Thee,
> But *chiefly* here my Soul is fed
> With Fullness of Immortal Bread.
> . . . .
> The Joy is more unspeakable,
> And yields me larger Draughts of God.[41]

The objective character of the Presence and the subjective Faith needed for its realization is well expressed in one of the devotional prayers:

> Great is thy Faithfulness and Love,
> Thine Ordinance can never prove
> Of none Effect and vain,
> Only do Thou my Heart prepare,
> To find thy Real Presence there,
> And all Thy Fullness gain.[42]

[37] No. 63.  [38] No. 71.  [39] ibid.
[40] ibid.   [41] No. 54.  [42] No. 66.

The somewhat confused and rather miscellaneous character of the hymns of this section[43] makes grouping—though there are indications of groupings—difficult for study. One may, perhaps, distinguish Hymns Nos. 82-94 as miscellaneous, autobiographical, controversial. They may well have been tagged on by Wesley after some self-questioning as to whether some of them were suitable for a devotional manual. I propose to treat the later controversial poems Nos. 86-92 in conjunction with the well-defined group of Nos. 54-70.

Hymns Nos. 54-62 are almost all of them argumentative religious poems; and Nos. 64-72 (hymns influenced by the thought of the earlier poems) are of the devotional character of which we read in the previous section. Nos. 72-86 are more mixed, but are rather of the devotional hymn type than the argumentative poem. Therefore, dealing with the argumentative hymns[44] it must be observed that they do not deal logically with successive points of Eucharistic controversy. They affirm, dogmatically, certain things which the Wesleys held to be truths about the Lord's Supper, and gave no reasons for believing them, beyond obedience to our Lord's commands. Indeed, they argue against attempts to give a rational account of these truths, because the grace conveyed is supernatural, and in that sense beyond reasoning. The hymns demand obedience to the command of Christ; claim that neither angels nor men can explain Sacramental power; and that it is not reasonable to expect that they should. The one appeal, confirmatory of the truths of Eucharistic grace, is the characteristic Methodist appeal to experience:

> Only this I know that I
> Was blind, but now I see.[45]

But they do face objections such as, Why is not faith alone sufficient?[46] Or,

> How can heavenly Spirits rise
> By earthly Matter fed?[47]

The questions Charles Wesley poses and answers are such as all intelligent men ask. Some arise specifically from the Moravian problems of Salvation by faith *only*, and others

[43] Nos. 54-92.   [44] Nos. 54-70 and 86-92.   [45] No. 59.
[46] No. 54.   [47] No. 57.

may be the reaction to Hoadley's rationalistic writings on the Sacrament; but they are not usually informed, except perhaps for two or three of the later controversial poems, by any very specific reasoning. One needs to feel something of the depth of Wesley's conviction and the fervour of his devotion to appreciate his standpoint and doctrine. Hymn No. 81, which may be classified as of general rather than particular significance:

> Jesus, we Thus obey
> Thy last and kindest Word,

if we compare it with two other similar hymns of the Memorial section,

> Let all who truly bear
> The Bleeding Saviour's Name,[48]

and

> Come all who truly bear
> The Name of Christ your Lord,[49]

—hymns of similar sentiment, and even phraseology (for instance, 'kindest word')[50]—the three may be treated as an introduction to the Sacramental and Instrumental character of the Lord's Supper as a means of grace. These hymns express the quality and feeling of Wesley's approach to the Table of the Lord and the joy and satisfaction and certainties of Eucharistic worship. Especially to be noted are the lines:

> Thy last and kindest Word,
> . . .
> We come with Confidence to find
> Thy *special* Presence here.
>
> Our Hearts we open wide
> To make the Saviour room:
> And lo! the Lamb, the Crucified
> The Sinner's Friend is come!
> His Presence makes the Feast.
> . . .
> His House of Banquetting is This,
> . . .
> He bids us drink and eat
> Imperishable Food,
> . . .

[48] No. 4.   [49] No. 13. (See pp. 44, 142, *infra*.)
[50] A recurring description of Charles Wesley's inference to the words: 'Do this in remembrance of me.' See Nos. 61–91.

> Whate'er th' Almighty Can
> To pardon'd Sinners give,
> The Fullness of our God made Man
> We here with Christ receive.[51]

The phrase 'keep his kindest Word' appears in Hymn No. 13, and the notable couplet which concludes the hymn is:

> And Fellowship with All we hold
> Who hold it with our Head.

Hymn No. 4 is remarkable for the verse of which the full significance belongs to the Sacrificial rather than the Sacramental hymns, but it is still the feast of No. 81 to which reference is made:

> This Eucharistic Feast
> Our every Want supplies,
> And still we by his Death are blessed,
> And share his Sacrifice.

Hymn No. 81, as fortified by several verses of Nos. 4 and 13, gives to us the expression of certitude and joy which must be kept in mind when Charles Wesley is impatient—sometimes fiercely so—with critics of the Lord's Supper: cold-hearted rationalists, unimaginative logicians, who do not enter into the joy of the Feast which he so rapturously experiences! The general teaching of these three hymns[52] is the basis of the argument to be found in his controversial and semi-controversial poems.

The group of sacred poems, with the addition of the later controversial verses, are perhaps the most important of the volume theologically, and indeed, of all Wesley's writings, for determining the value which the Wesleys gave to the Lord's Supper in its Sacramental meaning as apart from its Sacrificial significance, which is dealt with by them in Sections V and VI.

Hymns Nos. 54–62, can be considered consecutively, and indeed they show some continuity of thinking. Perhaps No. 55 is a better starting point than No. 54, as it reveals very clearly how much more the Lord's Supper is than a bare memorial devotion. The first line, indeed, might be a good motto for the whole section—' 'Tis not a dead external Sign'.

---

[51] No. 81.   [52] Nos. 4, 13, and 81.

The point of the little poem which it commences is that though Wesley seeks the Crucified, it is as one who is present that he seeks Him:

> Swift, as their rising Lord to find
>    The two Disciples ran,
> I seek the Saviour of Mankind,
>    Nor shall I seek in vain.

One of the best passages in Brevint lies behind those lines:

I want and seek my Saviour Himself, and I haste to his Sacrament for the same Purpose, that St. Peter and John hasted to his Sepulchre: because I hope to find Him there.[53]

So we come to Hymn 54, where the question all Protestants have asked some time or other is to be found:

> Why did my dying Lord ordain
>    This dear Memorial of his Love?
> Might we not all by *Faith* obtain.

Charles Wesley's answer is direct and simple:

> It seem'd to my Redeemer good
>    That Faith should *here* his Coming wait.

The word 'wait' is a direct echo of Wesley's answer to the Moravian Quietists, who argued that faith must be 'still' and wait for God's grace, without ever employing any 'means' of grace, particularly the Lord's Supper. John and Charles Wesley on the other hand, emphatically said we must wait for the Lord by using the Ordinances which he has provided; and particularly *here* at the Table of the Lord, the penitent Christian may wait in the hope that that Lord will honour his ordinance and promise. We receive outward signs, Charles Wesley argues, so that body, soul, and spirit may be inseparably joined to Jesus in His humanity, body, soul, and Spirit. There are many means of grace neglected by the Moravians, he argued; all are channels of grace, none are to be ignored, but

> *Chiefly* here my soul is fed
> With Fullness of immortal Bread.[54]

[53] Sect. IV, par. 1 (pp. 181–2).     [54] No. 54.

The word 'chiefly' recurs frequently in these hymns, and describes the centrality of Eucharistic worship in early Methodist devotion. The answer to Moravian criticism and to similar criticisms today is to be found in such phrases as:

> Come in Thy Appointed Ways;[55]
>
> Still in His Instituted Ways
> He bids us ask the Power.[56]

Hymn No. 62 is especially significant. More so if, as is possible, it was written by John Wesley. While faith is essential to reception of Sacramental graces, it must never be taken to mean that such faith is independent of the means of grace, because the Ordinances must be obeyed, and will be by persons who believe in His word. The objective value and power of the Sacramental Elements is brought out in Hymn No. 56 which is more nearly than most of the hymns a paraphrase of Brevint's argument, that the power of a curse in the Sacrament unworthily eaten also shows itself in corresponding power to bless when worthily received. But Wesley is here more careful than Brevint to insist that the grace implied 'through *Faith* is given'. He also guards his people with great care from magical interpretations of the Sacramental instruments, well aware as he was of the dangers of superstition among his fervent followers.

Hymns Nos. 57–9 deal with the mystery of the Eucharist. They face, though they do not attempt to answer the question:

> *How* the Bread his Flesh imparts,
> *How* the Wine transmits his Blood,
> Fills his Faithful Peoples Hearts
> With all the Life of God![57]

Two things are indisputable: the fact that God's thoughts are not our thoughts, that He is not only incomprehensible in His methods, but that we should expect Him to be. The answer is beyond human knowledge:

> Ask the Father's Wisdom *how*;
> Him that did the Means ordain!
> Angels round our Altars bow
> To search it out, in vain.[58]

[55] No. 63.   [56] No. 60.   [57] No. 57.   [58] ibid.

They may not presume to know the incomprehensible ways of God.

> *How* the Means transmit the Power
> Here He leaves our Thought behind,
> And Faith inquires no more.[59]

There is no answer to such questions. While Wesley evades any definition and commits himself to no theory, he has no doubts that the Sacraments are channels through which the grace of God flows, that virtue works through the Elements although consecration makes no apparent change to them. He writes:

> Who explains the Wondrous Way?
> How thro' these the Virtue came?
> These the Virtue did convey,
> Yet still remain the same[60]

He emphasizes the fact. He has no doubt that the Sacramental Elements and action are God-ordained vehicles of His power. They are definite, concrete channels through which blessings came. His only evidence is the typical Methodist appeal to experience; and a joy, the glad and conscious communion with God, of which his *Journals*, as well as the Hymns, give record, are the only evidence he offers or needs. How these 'creatures', these earthly things, were made:

> Organs to convey His Grace
> To this poor Soul of mine,
> I cannot the Way descry,
> Need not know the Mystery,
> Only this I know that I
> Was blind, and now I see.[61]

He no more doubts the fact than he understands the mystery. He is not so foolish as to try to answer the question,

> Who shall say how Bread and Wine
> God into Man conveys?[62]

But he himself knows that it does, and that all may know it. Nor is he so sure of Christ's presence in any other place, or so glad as at the Sacramental Altar. As he wrote:

[59] No. 59.   [60] No. 57.   [61] No. 59.   [62] No. 57.

> The Joy is more unspeakable,
>   And yields me larger Draughts of God,
> 'Till Nature faints beneath the Power,
>   And Faith fill'd up can hold no more.[63]

The foregoing poems express clearly Brevint's words:

In what manner this is done [Sacramental blessings conveyed] I know not; it is enough for me to admire. One thing I know . . . He laid Clay upon mine eyes and behold I see.[64]

That experience of a Caroline High Churchman is the essential Methodist experience witnessed to by the thousands of Methodists who thronged the parish churches. The hymns we have quoted and shall quote demonstrate clearly that Charles Wesley was one with Dr. Brevint when he said:

*This is my Body* promise(s) me more than a *Figure*; . . . this Holy Banquet is not a bare *Memorial* only, but actually conveys as many blessings to me as it brings curses on the profane receiver.[65]

Hymn No. 58 probably is in part autobiographical, like Hymn No. 80, but is well placed here because it indicates Charles Wesley's own relations before and after his conversion to Holy Communion. A favourite subject of his for preaching, according to his *Journal* of this period, was the Pool of Bethesda. Often his sermons can be traced through his hymns, where the thought is identical. A well-known long hymn of his on the Pool of Bethesda is an instance. No. 58 is another application of the same theme applied to the Sacrament.

> Thou seest me lying at the Pool,
> I would, Thou know'st, I would be whole;
> O let the troubled Waters move,
> And minister thy Healing Love

is closely parallel to verse 3 of the longer poem:

> See me lying at the Pool,
> And waiting for Thy Grace.[66]

---

[63] No. 54.
[64] Sect. IV, par. 3 (p. 182, *infra*).
[65] ibid.    [66] *Poetical Works*, Vol. II, p. 153.

Both hymns express his own experience. The words:

> In vain I take the broken Bread,
> I cannot on thy Mercy feed,
> In vain I drink the Hallow'd Wine,
> I cannot taste the Love Divine,[67]

are reminiscent of recorded experiences in his *Journal*, as is his hymn on the Means of Grace, in which he draws a vivid contrast between his pre-conversion and post-conversion communion:

> But I of *means* have made my Boast,
> Of *means* an idol made;
> The Spirit in the letter lost,
> The Substance in the Shade.[68]

Those lines are very different from his post-conversion experience:

> Here, *in thine own appointed Ways*,
> I *wait* to learn Thy Will:
> Silent I stand before Thy Face,
> And hear thee say, Be still![69]

But the mere letter of Scripture, the mere material bread and wine are not enough, and so just as the angel troubled the pool, he cries:

> Angel and Son of God come down,
> Thy Sacramental Banquet crown,
> Thy Power into the Means infuse,
> And give them now their Sacred Use.[70]

This, let it be noted, is not a prayer to the Holy Spirit for purity of the man, Charles Wesley, as in Hymns Nos. 5, 7, 16, but for the quickening of the Elements themselves. It is '*epiclesis*'. The significance of the prayer can best be understood when the verse is read in association with No. 61, a poem which is a literal paraphrase of an argument of Brevint's. The point of it is that God works by instruments chosen of His wisdom which are effective, notwithstanding that the choice, from one point of view, seems to be quite arbitrary. So in thrilling verses Wesley notes how the rod of Moses, the trumpets of Joshua,

---

[67] No. 58.    [68] *Poetical Works*, Vol. I, p. 234.
[69] ibid., p. 235    [70] No. 58.

the river of Jordan, worked miracles: 'If so thy Sovereign Will ordain.' Yet they are only instruments; not necessarily, of course, the only possible instruments.

> Yet not from these the Power proceeds,
> Trumpets, or Rods, or Cloaths, or Shades,
>   Thy only Arm the Work hath done,
> If Instruments thy Wisdom chuse,
> Thy Grace confers their Saving Use;
>   Salvation is from God alone.[71]

The definite expression of the Wesleys against a magical interpretation of the Sacraments cannot be over-stressed when Charles writes such words as:

> Thy Power into the Means infuse,
> And give them now their Sacred Use.[72]

I have called these words '*epiclesis*', and the description is confirmed by the verse which twenty years ago I claimed was an exact expression of the '*epiclesis*' prayer'[73] much discussed at the time—a claim now generally accepted. In the original the second line reads: 'realize the Sign.' But that active use of the word 'realize' has become archaic, so I ventured in quoting the verse to substitute 'real make' for 'realize'. The two verses are a little hymn of the devotional group appended to this cycle of argumentative poems.

> Come, Holy Ghost, thine Influence shed
>   And realize[74] the Sign,
> Thy Life infuse into the Bread,
>   Thy Power into the Wine.
>
> Effectual let the Tokens prove,
>   And made by Heavenly Art
> Fit Channels to convey thy Love
>   To every Faithful Heart.[75]

These verses suggest that the Sacramental Elements are consecrated by a direct action of the Holy Spirit of God. This, of course, has always been the doctrine of the Eastern Church,

[71] No. 61.    [72] No. 58.    [73] J. E. Rattenbury, *Legacy of the Wesleys*, p. 183.
[74] This archaic use of the word 'realize' is unfortunate. It would be much better to read 'real make'.
[75] No. 72.

but the Western has held that the recital of our Lord's words themselves by the priest consecrated the Elements as in the consecration prayer of the Anglican and Methodist liturgies. The question caused considerable divisions of thought in Christianity in past times, and is the basis of a long discussion by Dom Gregory Dix in *The Shape of the Liturgy*. It is unlikely that the Wesleys, who were well versed in the theology and the customs of anti-Nicene Christianity, could be ignorant of the controversy. I know of no evidence that the Wesleys were interested in this particular point, but it may be that they thought that the mere utterance of sacred words can become incantation, and that a direct prayer for the Spirit of God might in their view be necessary. Anyhow, it is important to realize that they expected the blessing to rest on and through the instruments of Holy Communion by the direct action of the Holy Spirit. They knew well that all means of grace could be idols if they were regarded as ends. Nothing is more important than to understand in what way and to what degree God manifests Himself by means of grace. They categorically denied that He was shut up in them. 'Salvation is of God alone.' But they are none the less firm in inculcating the observance of the divine Ordinances and especially this central act of worship. They believed both in the direct action of God upon a man's soul and His indirect actions, in the operations that is to say of the grace of God, both immediately and mediately.

That the emancipating experience of John and Charles Wesley and their followers of direct impressions on their hearts of the saving mercy of Christ created the Revival, is obvious. But Wesley was shocked by his Moravian friends when by their doctrine of stillness they neglected all normal means of grace and waited first of all for a direct experience. The danger of sheer individualistic fanaticism made itself clear, and Wesley was forced to re-orientate his personal experience to his older conception and practices of public worship. Corporate worship necessarily depends upon means of grace—media through which God works. John Wesley's sermon on this subject, the Sacramental Hymns, and the practice of worship, together illustrate my meaning. The insistence upon the use of means of grace secured the permanence of a worshipping society. Without such worship Evangelism would have lost its roots.

Hymn No. 60, one of the few corporate hymns in the first two sections of the Book—there are many later on—invites people to 'Come to the Feast' because,

> 'Tis here his closest Love unites
> The Members to their Head.[76]

Mediate and immediate relations to God are vital parts of the Christian religion. The Protestant stress on the immediate individual religion—even if in some ways disproportionately conceived—was a necessary reaction in Reformation times to the over-stressed mediate religion of degenerate Catholicism. While we cannot be too thankful for the Reformation assertion of personal relations to God which necessitate no intervening priest, it must not be forgotten that though Our Lord will cast out none who come directly to Him, that that does not mean that He will cast out those who come to Him mediately. Faith takes different forms. Jesus especially commended the Roman Centurion because of the simple directness of his faith when he said: 'Speak the word only'; but He did not turn away from the trembling woman who found help when she said: 'If I touch but the hem of His garment I shall be made whole.' Faith can be direct like the Centurion's, but like the woman's, it can turn common linen and woollen fabrics into sacramental vestments, into transfigured garments! To some minds the delicate imaginative faith of the timid woman is even more beautiful than the direct soldierly faith of the Centurion. The value of such garments is shown by the verses already quoted, yet Charles Wesley looked for a day when all mediate approach to God would be unnecessary—a day when he could see the Great Invisible.

> Without a Sacramental Veil,
> With all his Robes of Glory on.[77]

The centrality and importance of the Eucharist expressed by many of these hymns is never more emphasized than in the last hymn of the sub-section, inspired by words of Brevint's which compare the means of grace to stars differing in glory. I have often wondered whether this hymn on 'Ordinances Divine' may be of John Wesley's authorship.[78] Certainly

[76] No. 60.   [77] No. 93.   [78] No. 62.

the prosodic rules laid down by Dr. Bett would suggest this possibility. On the whole, however, it seems more probably to be from the pen of Charles, because he it was who illustrated Brevint's prose, although this does not of itself make it impossible that John in this case should have done so. Anyhow, the sentiment is that of both brothers.

> The Gospel-Ordinances here
> As Stars in Jesu's Church appear,
>
> .   .   .   .   .
>
> But first of the Celestial Train
> Benignest to the Sons of Men,
> The *Sacramental Glory* shines,
> And answers all our God's Designs.
>
> The Heavenly Host it passes far,
> Illustrious as the Morning Star,
> The Light of Life Divine imparts,
> While Jesus rises in our Hearts.[79]

While signs of controversy are not lacking, as we have seen, in this group of sacred poems, a few directly controversial hymns, in one case at least biting and satirical, are appended to this section.[80] Evidently Charles, so rich in his own experience of sacramental grace and joy, was angered at times by the sceptics and critics of this form of worship. A certain impatience is seen in No. 86, a poem in which he deals drastically with those who neglect the Eucharist because they do not *feel*. The people of whom he was thinking were evidently the Moravian Quietists who were perpetually quoting the words: 'Be still, and know that I am God.' They neglected, and sometimes seemed to despise, Holy Communion, because some of them enjoyed no direct experience of Christ through that devotion. Charles writes:

> Because He hides his Face,
> Shall I no longer stay,
> But leave the Channels of his Grace,
> And cast the Means away?[81]

And then, unfortunately, he becomes very sarcastic, and suggests that it is the devil who is tempting them when they

[79] No. 62.    [80] Nos. 86 and 89–92.    [81] No. 86.

54 EUCHARISTIC HYMNS OF JOHN AND CHARLES WESLEY

neglect the Lord's Table, and so addresses to him the words which the Moravians were always addressing to the Methodists.

> Get Thee behind me Fiend,
> On Others try thy Skill,
> Here let thy hellish Whispers end,
> To Thee I say *Be still!*[82]

Charles Wesley will listen to no argument against the Sacrament. 'Jesu hath said, *Do this!*'—that was enough for him:

> Let Others ask a Reason why,
> My glory is T'obey.[83]

In another hymn[84] he answers the question:

> Is the Memorial of your Lord
> An useless Form, an Empty Sign?

with the typical Methodist experience:

> With joy unspeakable we feel
> The Holy Ghost sent down from Heaven.

Perhaps when he writes:

> In vain the subtle Tempter tries
> Thy Dying Precept to repeal
>
> .   .   .   .   .
>
> Refine the Solid Truth away,
> And make us free—to disobey[85]

he is thinking of Bishop Hoadley.

More tenderly he reproves and admonishes those in another hymn,[86]

> Who slight thy dearest dying Word,
> And will not thus remember Thee

by the words:

> If chiefly here Thou may'st be found,
>     If now, e'en now we find Thee here,
> O let their Joys like ours abound,
>     Invite them to the Royal Chear,
> Feed with imperishable Food,
> And fill their raptur'd Souls with God.

[82] No. 86.  [83] ibid.  [84] No. 89.  [85] No. 90.  [86] No. 91.

## SYMBOL AND INSTRUMENT    55

The last hymn[87] of this section is one of popular controversy. The jubilant metre he uses is suitable to these forceful confident verses which joyously repudiate, because of the vivid experience of the singers, any notion that there is not validity in the objectives propounded by critics. The verses are almost defiant shouts of praise.

> Ah tell us no more
> The Spirit and Power
> Of Jesus our God
> Is not to be found in this Life-giving Food!

What nonsense it all seems to the men who knew by experience:

> With Bread from above,
> With Comfort and Love
> Our Spirit He fills,
> And all his unspeakable Goodness reveals.

> O that all Men would haste
> To the Spiritual Feast,
> At Jesu's Word
> Do This, and be fed with the Love of our Lord!

Little remains now to examine but the devotional hymns the verses of which were frequently sung at intervals in the service to enforce the teaching of these argumentative poems. Some are hymns of contemplation, and penitent devotion, suitable for any section of the book, but most of them make allusion in some form or other to the instrumental value of the Eucharist, such as Hymn No. 64:

> Thy Sacrament extends
> All the Blessings of thy Death.

Such a hymn as No. 67, is the cry of a penitent man coming to the altar. Nos. 74 and 75 are hymns of the Mixed Chalice treated earlier. A fine prayer for sincerity, quite possibly a hymn of John Wesley's, concludes with the words:

> Thy Blessings in thy Means convey,
> Nor empty send One Soul away.[88]

[87] No. 92.    [88] No. 76.

Nos. 78 and 79 which dwell on the historical facts of the passion might perhaps have been classified amongst the Memorial Hymns. No. 85 is of unknown authorship. Nos. 86 and 87 are indistinctive prayers for a blessing and penitence of no marked sacramental significance. Nos. 83 and 84 are choice little hymns which well might be sung at any non-Eucharistic service. The hymn on the Christian Passover interprets the sentiments of Brevint but concludes with a rather noteworthy verse:

> In this barren Wilderness
>    Thou hast a Table spread,
> Furnish'd out with richest Grace,
>    Whate'er our Souls can need;
> Still sustain us by thy Love,
>    Still thy Servants Strength repair,
> Till we reach the Courts above,
>    And feast for ever there.[89]

One other hymn,[90] a prayer of penitence for a despairing man, is worthy of note. It has, I think, an autobiographical accent, some remembered experience of suffering gives poignancy to the penitent plea he writes for a man despairing of himself:

> With Pity, Lord, a Sinner see
>    .    .    .
> A Blessing in the Means to find,
> My Struggling to throw off the Care
>    And cast them all behind.
>
> Long have I groan'd thy Grace to gain,
> Suffer'd on but all in vain:
>    An Age of mournful Years
> I waited for thy passing by,
> And lost my Prayers, and Sighs, and Tears,
>    And never found Thee nigh.
>
> Thou wouldst not let me go away;
> Still Thou forcest me to stay.
>    O might the Secret Power
> Which will not with its Captive part,
> Nail to the Posts of Mercy's Door
>    My poor unstable Heart.
>    .    .    .    .    .
> Now in the Means the Grace impart.
> Whisper Peace into my Heart.

[89] No. 84.     [90] No. 80.

What history lies behind these verses, which begin in despair and end in hope?

> Of all who to thy Wounds would fly,
> And let me have my One Desire
> And see thy Face, and die.

### (c.) THE REAL PRESENCE

In both parts of the book references are to be found to the 'real Presence' of Christ. Though some of the most important of these are to be found in the later sections, this seems to be a fitting place to examine the question. The use of the term 'real Presence' in *Hymns on the Lord's Supper* has been often referred to by Anglo-Catholics as implying a doctrine which the Wesleys never taught. There is no indication at all in their Hymns in such terms as 'real Presence' and 'special Presence' of the notion that that Presence is confined to the wafer. Indeed the Wesleys carefully say:

> No Local Deity
> We worship, Lord, in Thee.[91]

Their sense of the Presence of Christ was not of a hidden Christ, or of a Christ who underlay the bread which symbolized His body, but of a present, revealed, living Personality:

> We need not now go up to Heaven
>   To bring the long-sought Saviour down,
> Thou art to All already given:
>   Thou dost ev'n Now thy Banquet crown,
> To every faithful Soul appear,
> And show thy Real Presence here.[92]

The foregoing lines are certainly no description of a Christ in some mysterious way lying behind the wafer. The Presence that the early Methodists sought was the presence of One who 'crowned their banquet', both as their Host and in some sense their Guest. It was found not in the bread but

> In the Rite Thou hast enjoyn'd
> Let us now our Saviour find.[93]

It should perhaps be sufficient to say that John Wesley in the most emphatic way in his *Notes on the New Testament*

[91] No. 63.    [92] No. 116.    [93] No. 33.

expresses a sharp disbelief in transubstantiation, or any change made by Christ in the substance of the bread. But even an examination of these hymns makes it perfectly clear that any notion, such as that of the Roman theory, is entirely absent from the Wesleys' teaching.

It is, however, also clear that while they never identified Christ with the Elements, and that they disbelieved in His corporeal Presence in them, as Dr. Rigg rightly declares, they did believe that the Elements were the instruments of His power, and they did pray for a gift of the Holy Spirit that they may become such:

> 'Tis not a dead external Sign.[94]

They received what the hallow'd signs express.

> The Sign transmits the Signified.[95]

At the same time they detested the Zwinglian doctrine of the real absence of Christ from the Sacrament. It was never to them a mere memorial of the crucifixion of Christ 1,700 years before. But the presence in which they gloried was definitely the presence of a Person whose instruments were the sacramental Elements. His 'virtue' used them and worked through them, but the presence of the Lord Himself at work is one that they could realize.

> Only this I know that I
> Was blind, but now I see.[96]

Moreover, it is a 'special' Presence. Repeatedly Charles Wesley uses the words 'chiefly here' as when he says:

> *Chiefly here* Thou mayst be found[97]

—the Presence of a real Person who 'dost, ev'n Now, thy Banquet crown'—[98]

> His Presence makes the Feast.[99]

They came to the sacrament to find Christ there, as the Disciples found Him at the tomb:

[94] No. 55.    [95] No. 71.    [96] No. 59.
[97] No. 91.    [98] No. 116.    [99] No. 81.

> Swift, as their rising Lord to find
> The two Disciples ran,
> I seek the Saviour of Mankind,
> Nor shall I seek in vain.[100]

And, as we shall see in the following chapter, the eschatological hymns throb and thrill with the realized presence of Christ.

An examination of the hymns will result quite frequently in the discovery of allusions to the 'real Presence' of Christ, but it is always to a *personal* Presence.

It is quite clear that the sense of the Presence of the Divine Person as Wesley realized it, was very different from that of the Presence beneath or in the Elements, and implies that anything like the offering of Christ's memorial as a corporeal presence on the altar is an entirely impossible inference to make from Wesley's doctrine of the Real Presence. Even if John Wesley in his *Notes on the New Testament* and in his very strong words in *Popery Calmly Considered* (in both of which he categorically denies that there is any change in the bread) had not denied transubstantiation, these hymns, as we have seen, make it impossible to think that he held the Roman doctrine or any Anglo-Catholic equivalent. While he held that the Elements were not only symbols, but actual instruments, even material channels by which the justifying and sanctifying grace of God was communicated to believing men, he believed that the power of Christ—the 'virtue' as Calvin called it—was always exercised by the living personal Christ Himself, whose sacramental garments, it is true, might be so touched as to bring healing, but the virtue proceeded from the Lord.

> Sinner with Awe draw near,
> And find thy Saviour here,
> In his Ordinances still,
> Touch his Sacramental Cloaths,
> Present in his Power to heal,
> Virtue from his Body flows.[101]

If we try to place Wesley's doctrine in relation to those of the great Reformers, there can be little doubt that it is more akin to that of John Calvin than to that of Luther or Zwingli. Calvin taught the Real Presence and believed in the Eucharist, as Wesley did, as a means of grace. While he rejected Luther's

---

[100] No. 55.    [101] No. 39.

doctrine of the Ubiquity of Christ's body, he felt that he really gave a more philosophical account of what Luther believed but expressed in a blundering manner. When Calvin used the term 'Spirit' instead of the term 'the body of Christ' as Luther did, he did not use the word in any vague way equivalent to influence or aroma as it is so often used today; he thought in terms of personality.[102] This is also true of the Wesleys' conception of the Real Presence. It is important to realize that the Presence of Christ is the presence of the real Person, and although I do not mean to suggest that Wesley, who quite definitely says the words of Jesus mean: 'This symbolizes my Body', would have approved of the following statement, I doubt if he would have rejected it. May I suggest that when Jesus used the words, *This is my body*, they meant more than 'these signify my body'. May not our Lord have meant that just as the divine, human personality had a body of flesh and blood, which was His instrument while doing His redeeming work on earth, so, if you like quite arbitrarily, He made the bread and wine His instruments—in that sense His true sacramental mystical body.

But whether that be a true interpretation of the words or not, this is perfectly certain, that the Wesleys did believe and teach that Jesus Christ Himself kept His word, manifested Himself as He promised, to His disciples in all ages when they met together, and especially manifested Himself at the Meal where they did what Jesus bade them do. Nevertheless it would be a great mistake to suppose that the Wesleys taught that our Lord could be found only in the Sacrament. In all their fellowships they sang:

> Present we know Thou art
> But O Thyself reveal![103]

While the Presence of Jesus was sought and found repeatedly by the early Methodists, the Wesleys taught that it was 'chiefly' to be sought in His own ordained institution and repeatedly they called their own Methodist experience to witness that He kept His promise.

[102] For a brief statement of Calvin's views see Gregory Dix, *Shape of the Liturgy*, pp. 632-3; Brillioth: *Eucharistic Faith and Practice*, p. 169.
[103] *M.H.B.*, No. 718.

CHAPTER IV

## REALIZED ESCHATOLOGY

### THE SACRAMENT A PLEDGE OF HEAVEN

THE JOYOUS hymn,[1] controversial in character though it be, which was quoted in the preceding chapter, might well have been an introductory poem—because of its triumphant eschatological verses—to Section III. It throbs with expectation of the heavenly feast of which the Sacrament is both an earnest and pledge, and expresses joyously the triumphant spirit of the Evangelical Revival:

> O that all Men would haste
> To the Spiritual Feast,
> At Jesus's Word
> Do This, and be fed with the Love of our Lord!
>
> .   .   .   .   .
>
> Bring near the glad Day
> When all shall obey
> Thy dying Request,
> And eat of thy Supper, and lean on thy Breast.
>
> .   .   .   .   .
>
> Then, then let us see
> Thy Glory, and be
> Caught up in the Air
> This Heavenly Supper in Heaven to share.

Brevint's introduction to this section[2] is rather thin and pedantic, consisting largely of fine distinctions between the words 'earnest', 'pledge', and 'title', and is expressed in somewhat dry and legalistic terms. An 'earnest', he argues, is something given on account, in anticipation of the future; for instance, the graces of zeal, love, holiness, which remain our possession always and will not pass away. But a 'pledge' is taken back when the thing pledged is received. So, he argues,

---

[1] No. 92.    [2] His Section V.

the Eucharist will become meaningless in heaven when we see face to face the Christ whom it symbolizes. It is a pledge of future glory. We cannot partake of the Cup without realizing that one day we shall drink it with our Saviour when He drinks it anew in the Kingdom of His Father. Today we are unfit for eternal life. All we can do is to trust Him who, we are persuaded, can keep that safe which we have committed to His hands against that day. The Sacrament brings to our souls, even now, the graces which qualify for eternal life, but in addition, 'it is the most solemn instrument to assure us of it'. Brevint regards the Lord's Supper not only as an instrumental channel of grace, but as a legal instrument which gives us a 'title' to *mansions in the sky*. Houses and lands cannot be conveyed to a friend because in the nature of the case they are immovable; therefore, to make a design to give, sufficiently well-known, tokens and forms are necessary. Now Christ's estate, His happiness and glory, are not things that can be moved about any more than mountains can. As the kingdom of Israel was made over to David with the oil that Samuel poured on his head,

so the Body and Blood of Jesus, is *in full Value*, and Heaven with all its Glory, *in sure Title* made over to True Christians by that Bread and Wine which they receive in the Holy Communion[3]

—the tokens of the gifts to come.

One cannot but feel that these legal arguments, though illustrating important truths, are artificial, and that the illustration of David, for instance, is not very convincing. While Charles Wesley used quite freely the words 'earnest', 'pledge', and 'title', he generally used them in an allusive rather than an expository manner. One sentence of Brevint he glorified in one of the greatest of his hymns:

In the Purpose of God, his Church and Heaven go both together: That being the Way that leads to this, as the *Holy Place* to the *Holiest*.[4]

Brevint's arguments are summed up and treated by Wesley in several hymns:

[3] Sect. V, par. 6 (p. 185, *infra*).   [4] ibid., par. 2 (p. 184, *infra*).

Who in these lower Parts
Of thy great Kingdom feast,
We feel the *Earnest* in our Hearts
Of our Eternal Rest.[5]

He tasted Death for every One,
The Saviour of Mankind
Out of our Sight to Heaven is gone,
But left his *Pledge* behind.

His Sacramental *Pledge* we take,
Nor will we let it go;
Till in the Clouds our Lord comes back
We thus his Death will shew.

. . . . .

Now to thy gracious Kingdom come,
(Thou hast a *Token* given)
And when thy Arms receive us home
Recall thy *Pledge* in Heaven.[6]

Where Wesley in this section follows Brevint closely he is only less pedestrian than Brevint, but it is remarkable that he breaks loose from Brevint because the Evangelical Revival gave a note of triumphant joy to Sacramental devotions unknown to Caroline divines; the positively rollicking character was a novelty in Eucharistic worship. Wesley, through the medium of Methodist experience, realized that eternal life is present as well as future; that the Communion of Saints between those who are here and those who are gone before is a fact; that heaven, of which no doubt he thought as having a local significance, was also realizable on earth. None of these thoughts are to be found in Brevint's treatise. I do not mean that they contradict his teaching—Wesley never does that—but it is also true that he is never glued to it. The early Methodists realized as truly as the early Christians what is meant today by the phrase, 'realized eschatology', and found in the Eucharist a vivid joy which made them shout their praises, even if such songs disturbed the quieter reverence of the Anglican order at the sacred altar. The description which Dodd[7] gives of the eschatological Eucharist was certainly exemplified and experienced by the men and women who had been plucked out of a 'horrible pit' in the eighteenth century through the preaching of the Wesleys and their followers:

[5] No. 97.   [6] No. 100.   [7] *The Apostolic Preaching*, pp. 234-5.

In the Eucharist the Church perpetually reconstructs the crisis in which the Kingdom of God came in history. It never gets beyond this. At each Eucharist we are *there*—we are in the night in which He was betrayed, at Golgotha, before the empty tomb on Easter Day, and in the Upper Room where He appeared; and we are at the moment of His coming with angels and archangels and all the company of heaven, in the twinkling of an eye, at the last trump. Sacramental Communion is not a purely mystical experience to which history, as embodied in the form and matter of the Sacrament, would be, in the last resort, irrelevant. It is bound up with a corporate memory of real events. History has been taken up into the supra-historical without ceasing to be history.

It was all that, but it was also mystical; or perhaps it is truer to say it was Methodist; evangelical experience, vividly felt and experienced. A note of triumphant joy throbs in the outstanding hymns of this section which has more specific Methodist content than in any other part of the book. Early Christian Eucharists, as the name implies, were festivals of thanksgiving; but of thanksgiving, as Dom Gregory Dix shows, for creation as well as redemptive mercies. What he writes suggests a defectiveness in the later Wesleyans' narrowing of Eucharistic devotions to the mere facts of the Passion and death of Christ. It need not be questioned that Christian thanksgiving, the Christian Eucharist, should keep in mind Christ and all He stands for, and all that stands behind Him, as well as the mere fact of His crucifixion.

No doubt the Evangelical Revival was in some ways onesided, but the fact of redeeming love has never been more acutely felt than by the early Methodists. Their joy in deliverance as expressed by Charles Wesley is perhaps unparalleled, and certainly nowhere exceeded in Christian history. It is true that the goodness of God meant almost exclusively to them the redeeming love of Christ. In his 1779 collection of hymns, the basis of all Methodist Hymn-books, John Wesley classified no hymns on creation or providence under his title 'The Goodness of God'. The overwhelming 'goodness of God' is expressed by such hymns as: 'Would Jesus have the Sinner die?'[8]

The sense of deliverance from sin and fear caused the early Methodists to thrill with ecstatic wonder and joy, so they sang:

[8] *M.H.B.*, No. 173.

Amazing love! how can it be
That Thou, my God, shouldst die for me![9]

Or:

'Tis mercy all, immense and free;
For, O my God, it found out me![10]

Now, that this tremendous emphasis of redeeming mercy as manifested in the Cross of Christ gives a conception of God's goodness which is too narrow, may be admitted; but in fact it did create a quickening of the souls of these consciously redeemed people with a joy unspeakable and full of glory. Fortunately it found utterance in the poetry of Charles Wesley. He in his own private life, by his vivid experience of redeeming love, which delivered him from the prison in which, fettered by mere form and legalism, he had lain so unhappily for years, awoke and sang on that Whitsunday:

... The dungeon flamed with light;
My chains fell off, my heart was free,
I rose, went forth, and followed Thee.[11]

Dr. Henry Bett once claimed that the Wesleys 'evangelized' the Eucharist. If this phrase, capable of more than one interpretation, meant that their experience and hymns made it a festival of intoxicating joy, he was certainly right. Nowhere can the joy of the Evangelical Revival be more realized than in these Eschatological Hymns.

Perhaps it is worth while to consider that Methodism was really a revival, in some sense a repetition, of the realized eschatology which, according to Dr. Dodd, characterized the first Christians. The facts of Christian eschatology—the hope of heaven and the fear of hell—have often been misunderstood by non-believers, and occasioned the sort of criticism which was popularized by the Bolshevik Revolution that 'pie was always in the sky'. However true this may have been in certain eras—generally degenerate periods of Church history—the criticism of periods when eschatology has counted most must be challenged. The not unnatural logical deductions from propositions about future happiness which are made by sceptical outsiders assume that religion was nothing else than a mundane insurance against future evils. However true, and it is never wholly

[9] ibid., No. 371.   [10] ibid.   [11] ibid.

true, that may be of degenerate periods of Church life, it is not true of the vivid and powerful ages of Christian revival. Not long ago, Professor Laski told an English Court that it was well known to historians that the Methodist teaching about heaven interfered with social progress, or words to that effect. This is the sort of loose statement which does not apply of course to all historians, but when it does to some, reflects on the accuracy of their information or the soundness of their judgement.

That the Methodist Revival was a stabilizing and in some sense a conservative force is true, but the general comment of historical scholars has been that it saved this country from the sanguinary convulsions of the French Revolution. It does not follow because some Methodists were out of sympathy with early Trade Unionism that therefore they blocked social progress. In point of fact, many 'Primitive Methodists' were amongst the pioneers of that movement, and they were fervid enough in their religious beliefs, about heaven and hell. The truth is that the sort of advice Wilberforce gave to the poor— to be content with their poverty and to be sorry for the rich because their prospects of heaven were much less bright than those of the poor—was not typical Methodist teaching, and cannot be found in the writings of John Wesley, who was foremost among his contemporaries to further social reform. Forceful denunciations of social evils and anti-social wealth are to be found in some of his works.

When the question is analysed from every side it will be found that the Methodist Revival was a most fruitful source of social progress, even though some of the Victorian Methodists were much more anxious to improve mine and factory conditions than to join Trade Union organizations. One of the first causes of the success of Christianity, according to Gibbon, was the Christian hope of immortality. Bertrand Russell in his recent book, *Account of Philosophy*, says this opinion needs qualification, since other Eastern cults made the same claims and taught immortality without the same results, though it must be noted that now and again, in the same work—which by the way generally is markedly fair to Christianity—he does use this argument.

What further falsifies the argument of men like Laski and the Russian Bolshevist propagandists and others is, that the conviction about the future, the hopes and fears appealed to, is mingled with a conception of eternal life entirely outside the secular scope. In a word, it is not only the hope of another world which stimulates most Christian men, but its realization in time: that is realized eschatology. The genuine Christian is the man who has tasted the powers of the world to come. Dr. Dodd gives an impressive list of quotations from the New Testament which prove, beyond the shadow of a doubt, that the early Christian realized that the Kingdom had begun to come. Let me quote some of these impressive passages:[12]

'The kingdom of God has come upon you'—Matthew 12$^{28}$.
'This is that which was spoken of by the prophets'—Acts 2$^{16}$.
'If any man is in Christ then he is a new creature'—2 Corinthians 5$^{17}$.
'He has rescued us out of darkness and transferred us into the kingdom of the Son of His love'—Colossians 1$^{13}$.
'We are being transfigured from glory to glory'—2 Corinthians 3$^{12}$.
'The darkness is passing, and the real light is shining . . . it is the last hour'—1 John 2$^{8, 18}$.

To these might be added many more, for what does Paul mean but realized eschatology when he says 'to me to live is Christ'? Or, when speaking of our salvation by hope, he speaks of the possession of the first-fruits of the Spirit. A sense of the reality of the life of the world to come, of the unspeakable gift of God's grace, is stamped on all the accounts of Christian experience in the New Testament. The lives of these men as of generations of early Christians, who lived in times of persecution, were undoubtedly illuminated by the hope of heaven and quickened by the Spirit working in their minds which made them to know that the Lord, the King Himself, was with them always, till the end of the world, and was ready to sup with them, not in a future state, but here when they hear His voice and one of them opens to Him the door. In a word, the life of the early Church was not merely an eschatological hope, but an eschatological experience, which permeated and quickened love, joy, and peace.

Where in Christian history can be found a closer parallel to this realization of the presence of the world to come than in the

[12] *The Apostolic Preaching*, pp. 208-9.

Evangelical Revival? That movement is extraordinarily well documented, and however incredible the experience may seem to the modern mind, evidence abounds of the realized eschatology of the early Methodists; it was something experienced as well as hoped. 'He that hath the Son hath life' was the verdict of St. John—eternal life which is not a temporal and local process, but of an order independent of both, to be found in and through both. Charles Wesley was the man whose pen and voice best expressed the power, vitality, and joy of this experience and though often other hymns express it, nowhere can we discover the source and the definitely eschatological significance of this joy so well as in the distinctly Methodist experience of the eschatological Eucharistic Hymns.

Let us then examine the poems which tell of the experience of eternal life, which Brevint and most Christians of the eighteenth century thought of as a future event, but which the Methodists of the Evangelical Revival actually realized here in England.

The fact that the early Methodists, like the early Christians, realized eschatology does not mean that they exhausted its content. On the other hand, their realization was the ground of their confidence in the future and a wealth of heavenly experience of which they had only enjoyed the first-fruits. They had much joy in contemplating heaven because they knew so much by experience about it. To them it was not a problem or a query or a subject for discussion; it was their goal and experience. They travelled the Pilgrim Way singing:

> With songs to Zion we return.
> Contending for our native heaven.
>
> .    .    .    .    .
>
> Raised by the breath of love divine,
> We urge our way with strength renew'd.[13]

Charles Wesley who voiced in his hymns the heights and depths of their experience, was always happy at his people's burials. Few of his hymns are sublimer than his funeral hymns. There is no cant at all in his hymn beginning with the words,

> Rejoice for a brother deceased,[14]

---

[13] *M.H.B.*, No. 610.
[14] ibid., No. 973.

and that line, though perhaps repellent to modern ears, is the first line of one of the noblest funeral hymns he ever wrote, second only to that which many have felt to be one of the greatest in the language:

> Come, let us join our friends above,[15]

which develops, as we shall see later, some verses of this very section. The fact that the funeral hymns were often written in joyous anapaestic verse, apparently not very suitable on sad occasions, expresses the triumphant joy over death which his people felt. But this does not mean that the future exhausted his attention so that neither he nor his people could fix their minds on earthly duties. The more they thought about heaven, the more did they sing:

> From *Sion's* top the breezes blow,
> And cheer us in the vale below.[16]

Nothing is more significant in this series than that the 'earnest' in their hearts which they had already experienced was incredibly rich, and that their anticipations of the kingdom of God made death a triumph to them and not a tragedy.

It is the custom of Charles Wesley to use the double six-eight line metre for his noblest themes and this section begins with a fine specimen of its use. The thought of the hymn is suggested by Brevint's statement that the Sacramental pledge will be useless when the fulfilment of Christ's pledge becomes the experience of believers, so Wesley in the words already quoted on an earlier page[17] sings of the dazzling splendour of the heavenly King when no longer hidden under sacramental robes the vision of the universal God enables men in rapturous joy and love and praise,

> Him to behold with open Face
> High on His everlasting Throne.[18]

The glories of the heavenly vision are described in ever-ascending verses which indicate the ascent of the human soul.

[15] ibid., No. 824.  [16] *Poetical Works*, Vol. IV, p. 263.
[17] See p. 52 *supra*.  [18] No. 93.

> While we from out the Burnings fly,
> With Eagles Wings mount up on high,
>   Where Jesus is on *Sion* seen;
> 'Tis there He for our coming waits,
> And lo, the Everlasting Gates
>   Lift up their Heads to take us in![19]

But the verse particularly relevant to our theme is the next. How well it corresponds with Dodd's words. We may say at our Eucharist we are there ... at Golgotha, at the open tomb ... and we are at the moment of His coming with angels and archangels and all the company of heaven, in the twinkling of an eye, at the last trump.[20]

So Charles Wesley:

> By Faith and Hope already there
> Ev'n now the Marriage-Feast we share,
>   Ev'n now we by the Lamb are fed,
> Our Lord's celestial Joy we prove,
> Led by the Spirit of his Love,
>   To Springs of living Comfort led.[21]

The first verse gives wings to Brevint's rather pedestrian prose, and the last transcends all his devout but conventional thinking.

In the next hymn Wesley does make poetry out of some of Brevint's ideas, which he fails to do later. Here, Past, Present, and Future converge into a Now:

> O what a Soul-transporting Feast
>   Doth this Communion yield!
> Remembering here thy Passion past
>   We with thy Love are fill'd.
>
> . . . .
>
> It bears us now on Eagles Wings,
>   If Thou the Power impart,
> And Thee our glorious Earnest brings
>   Into our Faithful Heart.[22]

The distinctly Methodist note of experience enriches the prayer of verse 4 in a request that we may continually feel the 'Earnest', the communicated first-fruits of the Spirit, which bring peace and a well-founded hope of eternal bliss.

[19] No. 93. [20] *The Apostolic Preaching*, pp. 234-5. [21] No. 93. [22] No. 94.

One of the few hymns of which the reference is almost entirely to the future rather than to present eschatological blessing, especially dwells on the implications of the Cup:

> With mystical Wine He comforts us here,
> And gladly we join, Till Jesus appear,
> With hearty Thanksgiving His Death to record;
> The Living, the Living Should sing of their Lord.[23]

But the Cup is a pledge of future hope:

> The Fruit of the Vine (The Joy it implies)
> Again we shall join To drink in the Skies,
> Exult in his Favour, Our Triumph renew;
> And I, saith the Saviour, Will drink it with You.[24]

In Hymn No. 96 we find Charles Wesley at his best. Here it is that a phrase of Brevint's becomes glorified. The hymn expresses the concert between saints below and saints above. The sentiment of the second verse is expressed and developed in the great funeral hymn 'Come, let us join our friends above', the fifth line of which is:

> Let all the saints terrestrial sing.[25]

It is known all over the world in the version:

> Let saints on earth in concert sing
> With those whose work is done.[26]

The significant couplet for us is:

> Walking in all thy Ways we find
> *Our Heaven on Earth begun.*

But begun, it continues:

> The Holy to the Holiest leads,
> From hence our Spirits rise,
> And He that in thy Statutes treads
> Shall meet Thee in the Skies.

Further consideration of this hymn will be made later in relation to the Communion of Saints.

[23], [24] No. 95.   [25] *M.H.B.*, No. 824.
[26] *H.A.M.*, No 221.

The continuity of the Church on earth with that in heaven is well expressed in Hymn No. 97:

> Who here begin by Faith to eat
> The Supper of the Lamb.
>
> That glorious heavenly Prize
> We surely shall attain
> And in the Palace of the Skies
> With Thee for ever reign.

Our period of hope will be terminated by the second coming of Christ, as will Sacraments, but we can, in some sense, experience now the glorious event for which we wait.

> Faith ascends the Mountain's Height,
> Now enjoys the pompous Sight,
> Antedates the Final Doom,
> Sees the Judge in Glory come.[27]

Nowhere does Methodist joy sound out more clangorously than in Hymn No. 99: the joy of experience, the rapturous evangelical joy which accompanied the celebration of the Lord's Supper in the eighteenth century; and the secret that they knew meant that there

> Their heaven on earth begun.[28]

I will quote the first two verses, though the third clearly means that heaven can be realized here and now as well as when we feast for ever there.

> Whither should our full Souls aspire
> At this transporting Feast?
> They never can on Earth be higher,
> Or more compleatly blest.
>
> Our Cup of Blessing from above
> Delightfully runs o'er,
> Till from these Bodies they remove
> Our Souls can hold no more.[29]

Perhaps Methodists today would use language like this of some exhilarating revival meeting (or must I say of that of yesterday). But let them remember that the men who sang these joyous hymns were more ardent in Evangelism than we are, and sang them not in a revival meeting but at a celebration of

[27] No. 98.   [28] *M.H.B.*, No. 818.   [29] No. 99.

Holy Communion. Why? Because their religion was realized eschatology, and the glory of God had come down upon them. The heavenly feast was to them a refreshing stream, and at the Table of the Lord they found the source of their evangelical enthusiasm.

Hymn No. 100 is a rather unsuccessful attempt to make poetic use of Brevint's words 'pledge' and 'title'. Charles Wesley had a habit, particularly exemplified in his National Hymns, though often in others, of writing too many hymns on a single theme. Often these hymns are artist's studies rather than finished pictures. While there are less than usual of these in the hymns on the Lord's Supper, it would have been a great advantage both to Charles Wesley's reputation and to his readers if the 7,300 hymns he published had been reduced by some thousands.

He makes a glorious recovery from Hymn No. 100 in No. 101, which more than any other of the section establishes the claim of the realized eschatology of the early Methodists, and of the eschatological significance of the Eucharistic meal which they enjoyed. The content of the whole hymn is contained in the first couplet:

> How glorious is the Life above
> Which in this Ordinance we *taste*.[30]

Through the Lord's Supper, they sensibly experienced the joys of heaven, but what they experienced is but a taste and pledge of what will be, of 'That Fullness of Celestial Love'. The argument of Brevint is that eternal life is anticipated by the Eucharist, and Wesley acknowledges that our earthly vessels cannot contain it all, but the experience to which he gives testimony is so great, though only of a portion, that

> The Part which now we find reveal'd
> No Tongue of Angels can declare.

A taste! A part! But an angelical experience, unspeakably joyous. Surely this is actual experimental tasting of the powers of the world to come. The superlative expression of the eternal life and the infinite joy of what they had experienced though it is only part of the life eternal, is in itself a dazzling ray, and

[30] No. 101.

if only a drop of heavenly love, it overflows the soul 'And deluges the House of Clay'. It would have been difficult for any lord of language to have found expressions which conveyed the exceeding 'weight of glory' which overwhelmed those early Methodist partakers of the Lord's Supper more fittingly than Charles Wesley did in this great hymn. And yet what does such a dart of eternal Light, such a drop of unfathomable love involve? Are they not indeed pledges of ecstasies unknown?

> The Ray shall rise into a Sun,
> The Drop shall swell into a Sea.

Some very familiar lines of Charles Wesley, written later than these hymns, which contain doubtless a reminiscence of many Eucharists, sum up admirably the experience of Methodists when, time after time, they thronged the churches for Holy Communion:

> Yet onward I haste
> To the heavenly feast:
> That, that is the fullness; *but this is the taste*.[31]

The contemplation of God's love at the altar, the next hymn sings, is of a

> Love that turns our Faith to Sight
> And wafts to Heaven above![32]

They realized the heavenly vision. They tasted and saw how gracious the Lord is, and onward hastened to the heavenly feast. The second verse of Hymn No. 103 is a good summary of Brevint's teaching, which closes with Wesley's experience:

> Title to Eternal Bliss
>   Here his precious Death we find,
> This the Pledge the Earnest This
>   Of the purchas'd Joys behind:
> Here He gives our Souls a Taste,
>   Heaven into our Hearts He pours;
> Still believe, and hold him fast,
>   God and Christ and All is ours!

The short Hymn No. 111 also dwells simply but beautifully on God's pledge and token.

[31] *M.H.B.*, No. 406.  [32] No. 102.

Let us now return to Hymn No. 96 and consider it in connexion with Nos. 105 and 106. These verses suggest the real communion of saints, the concert, as it were, wherein heaven and earth conjoin:

> The Church triumphant in thy Love
>     Their mighty Joys we know,
> They sing the Lamb in Hymns above,
>     And we in Hymns below.
>
> Thee in thy glorious Realm they praise,
>     And bow before thy Throne,
> We in the Kingdom of thy Grace,
>     The Kingdoms are but One.[33]

The idea of this hymn, the Communion of Saints, is obviously present in the more developed verses of Wesley's, in his superb funeral hymn written some years later—the second quatrain of which as popularly sung reads:

> Let saints on earth in concert sing
>     With those whose work is done;
> For all the servants of our King
>     Both quick and dead are one.[34]

Then continues:

> One family, we dwell in Him,
>     One Church, above, beneath;
> Though now divided by the stream,
>     The narrow stream of death.
>
> One army of the living God
>     To His command we bow;
> Part of His host hath cross'd the flood,
>     And part is crossing now.

Now this expansion of thought in the Hymn No. 221 is of value because it shows what Wesley's idea really was. 'One Church, above, beneath' summarizes the content of the second and third verses of Hymn No. 96. The figure of the united family and unbroken army to which death is but a narrow ditch easily bridged, brings home with even greater force the oneness of the two sections—Militant and Triumphant—of the Church of Christ. This is a hymn of the concert of the heavenly and

[33] No. 96.
[34] The version given here is that of *H.A.M.*, No. 221; cf. *M.H.B.*, No. 824.

earthly children of God. The earthly Church meets with the heavenly, and the heavenly with the earthly, as this hymn is sung. The original words of Wesley are:[35]

> Let all the saints terrestrial sing
> With those to glory gone.

Heaven is begun on earth only to be continued as

> The Holy to the Holiest leads,
> From hence our Spirits rise,
> And he that in thy Statutes treads
> Shall meet Thee in the Skies.[36]

This conception of the Church at Holy Communion, as Brevint clearly shows, is more completely worked out in the sacrificial hymns, but here we note the concert between the two, both singing together: The earthly Church communicates with angels and archangels, and all the hosts of heaven. 'Holy, Holy, Holy! Lord God Almighty, heaven and earth are full of thy glory! Glory to Thee, O God Most High!'

Hymns Nos. 105 and 106 really enrich and more typically express the Communion of Saints, when communicants on earth are bidden

> Lift up your Eyes of Faith and see
> Saints and Angels join'd in One.[37]

The first couplet of a glorious versification of the *Preface to the Gloria*: 'Angels and Archangels and all the Company of Heaven laud and magnify Thy Holy Name, ever more praising Thee.' The following hymn which is a sequel, expresses in memorable words the joys of those hosts of God who have come out of great tribulation. There is a tradition, how well-founded I do not know, that this hymn was Charles Wesley's memorial to his father and mother. If it be true, its verses gain a new and tender significance. In all these hymns Wesley far transcends Brevint's prose. Never more so than in the words:

> What are these array'd in White
> Brighter than the Noonday Sun?[38]

---

[35] These are retained in the latest edition of *M.H.B.*
[36] No. 96.  [37] No. 105.  [38] No. 106.

The remaining hymns of this section require little notice. One is very good and one very bad. And the rest, while they are perhaps more than mediocre, are typically short hymns which Wesley wrote to be sung at intervals in the lengthy, crowded, communion services of the early Methodists. They are tender and simple verses, but not distinctly eschatological. They might be placed in any part of the book with equal propriety. But there are two to which attention must be called: a very bad hymn—No. 114—which makes a quite ridiculous and rather repulsive analogy between Adam's rib and Jesus' blood, the one issuing in the old Eve, the other in the new Eve—the Church of Christ. Why John permitted it to be printed under his name is a puzzle. But No. 109 is one of a few excellent hymns which has not gained a wide circulation for some unknown reason. It really ought to be sung. It brings to mind the hymn referred to in another chapter, 'Lamb of God, whose bleeding love',[39] with its refrain: 'O remember Calvary, And bid us go in Peace.' It is possible that the archaic language of the third verse has prevented its circulation:

> Let the bowels of thy Love
> Echo to a Sinners Groan.

These words are obviously impossible to sing. But if my amendment be accepted—

> Let the *music* of thy Love
> Echo to a Sinners Groan.

—then the sweet penitence, and the lilting music of the hymn would make it widely popular. The last lines especially bring 'O remember Calvary' to mind:

> One who feebly thinks of Thee
> Thou for Good remember me.

Why the hymn is placed amongst eschatological hymns cannot be explained, but one is thankful that it did not perish.

The section concludes with the Hymn No. 115, which brings us back to Eschatology and ends in a note of triumph:

> With joy we celebrate his Love,
>   And thus his precious Passion shew,
> Till in the Clouds our Lord we see,
> And shout with all the Saints, 'TIS HE!

---

[39] No. 20.

In summary of Part One of this book we may say of these Sacramental Hymns that doctrinally they dismiss as unsatisfactory the memorial theory of Zwingli and Cranmer; they assert emphatically that the Eucharist is more than a memorial, that it is a definite organ for the bestowal of present graces. They teach the 'Real Presence' of Christ not as being in any way identified with the Elements but as that of a person whose 'virtue' uses them and works through them in the souls of men. Part I concludes with hymns of realized eschatology which are reminiscent of apostolic times, and joyfully anticipatory of the heavenly feast, and contains the most distinctively Methodist of all the sacramental hymns.

# PART TWO

# THE CHRISTIAN SACRIFICE

CHAPTER V

# PRIESTHOOD AND SACRIFICE

### THE SACRIFICIAL HYMNS

THE POLEMICS of the Reformers of the sixteenth century against Roman Catholicism were based chiefly on the monstrous abuses of the Roman Mass. The practice of offering *meritorious* and *propitiatory* Masses for the living and the dead had issued in a most unscrupulous commercialization of the superstitions of the people. The sacrifice of the Mass, which was thought to repeat Calvary, and which made personal salvation in practice contingent on a well-paid priestly ceremony, could not have been too strongly abominated. Luther's language, though typically intemperate, gave expression to the inner feelings of thousands of good people:

Yes, I declare that all the brothels (though God has repressed them severely), all manslaughters, murders, thefts, and adulteries, have wrought less evil than the abomination of the Popish Mass.

Article XXXI of the Anglican Church is more balanced in expression, but not less condemnatory:

The offering of Christ once made is that perfect redemption, propitiation, and satisfaction, for all the sins of the whole world, both original and actual; and there is none other satisfaction for sin, but that alone. Wherefore the sacrifices of Masses, in the which it was commonly said, that the Priest did offer Christ for the quick and the dead, to have remission of pain or guilt were blasphemous fables, and dangerous deceits.

Even Anglo-Catholics of our own day, like Bishop Frere and Dom Gregory Dix, acknowledge that the Reformers had a strong case against these commercialized blasphemies, and mention the fact that the Council of Trent was troubled by them.[1] So great was the abuse of medieval propitiatory and meritorious sacrifices, that the Reformers, and even Cranmer, ridded the Eucharist of all sacrificial significance. So much so

[1] Frere: *The Anaphora*, p. 198; Dom Gregory Dix: *The Shape of the Liturgy*, p. 627.

that he in the 1549 Prayer Book—so Dom Gregory Dix shows—caused the offerings of the people to be placed in alms boxes and not offered at the altar, because 'in his nostrils', as Luther said, the offertory 'stank of oblation'.[2] In the later Prayer Books instruction was given for the offerings to be laid on the altar as in earlier times.

There is, however, another tradition in the Church of England. Bishop Lancelot Andrewes is quoted by Frere as writing: 'The Eucharist ever was, and by us is considered both as a Sacrament and a Sacrifice.'[3] Brevint, therefore, was following a sound tradition when he entitled one section of his pamphlet 'Concerning the Sacrament, as it is a Sacrifice', as were the Wesleys, when they entitled Section IV of their Hymn Book, 'The Holy Eucharist as it implies a Sacrifice'. The tradition has never quite died out in Methodism, and has recently found a new expression in Dr. Vincent Taylor's notable work, *Jesus and His Sacrifice* (pp. 322–3):

... no modern presentation of the doctrine of the Atonement is likely to be satisfactory which ignores, or deals imperfectly with, the doctrine of the Eucharist.... Before the Oxford Movement of the last century, it was recognized by John and Charles Wesley as their collection of *Hymns on the Lord's Supper* shows:

> This Eucharistic Feast
> Our every Want supplies,
> And still we by his Death are blest
> And share His Sacrifice.[4]

Here, then, is a difference between the Wesleys and Luther, though by no means the only difference.

Now let it be categorically asserted that both Brevint and the Wesleys were definitely anti-Roman. Brevint, indeed, wrote a book—*Missale Romanum*—in criticism of the Roman doctrine of Sacrifice, which Dean Waterland, by no means a narrow Churchman, commended in the strongest terms. Evidence is not lacking in the extract from Brevint's Preface of his anti-Romanism—

The offering of it (of Christ's sacrifice) therefore must needs be one only; and the repeating thereof, utterly superfluous.[5]

---

[2] *The Shape of the Liturgy*, p. 661.     [3] *The Anathora*, p. 24.
[4] No. 4.     [5] Sect. VI, par. 1 (p. 186, *infra*).

John Wesley's anti-Romanism has already been referred to, but it was quite frequently expressed in a variety of ways in his writings. Nothing could be more strongly anti-Roman than some expressions in the Hymns in the Sacrificial section of this book. The long hymn (No. 128),

All Hail, Thou Mighty to atone!

should be carefully read, since its anti-Romanism is as conclusive as its sacrificialism.

Charles Wesley, who is so often treated by Methodists as guilty of excessive ritualism, was in some ways an even stronger anti-Roman than his brother. This is very clear in many of his National hymns, and in his poem called 'An Epistle to the Rev. Mr. John Wesley';[6] his indignation with his son, Samuel, when he went to Rome was without bounds. Indeed, John Wesley's letters both to Samuel and to his brother Charles are much more charitable and tolerant to Romanism than anything Charles ever wrote.

Here then, having regard to the fact that the Reformers so hated the notion of Eucharistic sacrifice, we are presented with a problem which has perhaps never been carefully studied or solved in our immense Wesley literature, but rather evaded. Perhaps I can state it thus: While we repudiate as strongly, if more temperately than some of the Reformers, all notions of the Eucharist as a meritorious or propitiatory sacrifice—as a repetition of Calvary, made by priests on behalf of others, alive or dead, as though the Cross of Christ were not all-sufficient for salvation—is there any true sense or practical value in which the term Eucharistic Sacrifice can be used by Evangelical Christians? The answer is to be found in the sacrificial hymns of Charles Wesley, especially when they are considered in the light of early Christian worship.

To enter intelligently into an understanding of these hymns, we must examine what the Wesleys have to say about priests and sacrifices. *Hymns on the Lord's Supper* was published some time in 1745. We do not know the exact date, but obviously it was earlier than 30th December 1745, on which date John Wesley wrote a letter to his brother-in-law, Westley Hall, defining his views on outward sacrifice and outward

[6] *Poetical Works*, Vol. VI, pp. 53–64.

priesthood. Here are extracts from the letter which was written in response to a request by Westley Hall, then under the influence of the Moravians, that John and Charles should renounce the Church of England. John Wesley wrote:

(1) We believe it would not be right for us to administer either Baptism or the Lord's Supper unless we had a commission so to do from those Bishops whom we apprehend to be in a succession from the Apostles. And yet we allow these Bishops are the successors of those who were dependent on the Bishop of Rome.

(2) We believe there is, and always was, in every Christian Church (whether dependent on the Bishop of Rome or not), an outward priesthood, ordained by Jesus Christ, and an outward sacrifice offered therein by men authorized to act as Ambassadors of Christ and Stewards of the Mysteries of God.

(3) We believe that the three-fold order of ministers ... is not only authorized by its Apostolic institution, but also by the written word.

Yet we are willing to hear and weigh whatever reasons induce you to believe to the contrary.[7]

The rest of the letter is interesting because it expresses John Wesley's unchangeable devotion to the Church of England, with hints as to the limits to which it is given. But I do not quote it further because his remarks are not relevant to the question of priesthood or of outward sacrifice. It is important to note the date of this letter (30th December 1745), because three weeks later, Lord Chancellor King's *Account of the Primitive Church* led John Wesley to a change of view. It is true that the young man, King, when more mature, renounced the opinions he had published in his Work, but it is also true that Wesley never did. On the contrary, he was more influenced by Edward Stillingfleet's *Irenicum* even than by King's *Primitive Church*. Telford's note on Wesley's letter to Westley Hall reads:

Wesley still held his High Church views as to the succession and the 'outward sacrifice' offered. Three weeks later Lord King's *Account of the Primitive Church* led him to change his view [as to the succession].[8]

No reference, however, was made in the *Journal* to a change of view on the priesthood and the Christian sacrifice, but only of Apostolic Succession. Nor, so far as I can discover, was any such *renunciation ever made*.

[7] *Letters of John Wesley* (Standard Edition), Vol. II, pp. 55-6.    [8] ibid., p. 54.

PRIESTHOOD AND SACRIFICE 85

While John Wesley's conclusion that episcopal succession from the Apostles was an undemonstrable fable does involve also a renunciation of the belief with which he prefaced his letter of 30th December 1745, and by consequence of his belief in the *three orders*, it does not involve a repudiation of his belief in the outward sacrifice and outward priesthood, nor is there the least evidence that he ever repudiated these beliefs. Other evidences so far as they can be traced make for a contrary conclusion. The renunciation of the belief in Apostolic succession does, however, cancel the implications of a hymn— 'A Prayer for the Bishops'[9]—published in 1742, which Anglo-Catholics sometimes have quoted without giving proper value to its date, in which are found the words:

> The worthy Successors of those
> Who first adorn'd the Sacred Line,
> Bold let them stand before their Foes,
> And dare assert their Right Divine.

I challenged Mr. Telford on his note, but he could not give me any definite case of general retractation by Wesley of his High Church views. Some of them—for instance, Prayers for the Dead, and the Mixed Chalice—he actually defended in 1749 in his letter[10] to Dr. Middleton. It is almost incredible, if Wesley renounced his views on the priesthood and outward sacrifice, that he should not have said so publicly, as he did of Apostolic succession. Whatever else he lacked, he was not wanting in frankness, courage, and sincerity. It would be indeed inexcusable to think that the man who, in 1790, preached the Korah Sermon ever thought of himself as other than a priest. What is more significant is the fact that the *Hymns on the Lord's Supper* were published in 1745, and it will be admitted that the letter written on 30th December of that year could not have been written before their publication. Hence the date is important, as it shows that the hymns dealing with the Eucharistic Sacrifice must be judged as the products of men who believed that there were priests who made an offering of an outward sacrifice. Is it really credible that they should

[9] *Poetical Works*, Vol. II, pp. 341–2.
[10] *Letters of John Wesley* (Standard Edition), Vol. II, pp. 312–88. In his *Journal* (Standard Edition, Vol. III, p. 390) under 2nd January 1749, Wesley writes: 'Being much pressed to answer Dr. [Conyers] Middleton's book against the Fathers, I . . . spent almost twenty days in that unpleasing employment.'

have continued to publish these hymns and constantly to have used them without explaining that they no longer believed in the outward sacrifice as they did in earlier days? The fact that John Wesley changed his mind on episcopal succession cannot be made to prove that he changed his mind in relation to all other matters that modern Methodists think it would have been consistent for him to have done. The inference is purely subjective. As a matter of fact, though Wesley renounced episcopal succession he never did renounce all succession. In some sense he evidently believed that the orders that he received were orders that, as a Presbyter, he could transmit, and apparently held that ordination must be from a man who had received orders and therefore had a right to pass them on to other men.

### THE ANGLO-CATHOLIC CONTROVERSY

Although a detailed account of it would be irrelevant to our main theme, some reference must be made to the controversies between Anglo-Catholics and Methodists round about the year 1870. In 1871 a book entitled *The Eucharistic Manuals of John and Charles Wesley* was published by W. E. Dutton. This contained *A Companion for the Altar*, by Thomas à Kempis, Brevint's *Treatise*,[11] and *Hymns on the Lord's Supper*. The object of the publication was to attempt to prove that Wesley held High-Church doctrines on this Sacrament.[12] A book (*John Wesley in Company with High Churchmen*) by H. W. Holden was published in 1869. Other writers of similar works were R. D. Urlin, and Frederick Hocking. These contentions of the Anglo-Catholics that John Wesley was a High-Churchman whose teaching their contemporary Methodists ignored, caused a good deal of controversy. Acrimonious magazine articles reveal the deep resentment of the Methodists of that time on account of the attack made on their loyalty to their Founder. While Anglo-Catholic views, generally speaking, upon Wesley's Sacramental teaching have never been successfully met by Methodist denominational controversialists, it is true that they did interpret many of the sayings of the Wesleys unfairly and read into them nineteenth-century ideas. Undoubtedly they saw Wesley's churchmanship

[11] As abridged by Wesley.
[12] Richard Green: *Wesley Bibliography*, p. 44.

out of relation to his great evangelical mission, which dominated all that he did. These exaggerations and misunderstandings were not difficult to answer, but unfortunately the Methodist controversialists, particularly Dr. J. H. Rigg, were as extreme in their denials of Wesley's High-Churchmanship as the Anglo-Catholics were in their assertions. Dr. Sparrow Simpson, himself an Anglo-Catholic, published in 1934 his *John Wesley and the Church of England*, which in many ways is the fairest putting from both sides of Wesley's churchmanship with which I am acquainted. His verdict on the controversy is worth quoting:

During the nineteenth century, the tendency on the Anglican side was to over-stress the identity between John Wesley's teaching and that of the Church, and on the Methodist side to over-stress the differences.

There can be no doubt that what Wesley once called 'an overgrown fear of Popery' influenced the minds of nineteenth-century Methodists, because of the fears created generally amongst English people by the Oxford Movement that there was a real danger of a revival of Romanism in this country, which naturally made Methodists, whose Sunday reading was often Fox's *Book of Martyrs*, somewhat frightened. One cannot help noting as one reads the biographies of Wesley that the early biographers were not much troubled about his so-called High Churchmanism. But as the century went on, the Methodist authorities became more and more perplexed. Tyerman, for instance, who was a perfectly honest historian of the Methodist revival, referred to what once he called 'John Wesley's High Church nonsense' but had to acknowledge (because, as he says, his business is to tell the truth) that some of these practices and notions which he affirmed were characteristic of the Oxford and Georgia days of Wesley, always persisted.

One of the results of the controversy seems to have been the formulation of two myths which ought to have exploded long ago: one may be called the Methodist Myth of the Conversion, and the second the Myth of the 'rags of Popery'. More than any other man, Dr. J. H. Rigg is responsible for both of them, but the crude view, occasionally expressed even to these days, that Wesley's conversion changed his ecclesiastical opinions and practices, was too obviously absurd to be seriously advocated without considerable qualification by a man of Dr. Rigg's culture and ability; and so the Methodist Myth of Conversion was developed by him into what I call the Myth of the 'rags of Popery'—an expression which I heard on the lips of a theological tutor in my youth when I talked to him about some views of Wesley's on the Sacraments which had surprised me. Dr. Rigg expresses himself in these words:

> Wesleyans admit that up to 1738 Wesley had been a High Church ritualist, but they insist that all his life afterwards he taught the evangelistic doctrine of salvation by faith: that before long, and once for all, he discarded the fable, as he called it, of Apostolic succession, and that he presently gave up all that is now understood to belong to the system, whether theological or ecclesiastical, of High-Church Anglo-Catholicism. The graveclothes of ritualistic superstition they say still hung about him for awhile, even after he had come forth from the sepulchre, and had, in his heart and soul, been set loose and free, and he cast them off gradually; but the new principles he had embraced led, as they affirm, before long, to his complete emancipation from the principles and prejudices of High-Church ecclesiasticism.[13]

Now this relatively careful statement goes far to justify the Methodists who say, without qualification, that the conversion of Wesley changed his ecclesiastical beliefs and practices. As a matter of fact, while his conversion was the most important and revolutionizing fact of his religious experience, it made very little distinctive or ascertainable change to his ecclesiastical views. The argument usually propounded is, that before his conversion, when he was in Georgia, he was guilty of many ritualistic extravagances of which he was not guilty after his conversion.[14] This totally misreads the situation. Wesley's common sense had quite as much to do with his change of opinion as his conversion. He was not merely a High-Church ascetic when he went to Georgia, but an Oxford Don who had plunged deeply into the records of the Early Church and had formulated for himself, out of touch as he was with ordinary human beings, a theory which he tried to put in practice in Georgia. His contact with the rough Colonials proved to him how mistaken many of his practices were, as

[13] *The Churchmanship of Wesley*, pp. 60–1.
[14] See J. E. Rattenbury: *Conversion of the Wesleys*.

PRIESTHOOD AND SACRIFICE 89

may be seen by a letter that he wrote *before* his conversion when he was reviewing the catastrophe of his Georgian ministry. Even Dr. Rigg quotes the letter in which Wesley confesses the mistakes that he had made:

> I bent the bow too far the other way: first by making antiquity a co-ordinate rather than a subordinate rule with Scripture; second by admitting several doubtful writings as undoubted evidence of antiquity; third by extending antiquity too far, even to the middle or end of the fourth century, by believing more practices to have been universal in the ancient Church than ever were so. Sixth, by considering that the most of those Decrees were adapted to particular times and occasions, and consequently when the occasions ceased must cease to bind.[15]

Here we have a clear expression of Wesley's acknowledgement of his own errors in Georgia. Whether his rigid discipline and extravagant ritualism had been attempts to set up a modern expression of the early undivided Church, or whatever part his conversion played in the change of his conduct later—and no doubt the effect of his conversion was so great as to be incalculable—it is quite clear that his widening experience of life altogether apart from his conversion, made him see the absurdity of his extravagances in his first parish at which in mature life he smiled, as when thinking of his refusal to give the Sacrament to Bolzius; he wrote: 'Can anyone carry High-Church zeal higher than this? And how well I have been beaten with mine own staff.' Very often what is attributed to Wesley's conversion is plainly attributable to his common sense and his expanding vision through the normal experiences of life and men.

Evidences by which the conversion myth are established are such as these: In Georgia Wesley refused communion to Dissenters and insisted on rebaptizing them, and after his conversion we are told that he gave communion under certain circumstances to Dissenters. But the conversion must have worked rather slowly because it was after their conversion that John and Charles Wesley got into trouble with the Bishop of London for rebaptizing Dissenters! Wesley always held, at least until 1777, that Baptism, like Holy Communion, could only be administered by an ordained priest. One of the errors of Rome, according to him, was the teaching that Baptism

[15] *The Churchmanship of Wesley*, p. 25.

under certain conditions by laymen, women, and heretics was valid. Modern Methodists in this matter are much more Roman Catholic than Wesley.[16] Sometimes it is said that Wesley, because he regarded Holy Communion as a means not only of sanctifying but of justifying grace, made this statement as a result of his conversion.[17] As a matter of fact, as the statement on pages 9 and 10 *supra* shows, it was through the consideration of other people's conversions, like that of his mother and the Early Methodist Preachers, that he came to this conclusion. Wesley's outlook undoubtedly widened as his ministry widened, but it is no evidence against his sacerdotal views of priesthood and outward sacrifice that he gave to Eucharistic worship a wider appeal.

My friend T. H. Barratt, whose article in the *London Quarterly Review* of July 1923 was as valuable as any contribution ever written to the understanding of the Sacramental practices of John Wesley, is rather unfortunate when in his contention that Wesley was not a sacerdotalist he quotes the following verse from the Sacramental hymns:

> Lord, I have now invited All,
> And instant still the Guests shall call,
> Still shall I All invite to Thee:
> For O my God, it seems but right
> In mine, thy meanest Servant's Sight,
> That where All is there All should be.[18]

This verse is George Herbert's and not Wesley's, and by a curious irony is extracted from a hymn which Dr. J. S. Simon regrets was ever published in *Hymns on the Lord's Supper*, because he thinks that its High-Church views are the chief cause of objection amongst Methodists to the book.[19] One suggestion that Mr. Barratt made impressed me very much when I first read it, namely, that a subtle change came over Wesley after his conversion so that in his Office of Holy Communion he changed the form of absolution into a prayer. But on reflection I feel that the change if subtle was very slow, as it happened in 1784 in Wesley's abridged prayer-book for the American churches. After all, it must not be forgotten that when the Early

---

[16] See pp. 9, 10, *supra*.
[17] *Popery Calmly Considered*, *Wesley's Works* (3rd Ed.), Vol. X, pp. 140–58.
[18] No. 9.  [19] See p. 15, *supra*.

Methodist Preachers read Morning Prayers, as they must have done, they were never permitted to pronounce the Absolution, because that could only be said by an ordained priest. Does this not rather suggest sacerdotalism than anti-sacerdotalism? But there is no doubt a difference between Morning Prayer and Holy Communion. Why Wesley changed the pronouncement into a prayer in the American office, and afterwards in the English, it is very difficult to say, but it may quite well be that special American conditions accounted for the alteration. However that may be, Wesley certainly used the form of absolution himself, and definitely, in 1777, defended this declaratory form of absolution.

The popular treatment of these views is illustrated by the writing of Stephenson. Referring to the *Hymns on the Lord's Supper*, he says:

It is important to note that some of the hymns refer to what is called the 'real Presence', hence the ritualists of the present time claim Charles Wesley as the advocate of one of their prominent but erroneous doctrines. Two remarks are necessary to explain the admission of that opinion into a few of the hymns: the first is in those hymns where he was expressing in verse the sentiments contained in Brevint's treatise rather than conveying his own views on that doctrine. The second is during the year in which the book was issued, John and Charles read Lord King's work on *Primitive Church*. Up to that time both brothers Wesley maintained all the dogmas which distinguish High Churchmen, such as the Apostolic Succession, Baptismal Regeneration, and probably the Real Presence of Christ in the Sacrament of the Lord's Supper. Lord King's work entirely changed the views of John Wesley on all the points, and so far modified the views of Charles that in none of his poems can any of these opinions be found. From being the rigid Episcopalian and an earnest advocate of High Church principles, John Wesley became a convinced advocate and believer in Presbyterate principles.[20]

A completer catalogue of what, in charity, I will term errors it would be impossible to imagine. Stephenson did excellent work, for which Methodists are grateful by means of the information he collected about the Wesley family, but he was not a theologian, and though he collected a number of edifying anecdotes about the value of Wesley's hymns to dying people, and published them as a commentary on the *Hymn Book*, he obviously knew little about the *Hymns on the Lord's Supper* as is

[20] *Memorials of the Wesley Family*.

clear from the fact that he copied a misprint in Jackson's *Life of Charles Wesley* which says there were 66 of these hymns, when even a casual reader would have discovered there were 166.

It is not necessary to answer the paragraph I have extracted from Stephenson's book, but merely to state that obviously the reason that Wesley's abridgement of Brevint's treatise was published with the hymns was that it was Wesley's opinion. The first reference we have to Lord King's book is in 1746, not 1745. It is simply false to say that the Wesleys rejected the doctrine of baptismal regeneration or changed their minds on all the dogmas which distinguished High Churchmen. It is quite unlikely that they ever held the Lutheran doctrine of the Real Presence, but if they did, there is no reason to suppose that they ever changed their views, or that Charles Wesley wrote no Sacramental hymns later, which in point of fact is not true, although it would not be a matter of surprise if he had not, since he had already composed 170—a number that might be said to satisfy any man. Moreover, the modified acceptance of presbyteral orders did not cause Wesley to regard Anglican bishops as in practice, undesirable, and certainly did not mean that he adopted Presbyterian principles, such as Calvinism, as a consequence. He never regarded himself as a Presbyterian.

Dr. Rigg, of course, was too able a man to commit himself to any such unqualified statement. He says that instead of being an ecclesiastical High Churchman, Wesley preached always 'salvation by faith'. It must be observed that this statement is both *suggestio falsi* and *suppressio veritatis*. The suggestion in it to many minds is that he preached salvation by faith *only*. Of course he preached salvation by faith. It may be that in the first year of his conversion he almost went so far as to support the Lutheran mistranslation of Romans $5^1$, and preached salvation by faith *only*. As everybody knows, he said some very foolish things about his conversion at that time, which he repudiated when he republished his opinions between 1771 and 1774 in his *Collected Works*. Very soon he came up against the Moravian Quietists who emphasized that word *only*, and consequently denied the necessity of means of grace. Wesley was compelled to re-orientate his new evangelical experience to the old beliefs of his Anglican training. While there never was a time when he did not preach salvation by faith, it is very certain, especially from his writings in 1769 and 1770 and the great Calvinist controversy that ensued, that he qualified his more extreme expressions of that doctrine.

Dr. Rigg allowed that Wesley divested himself of the graveclothes, or as I call them, the 'rags of Popery', very gradually. Sometimes the date is 1746, eight years after his conversion, when he renounced apostolic succession. Sometimes it is 1747, because in the Conference of that year he made certain perfectly good criticisms of the Church of England and affirmed his belief that the New Testament did not settle for all time the constitution of the Church. Really, Rigg should have said 1750, as the letter which affirms some of his so-called Popish practices to Dr. Middleton was written in 1749. But the best date of all would be 1791, when he went to heaven and learned for the first time what a good old-fashioned Methodist ought to be!

While the Methodist controversialists had little difficulty in replying to the exaggerated and disproportionate statements about some of Wesley's sayings, to which it was possible to give even a Roman interpretation, it is on the Sacraments that Dr. Rigg is most unsatisfactory. He says, for instance, quite definitely that the only statement on the subject in the *Standard Sermons* is that in the sermon on 'The Means of Grace',[21] which he does not quote, but affirms that it contradicts Anglo-Catholic beliefs. I do not believe that any modern Anglo-Catholic would object to these words, though, of course, he might add others to them, as we shall presently learn Wesley does in the *Hymns on the Lord's Supper*. It is extraordinary that Rigg should assert that this is the only reference to Holy Communion in the *Standard Sermons*, and forget the striking words by which Wesley obviously embraced the opinion of the Fathers of the Early Church in his sermon on 'Daily Bread', where the Lord's Supper is called '*the grand channel* whereby the grace of His Spirit was conveyed to all the souls of the children of God'. While Dr. Rigg gave, in a qualified way, his assent to the fact that Wesley taught baptismal regeneration, and affirmed his belief that probably Wesley never held a doctrine of transubstantiation, even in his Oxford and Georgia days, it is perhaps better to describe than to characterize the treatment which he

[21] For full quotation see p. 9, *supra*.

gave to the *Hymns on the Lord's Supper*. John Wesley sanctioned in his middle age, he writes:

the publication of extracts from Brevint's tractate on *The Christian Sacrament and Sacrifice* as a preface to his brother Charles' Hymns on the Lord's Supper.

He *sanctioned*—permitted—it is suggested, his ritualistic brother Charles to use extracts from Brevint's tractate on *The Christian Sacrament and Sacrifice*. Is this even honest dealing? Rigg must have known that the extract was made by John Wesley, not by Charles; he must have known that that extract was not only published with the Hymns, but was also published separately; he must have known that, as Tyerman says, it must be regarded as Wesley's own opinion. Indeed, it was the only expression of his sacramental views which was generally and repeatedly published and circulated amongst the Methodist people. Sanctioned, indeed! Rigg plainly implies that John Wesley was reluctant to publish this extract, but does not explain why it was republished nine times during his lifetime, and always under the authority both of John and Charles Wesley.

Brevint's words were published simply because they expressed John Wesley's opinion: nothing can be clearer than this. He abbreviated 132 pages of Brevint to thirty, and when the extract was made, it obviously was John Wesley's rather than Brevint's. The book was two-fold: 'Sacrament' and 'Sacrifice'. And it is the second part of the book—Sacrifice—that gives offence today to some Protestants, and much joy to Anglo-Catholics. As to the first part, the Sacramental sections, he quotes Brevint's own words that the Sacrament was to 'convey the first Fruits of these Sufferings, in Present Graces, whereof it is a means'.[22] As to the crucial point, he says, Brevint explains himself more precisely:

... his Body and Blood have every where, but especially at this Sacrament, a true and Real Presence. ... And since he is gone up, he sends down to Earth the Graces that spring continually both from his everlasting Sacrifice, and from the continual Intercession that attends it.[23]

Rigg thinks that this passage may possibly be interpreted as evidence that Brevint accepted the Lutheran doctrine of

[22] Sect. II, par. 1 (p. 176, *infra*).   [23] Sect. IV, par. 5 (p. 183, *infra*).

Ubiquity, but makes it evident that he did not believe in the real corporeal presence under the elements of bread and wine in virtue of priestly consecration.

Brevint's doctrine of the Real Presence Charles Wesley transformed into ecstatic hymns which, however, contain no trace of any doctrine equivalent to the corporeal presence of Christ. On the whole, as will be seen in a later chapter, Rigg's statement of Part I of Brevint's treatise is quite fair.

What, then, is so offensive in Rigg's propaganda? It is the almost incredible fact that he makes no reference whatever to the sacrificial beliefs of Brevint, or to Wesley's sacerdotal hymns. He treats Part II as if it were non-existent. This is really monstrous. Although the question of the Real Presence is no doubt important—but even then, the most memorable expressions of it are to be found in the sacrificial hymns—it is relatively unimportant in comparison with the sacrificial hymns themselves, and indeed, the entire second part of the book. Having regard to the fact that *after* this book was published, Wesley definitely expressed his belief both in the outward priesthood and the outward sacrifice, it is impossible to evade the conclusion that priestly consecration, at that time of his life at all events, did, at least, mean something, and that the reference to the Eucharist as 'the Holy Sacrifice'—'the Daily Sacrifice'—was more than a mere conventional description, as Rigg describes it, of the Lord's Supper.

The problem as to whether or no the Wesleys regarded themselves as sacrificing priests is of vital importance, and must not be evaded. The evidence that in some sense Wesley believed that he was such a priest, at the time the Hymn Book was published, is clear. It is no answer at all to say vaguely that his conversion altered his opinion on this subject. That happened seven years earlier, all of them years of revival, years in which Methodism was really established in pagan England. These were the years in which he was wearing his 'Roman rags'—his 'graveclothes'! Can any such view be regarded as other than preposterous? It must therefore be clearly stated that there is no evidence whatever that Wesley altered his opinion upon the priesthood and the outward sacrifice. That he repudiated other rituals is only an inference made from modern Methodist opinion of what *a priori* should have been the logical result of his evangelical conversion. It is not sufficient to say where proof is lacking (and what evidence there is seems to be contrary to these views), what an inconsistent man John Wesley was!

The inference on which the 'rags of Popery'[24] theory is built is made, no doubt, from the fact that Wesley renounced in 1746 his belief in episcopal succession. The inference would be much stronger if it were true that when he rejected that dogma, he rejected all idea of succession. But Wesley believed that ordination was given by a man who had received ordination, which obviously implies succession, though not necessarily *episcopal* successors.[25] He certainly did not renounce his belief in succession when he repudiated his belief in the Apostolic succession of Bishops. He did not believe that a Church by a majority vote could give ordination to one of its members to administer Sacraments. I am not writing this in order to defend my own beliefs, since I do not personally agree with Wesley in these matters, but only because it is necessary that we understand what Wesley thought, and do not suppose that he is really the son of his own children, which is so often the lot of a founder of a great movement. He believed that as a Presbyter he could make other Presbyters, and he always believed in a priestly order.[26] There is nothing new whatever in the views he expressed in his Korah sermon of 1790. They are quite consistent with his whole relation to lay preachers whom he never authorized, as lay preachers, to administer sacraments but always ordained, if and when they had permission to administer. It was not that he looked down on the vocation of a preacher. Both Charles Wesley in his Hymns on the functions of the Methodist Preachers (as the early Itinerant as well as the Local Preachers were described)[27] and John Wesley in his letters to them, especially to Nicholas Norton in 1756,[28] expressed quite clearly their sense of the magnificent vocation which the lay preachers of Methodism responded to, but not less definitely did Wesley say in that same letter to Norton that he held that it would be wrong to permit lay preachers to administer sacraments.

---

[24] *Popery calmly Considered*, *Wesley's Works*, Vol. X, p. 143–58.
[25] See pp. 84–5, *supra*.   [26] See p. 144, *infra*, and Addendum, pp. 150ff., *infra*.
[27] *Poetical Works*, Vol. VI, pp. 97–108.
[28] *Letters of John Wesley* (Standard Ed.), Vol. III, pp. 185–92.

## PRIESTHOOD AND SACRIFICE

Now what was the reason that Wesley refused to give to these men, whose work he so much admired, permission to administer sacraments—what could it have been except that he believed in a priestly as well as in a preaching order? And in some sense the priestly order meant to the Wesleys the outward priesthood which was necessary for the offering of an outward sacrifice. What content they gave to the words 'sacrifice' and 'outward' may be a matter for discussion, but it is certain that they did not give them a Roman content. That the question of sacrifice was in their minds is made clear by a remark of Edward Perronet[29] to which too little attention has been given.

The Perronet family was one of the most interesting in early Methodism. Edward has won enduring fame by his great hymn, No. 91 in the *Methodist Hymn-book*:

All hail the power of Jesu's name.

He was one of two sons of Vincent Perronet, the Vicar of Shoreham, who for long years was the most trusted counsellor of John and Charles Wesley, and was called by them the Archbishop of Methodism. Edward and his brother Charles did not, as their father did, take Holy Orders, but joined the brotherhood of the Wesleyan lay preachers. Edward itinerated, but Charles seems to have been half itinerant and half local, probably because of his ill health. They were, through birth and education, naturally friends of John and Charles Wesley as the other preachers were not. But as a letter of John shows, they were not a very submissive pair. 'Charles and you', he writes to Edward, '*behave* as I want you to do; but you cannot, or will not, preach *where* I desire.'[30] More and more they showed a rebellious spirit; they ministered irregular sacraments,[31] and unquestionably stirred up the other lay preachers to claim this right. Charles Wesley and Charles Perronet were ecclesiastically poles apart. Wesley's conversation with the preachers in 1755 resulted in a promise from those who were present that they would not minister sacraments since, whether lawful or not, it was inexpedient to separate from the Church of England, which inevitably would be the result of such a practice. Neither

---
[29] See p. 99, *infra*, where this point is further discussed.
[30] Tyerman, *The Life and Times of John Wesley*, Vol. II, p. 85.
[31] ibid., p. 211.

Charles Wesley nor Charles Perronet was satisfied, as John in a letter to his brother says: 'Here is Charles Perronet raving because his friends have given up all: and Charles Wesley because they have given up nothing.'[32]

Charles Perronet seems to have been quite a saintly man who did not succumb to contentions and bitterness as, unfortunately, Edward did. Edward Perronet entertained an almost incredible hatred and contempt for the Church of England. He published what Tyerman calls a withering satire on the National Establishment, entitled *The Mitre*. This book infuriated John Wesley, who demanded its immediate suppression. So thoroughly was this command carried out that it is believed not more than thirty copies ever got into circulation. One copy can be seen today in the British Museum, I do not know whether any others have survived. The quotations which Tyerman makes from the book are certainly witty, but also scurrilous libels. It is not surprising that soon after this Edward broke his connexion with the Wesleys, and after a brief association with Lady Huntingdon's work, he became the minister of a little Independent Church in Canterbury until his death.

Charles Wesley, on 16th November 1776, wrote to his brother about Perronet's *Mitre* to express his agreement with the summary action John had pursued and strongly to criticize his conduct as a Methodist preacher. The following note is interesting:

At Canterbury I saw our sacramental hymns which Ted has scratched out and blotted, hardly leaving twenty entire leaves.[33]

Even if Charles Wesley exaggerates somewhat, one must agree when he writes: 'How can two walk together except they be agreed? How can he pretend to labour with us?'[34] A note of Edward Perronet makes one wonder that he ever did agree with them—

I was born and am like to die [he writes], in the tottering communion of the Church of England, but I despise her nonsense; and thank God, I have once read a book [presumably he meant the Bible] that no fool *can* answer and that no honest man *will*.

[32] See Tyerman, Vol. II, pp. 240-4, 264, 265.
[33] Atmore, *Methodist Biographies*, p. 300.
[34] For a good summary see Dr. Grosart's article in Julian's *Dictionary of Hymnology*, pp. 889ff.

Now, in his satire *The Mitre*, one statement of Perronet's in my opinion is of great importance, because it shows what was the real problem in Wesley's mind in his refusal to permit laymen to administer sacraments. In a note in this book Perronet denounces the doctrine of the Lord's Supper as 'a sacrifice' and says '*so long as this delusion is maintained, the sacrifice must be administered by priests and priests only*'. On page 128 of his book, he writes:

Only reduce this *simple* institution to its *primitive* and scriptural standard and then a handful of private individuals, or a single family, may communicate, as the Christians did of old, and the *sacrament* (so-called) become once more *literally* a daily sacrifice of *praise and thanksgiving*.

No doubt, whether intentional or not, Perronet here is controverting the opinion of the Wesleys. Many modern Nonconformists are more likely to agree with Perronet than with Wesley, but the fact remains that it was the Wesleyan belief in the sacrifice and the priesthood which made it impossible for them to sanction lay administration. They never withdrew their expressions of belief in either, and the hymns which were circulated throughout their lives, and which they made Methodists everywhere sing, were written at a time when no one denies their belief in outward priesthood and outward sacrifice. Their attitude to orders, and their refusal to give them, or to permit sacramental administration to anyone lacking them, even though their preaching might do more good (as the letter to Norton shows), are facts which demonstrate their permanent belief that sacrificing priests at the altar, for so they commonly described the Communion Table—offer a holy sacrifice, which they wished to be a daily one, as in early Christianity; so they sang:

> O wouldst Thou to thy Church return!
> For which the faithful Remnant sighs,
> For which the drooping Nations mourn,
> *Restore the daily Sacrifice.*[35]

Now while impartial persons will admit that the Wesleys never denied their expressed belief in outward priesthood and outward sacrifice, there is another question much more difficult

[35] No. 166.

that awaits an answer: What do they mean by these terms when they use them? We can at least say categorically that they do not use them in a Roman sense, or in what they considered a Roman sense. All that we can examine is the sacrificial hymns; there seems to be no other clue to the meaning they attached to the word 'sacrifice' than these hymns and the writings of Brevint. The fact that the hymns were continually being produced and constantly used is unevadable, and forces us to consider them as the normal teaching of the Wesleys. All we can do is to follow Luke Tyerman's example, without necessarily agreeing with his adjectives. When he refers to the outward priesthood and outward sacrifice, he says:

An extract from Brevint which, by publishing, Wesley made his own, will help to explain his meaning in the objectionable phraseology he employed in his letter to Westley Hall.

He then quotes Brevint's description[36] of the Sacrament. What he read comforted him, and he felt that Brevint's and Wesley's words about the Sacrament were quite convincing; he probably found comfort even as to the Sacrifice in the thought that the Eucharist, after all, was not in their opinion a Roman propitiatory Mass, but only a *kind* of sacrifice. Let us now pursue the Methodist historian's method and try to find out by careful examination of the hymns what kind of sacrifice it was.

[36] For quotation see Chapter 6, p. 105, *infra*.

CHAPTER VI

# SACRIFICE AND THE ALTAR

I

THE KEY passage in Brevint to an interpretation of his teaching about the Eucharistic Sacrifice and to Charles Wesley's hymns in which he follows Brevint more closely than in any section of the book (though they are always stamped with Wesley's individuality) is to be found in Section II (paragraph 7)[1] of his treatise. It is the passage in which he so vigorously dissociated himself, as we saw earlier, from mere memorialism.

The main Intention of Christ herein, was not, the bare *Remembrance* of his Passion; but over and above, to invite us to his Sacrifice, not as done and gone many Years since, but, as to Grace and Mercy, still lasting, still *new*, still the same as when it was first offer'd for us.

These words inspired some of the greatest of Charles Wesley's hymns of which we have postponed our consideration. Brevint's teaching is through and through soaked with the sacrificial idea, as a second quotation from another section which is paraphrased by Charles Wesley in the hymn which many people think his greatest contribution to Eucharistic thought (No. 116) shows. It is the first hymn of the Sacrificial Section to which he rightly regarded Brevint's earlier paragraph as relevant. Brevint writes:

This Victim having been offered up in the Fulness of Times, and in the midst of the World, which is Christ's Great Temple, and having been thence carried up to Heaven, which is his Sanctuary; from thence spreads Salvation all around, as the Burnt-offering did its Smoke. And thus his Body and Blood have every where, but especially at this Sacrament, a true and Real Presence. When he offered himself upon Earth, the Vapour of his Atonement went up and darkened the very Sun: And by rending the Great Veil, it clearly shew'd, he had made a Way into Heaven. And since he is gone up, he sends down to Earth the Graces that spring continually

[1] p. 178. *infra*.

both from his everlasting Sacrifice, and from the continual Intercession that attends it. So that we need not say, *Who will go up into Heaven?* Since without either ascending or descending, this sacred Body of Jesus fills with Atonement and Blessing the remotest Parts of this Temple.[2]

Probably it was this last sentence that persuaded Dr. Rigg that Brevint may have shared the Lutheran doctrine of the Ubiquity of Jesus. This, however, is not necessarily correct, though a possible inference, since what fills the earth is not the body of Christ, but 'Atonement and blessing'. Anyone who reads the passage carefully and compares it with Hymn No. 116 will see whence Wesley's metaphors issued and how gloriously he gave wings to them. 'Victim divine'—'the Great Temple here below'—the enriched content of Brevint's word 'Sanctuary', with the continual 'Intercession' made unto God, are, with other symbols, found in Wesley's verse:

> Thou didst for All Mankind atone,
> And standest now before the Throne.
>
> Thou standest in the Holiest Place,
> As now for guilty Sinners Slain.[3]

The obscure words, 'the Smoke of thy Atonement', become full of meaning when the figure of Brevint, which they paraphrase, is read. Wesley's words made the *new* way to heaven appear and showed the Great Invisible, and in the next verse the line—

> He *still* respects thy Sacrifice,

nobly expands and expresses Brevint's meaning. Then the final, the best-known, and most quoted verse of all, gives winged utterance to the well-chosen words of Brevint:

> We need not now go up to Heaven
>   To bring the long-sought Saviour down,
> Thou art to All already given:
>   Thou dost ev'n Now thy Banquet crown,
> To every faithful Soul appear,
> And shew thy Real Presence here.

Hymns Nos. 3 and 4 respectively postponed for our consideration from Section I, emphasize most of all the *newness* of the sacrifice and its perpetual continuation:

[2] Sect. IV, par. 5 (p. 183, *infra*).  [3] No. 116.

But Jesu's Death is ever New,
He whom in Ages past they slew
Doth still as slain appear.[4]

This emphasis of the newness of the sacrifice is related definitely to the Eucharist in Hymn No. 4:

> Our Passover was slain
> At *Salem's* hallow'd Place,
> Yet we who in our Tents remain,
> Shall gain His largest Grace.
>
> This Eucharistic Feast
> Our every Want supplies,
> And still we by his Death are blest,
> And share his Sacrifice.

That is to say, the work of Calvary, if a finished work in the sense that Christ dying once would die no more, was still unfinished; He was not dead but risen, ascended at God's right hand. The High Priest was the Lamb of God, raised up from the dead to be the Great Shepherd of the Sheep. He is the Priest-Victim. The metaphor of 'sheep' and 'shepherd' seems curiously mingled in the words of the Apocalypse: 'For the Lamb which is in the midst of the throne shall be their shepherd, and shall guide them unto fountains of waters of life' (Revelation 7$^{17}$, R.V.). This strange combination of metaphors, as a matter of fact, is fundamental to an understanding of Wesley and Brevint, and really of any doctrine either of Eucharistic sacrifice or of the Atonement of Christ. The conception of the Priest-Victim is best expressed by Hymn No. 5 which contains in substance the doctrine which lies behind, and is assumed in all Wesley's Sacrificial teaching. The hymn is one of the most noteworthy of all Charles Wesley's poems:

> O Thou eternal Victim slain
> A Sacrifice for guilty Man,
> By the Eternal Spirit made
> An Offering in the Sinner's stead,
> Our everlasting Priest art Thou,
> And plead'st thy Death for Sinners now.

---
[4] No. 3.

Thy Offering still continues New,
Thy Vesture keeps its Bloody Hue,
Thou stand'st the ever slaughter'd Lamb,
Thy Priesthood still remains the same,
Thy Years, O God, can never fail,
Thy Goodness is unchangeable.

O that our Faith may never move,
But stand unshaken as thy Love,
Sure Evidence of Things unseen,
Now let it pass the Years between,
And view Thee bleeding on the Tree,
My God, who dies for Me, for Me!

When Wesley entitled his section 'The Holy Eucharist as it implies a Sacrifice', it must not be thought that he meant something Brevint did not mean when the latter used the title 'Concerning the Sacrament, as it is a Sacrifice. And first, of the Commemorative Sacrifice.' They really mean exactly the same thing. What then does the word 'commemorative', which Wesley does not use, signify in Brevint? That it means more than a mere memorial of Calvary is plain, not only from the first quotation and the hymn, but from the text of the section. What is not so easy to be dogmatic about is, whether there is some expansion of the meaning of the New Testament word '*anamnesis*', which is always translated 'in memory', or better, as 'a memorial of'—*eis anamnesis* 'of me'.

We must return again to the Greek word *Anamnesis*, which is defined by Liddell and Scott primarily as meaning 'a call to mind'. The phrase 'call to mind' occurs several times in the hymns and may well be, as Wesley was very familiar with New Testament Greek, a deliberate translation of the term. Generally speaking, it obviously means recalling what is distant in time, that is, recollecting, remembering. But whether it can be used to call to mind what is distant in space or invisible I am insufficiently qualified to say. What is evident is, that it is in such a way that Brevint and Wesley apply the term when they quote: 'Do this as a memorial of Me.' They thought of the Crucifixion as a past event and never failed to call it to mind, but when they used the word 'memorial' they were thinking of Jesus as He is represented in the Epistle to the Hebrews and the Apocalypse—as the slaughtered Lamb who was also the Great High Priest, eternally living and pleading, by His wounds and suffering, the cause of sinful men for whom He died. After all, it was Jesus, and not primarily His crucifixion which our Lord told us to call to mind when He said: 'Do this in remembrance of Me.' And although doing this always involves a memory of Calvary, always shows forth the Lord's death till He come, it is Christ crucified, not the crucifixion of Christ which we are told to call to mind. It was impossible to men who believed that Jesus Christ was risen, ascended, at the right hand of God—to think only of the historic fact of His death. He was to them the crucified Christ who was the same yesterday, today, and for ever. Always risen, though always crucified. Always by His 'glorious scars' manifesting His great love for us, always, it might be said of Him:

> He ever lives above
> For me to intercede,
> His all-redeeming love,
> His precious blood, to plead.[5]

The sentences of Brevint relevant to the whole subject which comforted poor Tyerman when he was so worried by what he thought were the 'objectionable' claims of the Wesleys to be outward priests who offered an outward sacrifice read:

The Holy Communion alone brings together these two great Ends, Atonement of Sins, and acceptable Duty to God, of which all the Sacrifices of old, were no more than weak Shadows. As for the Atonement of Sin, 'tis sure the Sacrifice of Christ alone was sufficient for it: And that this great Sacrifice, being both of an infinite Value, to satisfy the most severe Justice, and of an infinite Virtue, to produce all its Effects at once, need never more be repeated.[6]

Indeed, he argues that it would be a great offence against Christ to question its *infinite* worth, so repetition would obviously be foolish and superfluous, as well as offensive to Christ; and continues:

Nevertheless this Sacrifice, which by a *real* Oblation was not to be offered more than once, is by a Devout and Thankful Commemoration, to be offered up every day. This is what the Apostle calls, *To set forth the death of the Lord*; To set it forth as well before the Eyes of God his Father, as before the Eyes of Men; And what St. Austin *explained*, when he said, The Holy Flesh of Jesus was offered in three

[5] *M.H.B.*, No. 368.   [6] Sect. VI, par. 1 (p. 186, *infra*).

Manners; By *pre-figuring Sacrifices* under the Law, before his Coming into the World, in *real Deed* upon the Cross, and by a *Commemorative Sacrament* after he ascended into Heaven. All comes to this,

1. That the *Sacrifice* in itself, can never be repeated; 2. That nevertheless, this Sacrament, by our Remembrance, becomes a *kind*[7] of *Sacrifice*, whereby we present before God the Father, that precious Oblation of his Son once offered. And thus do we every Day offer unto God, the meritorious Sufferings of our Lord, as the only sure ground whereon God may give, and we obtain the Blessings we pray for.[8]

Brevint reiterates:

Now, there is no Ordinance or Mystery, that is so blessed an Instrument to reach this everlasting Sacrifice, and to set it solemnly forth before the Eyes of God, as the Holy Communion is. *To Men* it is a *sacred Table*, where God's Minister is order'd[9] to represent from God his Master, the Passion of his dear Son, as still fresh, and still powerful for their Eternal Salvation. And to *God* it is *an Altar*, whereon Men mystically present to him, the same Sacrifice, as still bleeding and sueing for Mercy.[10]

If the words 'commemoration' and 'memory' are read in conjunction with his last sentence, as they must be, to make the earlier quotations from Brevint and Wesley of the hymns intelligible, it will be clear that in their minds more than a commemoration of a past event is implied, although the word might be properly explained as referring to Calvary, which cannot but be called to mind even when those who behold the Lamb, whose sacrifice is always new, are singing:

> He ever lives above
> For me to intercede.[11]

Now, while the Eucharist is, as Charles Wesley in an early hymn called it, the 'unbloody sacrifice', whereby the Church calls to mind the shed blood of the Slaughtered Lamb which speaketh better things than the blood of Abel, it is first of all supremely necessary to realize what that sacrifice, continually pleaded in heaven, meant to Brevint and Wesley. Brevint expresses his conception of it in the devotional language of a scholar and theologian. But Wesley sees where Brevint thinks, and the second mode, the poet's mode, is not less important for the presentation of truth. What, then, did Wesley visualize?

---

[7] Italics mine.     [8] Sect. VI, par. 2 (pp. 186–7, *infra*).
[9] 'Order'd', probably in the sense of ordain.     [10] ibid. (p. 187, *infra*).
[11] *M.H.B.*, No. 368.

As we have already learned from the sacrificial hymns of earlier sections, the conception of the Priest-Victim is that of the Epistle to the Hebrews. But Wesley's visualization of the heavenly scene also depends upon the metaphors of the Apocalypse. The picture of Revelation 4 and 5 though not explicitly referred to, is obviously in the background, and the great High Priest appears to him as the Lamb of God Slain from the foundation of the World. The hymns already quoted give a much more graphic picture of the Priest-Victim than that of Brevint's prose. The difficulty of thinking at one and the same time of the Lamb of God as Shepherd of the Sheep, as both Victim and Priest, probably did not very greatly trouble Wesley, who thought of Him also as the Aaronic Priest, clad in hieratic robes, with breast-plate of gems and glittering shoulder straps, and at the same time as the Slaughtered Lamb of God. The different figures in Brevint are rather successive than simultaneous in his more logical expression of the truth. The standing posture of the priest, which so often occurs in Wesley's hymns, is not authorized by the actual words of the Epistle to the Hebrews, where He is spoken of as 'sitting down' at the right hand of God. But surely, it is hypercritical to object to this application of the symbol of the priesthood of Christ. Anyone who reads Hebrews 10 can hardly be surprised that the priest should be pictured by Wesley as standing, though the posture is never actually affirmed there. While he worked out the metaphor of the priest in his own way, it must be remembered that it is a complex of the figures both of the Epistle to the Hebrews and of the Apocalypse. More conspicuous in the thought of Welsey than the figure of the Priest is that of the Slaughtered Lamb. The wounds of the Lamb slain are the silent pleaders for God's mercy. Hence the Lamb is the Priest. Though he does not express it exactly in words, the hymns of this section seem to be echoing:

Worthy is the Lamb that was slain.[12]

Wesley thinks of Jesus as a spectacle, and often calls upon His Father to look upon Him, the Slaughtered Lamb. Brevint, indeed, once prayed: 'Look upon the Sacrifice of Thy dear Son, once offered for my sins.'[13] This petition became a passionate cry in Wesley's hymns:

[12] Revelation 5$^{12}$.   [13] Sect. VI, par. 7 (p. 187, *infra*).

> Father, God, who seest in me
> Only Sin and Misery,
> See thine own Anointed One,
> Look on thy beloved Son.
>
> Turn from me thy glorious Eyes
> To that bloody Sacrifice.[14]

The spectacle of Our Lord's suffering is never better expressed than in the great hymn:

> Oh God of our Forefathers hear,
>
> . . .
>
> Father, behold thy dying Son,
> And hear his Blood that speaks above.[15]

The glorious scars of Jesus plead with a silent eloquence richer than words; the thought is better expressed in a hymn not of this book but written later:

> Entered the holy place above,
> Covered with meritorious scars,
> The tokens of His dying love
> Our great High-priest in glory bears;
> He pleads His passion on the tree,
> He shows Himself to God for me.[16]

The imagery of blood sacrifice stamps all these hymns, and however much the other metaphors of Brevint are used—Aaron's ephod particularly—the dominant thought of Wesley is the precious blood of Christ, which in some way is implied or described in every hymn of the section. To quote a few phrases:

> Thy Blood of Sprinkling speaks, and prays
> All-prevalent for helpless Man,
> Thy Blood is still our Ransom found,
> And spreads Salvation all around.[17]
> His Body torn and rent
> He doth to God present.[18]

The bloody sacrifice—the Victim slain—pouring out his precious blood, of Hymns 119 and 120.

> Look thro' Jesu's Wounds on me.[19]
>
> That precious, bleeding Sacrifice.[20]

[14] No. 119.  [15] No. 125.  [16] *M.H.B.*, 232.  [17] No. 116.
[18] No. 118.  [19] No. 120.  [20] No. 125.

All the hymns contain such expressions or suggestions. The fact must not be overlooked that the Lamb of God who takes away the sins of the world is the central reality of heaven—the *Slaughtered* Lamb. And the figure is used in the most realistic way possible till at times, if we are to be quite frank, it becomes positively repulsive to modern readers. A phrase like 'Look thro' Jesu's wounds on me' does rather disgust one; and can we read the following lines without a shudder?

> Still the Wounds are open wide,
>     The Blood doth freely flow,
> As when first his sacred Side
>     Receiv'd the deadly Blow:
> Still, O God, the Blood is warm,
> Cover'd with the Blood we are.[21]

Now the realism of all this is terrible, but it brings out with unequivocal force Wesley's sense of the continuing sacrifice of Christ in heaven which is basal to all Eucharistic worship regarded in its sacrificial aspects. The problem that it presents to the modern Christian who shrinks from this odious realism cuts very deep, and some consideration seems necessary in order that we may appreciate what lies behind these crude expressions. Doubtless our repulsion has much that is good in it, though perhaps we may find, on analysis, that the realization of Christ's sacrifice for sin is one of the greatest *desiderata* of the days in which we live. How much might we be confirmed in our faith, as were His disciples, if we had a clearer vision of those wounded hands and feet which He showed to His disciples to confirm their faith after He had risen from the dead.

While admittedly it is true that repulsive descriptions of blood sacrifice outrage the aesthetic sense of modern man, as they did that of the Greeks and the Jews when they first heard of the message of the Cross, it can be shown that a new realism is desirable today. Decent people in the first century were shocked by Calvary. The greatness of St. Paul's boast is only realized when we see that he actually gloried in what horrified his contemporaries: 'God forbid that I should glory save in the cross of Our Lord Jesus Christ.'[22] But even then we may ask about Charles Wesley's hymns whether some of the expressions are really Christian at all. This dwelling on the blood of Christ,

[21] No. 122.   [22] Galatians 6¹⁴.

plunging into it, and so forth, are not expressions which seem to have any justification in the New Testament.

Some twenty years ago, I visited the ancient Church of San Clemente in Rome, and was taken down to the subterranean floor—probably of the first century—where I saw in one part a Christian altar, and in another a temple of Mithras, the roof shaped like a cave. In the temple there still stood the ancient structure whereon the *taurabolium* (the slaying and sacrifice of a bull) was performed. Underneath was a shelf on which Mithraic worshippers lay, under the bull, the blood of which came through an aperture still visible, so that they were bathed in the blood of the bull. A repulsive sight indeed, but it was impossible, as one stood in that temple of Mithras, not to call to mind hymns Evangelical and Catholic, which treat of the blood of the Lamb in very similar terms.

An examination of Scripture will show that it is only by straining metaphors out of their normal meaning that any sort of justification can be found for this sort of language. Unquestionably many of the uses of the term 'blood of the Lamb' have been derived from the pagan use of the term 'blood of the bull'. The Old Testament never justifies such expressions as plunging into fountains of blood and the like. There are lines of Charles Wesley which are evidently influenced by Mithraism; probably even the familiar, though to my mind meaningless words

> My Jesus to know,
> And feel his blood flow,
> 'Tis life everlasting, 'tis heaven below.[23]

The learned Irish monk who was our guide quite frankly told us that he found no study more interesting than the influence of Mithraism on early Christianity and the influence of Christianity on Mithraism. Therefore it is only fair, when one thinks of Wesley's use of these metaphors, to distinguish between what is Mithraic and what is Christian. It must also be admitted that a few of Wesley's hymns suggest that he held the crude anthropomorphic theory that justice is to be identified with the Father and mercy with the Son. This is not characteristic, but it ought to be noted. In Hymn No. 36, for instance, we read:

[23] *M.H.B.*, No. 406

His Blood procur'd our Life and Peace
And quench'd the Wrath of hostile Heaven.

However, it should be remarked that there is quite another side to Wesley's beliefs in this matter, as can be discovered by reading his hymns on the Trinity, where it is plain that he realizes there can be no competition between the Father and the Son as illustrated by identifying the one with justice and the other with mercy. On the whole, I conclude in the hymn quoted he is simply using a convention without much reflection.

While there are repulsive elements not genuinely Christian in some of Wesley's metaphorical uses of blood symbolism, as also in many Medieval and Protestant pietisms, both pictorial and written, we must realize the truth that underlies sacrifice; namely, the tragic helplessness of human beings to quieten their own consciences and to overcome the evil spirit that lurks in them. The modern repulsion to blood sacrifice has been expressed in very powerful English, as forcibly as anyone, by Mr. Bernard Shaw, in his *Search of the Black Girl for God*, and other works. The horror of ancient sacrifices which he expresses cannot but gain the sympathy of people who have any imagination. The cruelty and bestiality of ancient holocausts of thousands of cattle and sheep, the temples reeking with blood, the horrifying fact that behind these repulsive sacrifices there stands the sacrifice of human beings—strong men, fair maidens—make the ancient temple worship an almost incredible nightmare to modern men, so to men like Bernard Shaw, the sacrifice of Jesus—the worship of the Slaughtered Lamb, with its obvious relation to the sacrifices of ancient times—is too nearly related to the blood sacrifices of earlier ages to be credible or tolerable today!

Now while one cannot deny the truth of much of what Mr. Bernard Shaw says about the foulness and immorality of ancient sacrifices, no fair-minded man can deny that his treatment of the subject is both one-sided and superficial. Why does it never occur to him and to others that there must be some explanation of the universal instinct of human beings to offer sacrifices? Such sacrifices have always been costly, both economically and affectionally. Men have paid dearly in tears as well as in money for the precious things that they have offered to God. Are these sacrifices merely the result of superstitious fears or of the commercial rapacity of unscrupulous priests? Surely, the universality of sacrifice in all nations in every part of the world requires more careful thought and treatment when one penetrates beneath the obvious superstitions of many of them. Is there not something at the bottom of them all which belongs almost to the constitutional nature of a human being? Surely, there was some primitive instinct that the wrong that men did needed righting; that there must be some way of satisfying the conscience of human beings outraged by their own wrong doing; some way of expressing the aspirations that were frustrated by sin. These reeking sacrifices, loathsome as they were, cannot be explained except by the human conscience. They were horrible indeed, but then sin is horrible, and the sacrificial system is one of the ways of emphasizing its horror.

The ancient story, almost the oldest in the Bible, of Cain and Abel, is a most significant expression of the moral significance of sacrifice as it was seen by the ancients, and what is more, it is a very modern story. Cain was the pioneer of modern culture—Agriculture—the only culture possible to such a man. By the sweat of his brow, manual effort, and intellectual application, he tilled the earth and caused it to bring forth fruits and flowers. He was proud of the result, but felt that it was not altogether due to him, because he had the co-operation of some power that was not himself; and so he made his offering of flowers and fruits—an offering, it may be called, of praise and thanksgiving to that Someone Else. But in the moment of his worship of God, and mingled with congratulation of himself, he forgot one thing—sin, couching at the door. And so the couching beast sprang upon him and made him the instrument of its own murderous fury as he put his brother Abel—righteous Abel—to death. When he offered the sacrifice, the result of his culture, he forgot sin. But Abel, on the other hand, offered a sacrifice, not beautiful, like the flowers which Cain offered, but ugly, repulsive—a slaughtered lamb, because he did not forget that sin couched at the door, and expressed his horror of sin in a horrible thing. The story of that slaughtered lamb as it has been told to us was undoubtedly told by men who inherited a tradition of sacrifice from prehistoric eras, but its significance is inescapable: Man may not forget sin. No culture will avail him if he forgets sin. And in the awful presence of God, whether the reality of God has been brought home to him by revelation or whether it in some sense is the projection of his own conscience, man cannot say: 'Lord, what wonderful things I have done with thy help'—but: 'God be merciful to me a Sinner.' To forget sin is fatal.

And so we come to the sacrifice of Christ, acknowledging that it is linked with the sacrificial system of the past and that it was horrible. We have too much sentimentalized, through our love of Christ and gratitude for His mercy, the slaughtered lamb. The actual Cross of Calvary was a stumbling block and an offence to the cultured Jew and Greek of the first century. It was a horrible, loathsome, repulsive thing. And the slaughtered lamb is eternally horrible, because sin is horrible.

The Cross ought to shock people. When one looks upon the Lamb of God slain, one can only say: 'That is what sin did; innocence was no guard against its foulness.' And it is only as men realize the tragic character of sin that there is any real hope for the future of humanity. The tragic character of sin is manifested in the sacrifice of the lamb. But then there is a vast difference between this sacrifice and all the other sacrifices it makes unnecessary. For while it displays the horror of human sin, it also displays the love of God. The lamb slaughtered was the Lamb of God, the Son of God; and to have any meaning at all, we must accept the Christian story that God in His Son came into this world, was made like unto His brethren, suffered the consequences of sin by being identified with sinful men, inevitably bore the sins of the race, and because He was a God of Love and power, bore them away. The blood of Christ says two things. It says sin is horrible, it puts innocence to death. But it also says what Wesley sang, that the blood of Christ

> ... through earth and skies
> Mercy, free, boundless mercy! cries.[24]

There is nothing that matters more to the world today than that it should have a new realization, however shocking the method be, of the horror and tragedy of sin. This is continually brought home to the minds of men who contemplate the Lamb of God which taketh away the sin of the world, and the plea

[24] *M.H.B.*, No. 375.

made continually by Him at the throne of God. But men harden their hearts and turn away from God in a vain hope that culture will save them. That hope found its highest expression in the nineteenth century, when it became incredible to the rationalists of the time that such a thing as war on a world scale should ever break out again. One confirmation (and there are others of this), is to be found in Buckle's *History of Civilization*, and its glorification of Rationalism in contrast with Religion. There we read that at the time when war was taking place between Russia and Turkey, such a war was impossible to the more educated and cultured nations of Europe, and that it was significant that it took place between the least rationally developed of European peoples—and then we think of what has actually happened! Two holocausts, more bestial, more brutal, more fatal in this century, not of animals but of men in millions, in comparison with which the sacrifices of the past pale into insignificance. What do they mean?

It is true that millions of people have died very much as the animals died in the ancient temples, without thought and without understanding. But in these wars it is equally clear that sacrifices of the highest have been given. Men in thousands, who felt it was better to die than that their country should perish; and many, many men, who felt that the beliefs of humanity were something to die for, and who laid their lives down willingly in order that civilization might be saved, and that there might be hope for future generations of mankind. How is it that in this world of ours we should be forced to make the filthy sacrifices of world-war? The reason is that men are the victims of every sort of sin, and in the complex of society often the highest can only make their witness by dying.

But men harden their hearts; only a month or two ago, an amiable and honourable philosopher on the Brains Trust listened to some statement about sin and said: 'Talking about sin will not get us very far.' There is certainly no real prospect of solid progress for the human race if it does not remember that sin lies couching at the door. The scientist makes his apology for the invention of lethal weapons by saying that the quest of knowledge must be pursued at all costs. He really believes that light is the life of men and not with St. John that life is the light of men. What is it that makes people fear the atom bomb today, and the other products of modern culture? Can anyone object to scientific discovery? Who has not benefited by it? Nobody would have any fear at all of the uses of atomic energy if it were not that men and nations are sinful and cannot be trusted with it.

Surely, some check should be put upon communications of knowledge to people who are too criminal to know how to use it. We should hang a parent who allowed his child to play fatally with a razor, or permitted a child to drink poison from a bottle because it liked the look of it: yet we have no reproach to give to men who deny all sense of responsibility for the criminal use of an invention which they know will be exercised for ill if it gets into the hands of people who are not merely undeveloped children but are of criminal minds.

The menace of society is sin, and culture can do no more than the flowers and fruits of Cain's sacrifice to save the world if people forget that, like a wild beast, it coucheth at the door. Sin is horrible. However much some extravagant doctrines of total depravity have misled men, the fact of our stained and warped nature cannot be ignored. Nothing brings this home to men more vividly than the Cross of Calvary; that murder of the Highest. When men shrink from crude expressions of the Christian Atonement, they should think with realism of the cruelty of the modern battle-front. The Slaughtered Lamb of God is tragic, but the significance of it is that sin is tragic. The realism of Charles Wesley's hymns has no note of artificiality; he, like his brother—saints as they were, and perhaps because they were saints—saw and felt the loathsomeness of sin. They struggled for years with it, and gained liberation by their trust in Christ to forgive them their sins. However strange and unaccountable they may seem to modern men, however fanciful their theories may seem, they were the realists. For there is a great lack of realism in many who turn their eyes away from the horrors of life and imagine that all that is needed is to cover ugly things with flowers and to ignore the couching beast—the beast which the chains of culture cannot keep captive, which every now and then springs out of the deep abyss of human personality and ravages the world with slaughter and foulness.

The fact of the Slaughtered Lamb visualized in the Wesleys' hymns is to be found in the Epistle to the Hebrews and the

Apocalypse, of which they did not think as if it were an interesting Platonic speculation, but as an account of what actually was happening all the time. In our own days our minds have been turned to think about the Jesus of history. This has been the main characteristic of twentieth-century teaching from the pulpit. There is much, no doubt, that is good in all truer thought about the greatest Figure in the history of the world. So far as the contact of men with a real historic character was a reaction from a religion of abstractions and dogmas, we cannot but be thankful for the truer picture of Jesus that modern scholars have given to us. But how limited when the history of Jesus finishes with the tragedy of the Cross a teaching about Jesus is! The conception which people have of Jesus is often sub-Christian, for the Jesus of history is a much less figure than the Christ of the creeds and of experience, who includes the Jesus of history, since the whole is greater than its part. The Saviour of Mankind is not merely the lovable Galilean, but the Son of God who has risen again from the dead and ascended into heaven and who is always with His Church; in whose hands are the keys of life and death. He is Alpha and Omega, the Beginning and the End. That is the Christ who made Christianity and who can sustain it. And there is no other name but His whereby men can be saved. Nothing is so needed either in the Church or the world today as the realization of this powerful, living Christ, who is powerful and living because he bears in His hands and feet and side the scars of death.

A man writing as I am, in his seventy-seventh year, brought up in an Evangelical household, cannot but realize the immense change that an altered Christian teaching has made to our approach to the Atonement and the Atoning Lord. As I look back on a childhood nearly seventy years ago, the difference of the modern Methodist approach from that of my early days is amazing. I suppose most people brought up as I was have memories of children's hymns that they learned, possibly at their mother's knee, and yet, though some of these hymns remain an abiding impression, there is one hymn which I was never taught, but often heard sung, which has impressed itself upon my memory as very few others ever did, and it sums up all that I have written. Moreover, it expresses more perfectly than any of the Eucharistic hymns what all of them together teach. It was published in 1742, and I feel its significance so great that I have added it to the Sacramental Hymns published at the end of this book.[25] It may seem strange that any child should have been impressed by such a hymn. No one would think of teaching it to a child today. It is rarely sung in our public services now, whereas in my childhood it was repeatedly sung. As I have in my Fernley-Hartley lecture given a careful exposition of it, which I shall not repeat here, I will write down the central verse which has been in my mind all my life:

> Five bleeding wounds He bears,
> Received on Calvary;
> They pour effectual prayers,
> They strongly speak for me:
> Forgive him, O forgive! they cry,
> Nor let that ransomed sinner die.

That is the picture of the Lamb of God whose wounds perpetually plead with the Father for sinful men.

> Before the throne

so it runs:

> my Surety stands;
> My name is written on His hands.

What did it mean, I used to ask myself as a child? How could everybody's names be written on one pair of hands? Were they tattooed, I asked myself? A child's problems are obvious enough. But the picture of this interceding Saviour in heaven has remained with me all through my days, and I am profoundly thankful for it. For I remember with what confidence in my childhood, when (like many children I had an acute sense of sin) I used to sing:

> My God is reconciled,
> His pardoning voice, I hear;
>
> . . .
>
> I can no longer fear;
> With confidence I now draw nigh,
> And Father, Abba, Father! cry.

No one would wish, I believe, to teach their children this or any other hymn if they could not teach it sincerely, but how

[25] See p. 173, *infra*.

much the child loses; the 'green hill' is often too far away. The modern approach to Jesus exclusively through the Gospel narrative undoubtedly has its great values, but for the future nothing matters so much as that the children should realize that

> There was no other good enough
> To pay the price of sin;
> He only could unlock the gate
> Of heaven, and let us in.[26]

Well, this, then, is the scene in heaven: the Lamb of God whose death 'is ever new', and whose sacrifice is a fundamental truth of all Evangelical religion. To think of this sacrifice and to celebrate it is not a Roman error, but the central reality of the Protestant Reformation. The thing that matters to us all most is the sacrifice, a sufficient sacrifice and oblation for the sins of the whole world. There is far greater danger to modern Protestantism in the rationalism that forgets the death of Christ than in the Roman abuses that some people foolishly fear when Eucharistic devotion is emphasized. It might be well for some who criticize Eucharistic worship to ask themselves how far their criticism is due to their dislike of or disbelief in the fact of Christ's Atoning Sacrifice which is fundamental to deep sacramental worship and without which the Wesley's devotion is unintelligible.

'Behold the Lamb of God which taketh away the sin of the world.'

II

But now we leave the heavenly scene and direct our attention to its re-presentation on earthly altars. As Brevint, speaking of the earthly worship, says that the Holy Communion '*to God is an Altar*, whereon Men mystically present to him, the same Sacrifice, as still bleeding and sueing for Mercy';[27] which means, of course, that they present the heavenly sacrifice, and by the offering of the bread and wine, typify the Lamb of God which taketh away the sin of the world. The correspondence and distinction of the two offerings are clearly set forth in Wesley's hymns. While the earthly offering is symbolical, 'a

[26] *M.H.B.*, No. 180.   [27] Sect. VI, par. 2 (p. 187, *infra*).

*kind* of offering', it must not be forgotten that in the hymns of the earlier sections of the book we have seen that the Elements are regarded as instruments of grace, and so they must be regarded when they are thought of as offerings.

Two quotations from the hymns are specially descriptive of what I mean. One makes a reference to Christ as the heavenly Aaron in a figure which will be interpreted later, on whose breast-plate the Father reads our names:

> All our Names the Father knows,
>   Reads them on our *Aaron's* breast.
>
> He reads, while we beneath
> Present our Saviour's Death,
>   Do as Jesus bids us do,
> Signify his Flesh and Blood,
> Him in a Memorial shew,
>   Offer up the Lamb to God.[28]

Another hymn[29] confirms the claim of these verses, but more vividly contrasts the heavenly and earthly sacrifices and shows the difference between the sacrifice in heaven and the earthly 'Image of his Sacrifice':[30]

> Angels and Men might strive in vain,
> They could not add the smallest Grain
>   T'augment thy Death's Atoning Power,
> The Sacrifice is all-compleat,
> The Death Thou never canst repeat,
>   Once offer'd up to die no more.
>
> Yet may we celebrate below,
> And daily thus thine Offering shew
>   Expos'd before thy Father's Eyes;
> In this tremendous Mystery
> Present Thee bleeding on the Tree
>   Our everlasting Sacrifice.[31]

Our oblation however means much more as is shown by the words:

> To us Thou hast Redemption sent;
> And we again to Thee present
>   The Blood that speaks our Sins forgiven,
> That sprinkles all the Nations round;
> And now Thou hear'st the solemn Sound
>   Loud-echoing thro' the Courts of Heaven.[32]

[28] No. 118.   [29] No. 124.   [30] No. 118.   [31] No. 124.   [32] No. 121.

The silent offering on the earthly altars appeals to the heavenly Father to

> Turn from me Thy glorious eyes
> To that Bloody Sacrifice.
>
> .      .      .
>
> To the tokens of His death
> Here exhibited beneath.[33]

In an earlier hymn[34] we read: 'The Holy to the Holiest leads'—a thought which is developed in the verses:

> To Thee his Passion we present,
>   Who for our Ransom dyes,
> We reach by this great Instrument
>   Th'eternal Sacrifice.
>
> The Lamb as crucified afresh
>   Is here held out to Men,
> The Tokens of his Blood and Flesh
>   Are on this Table seen.
>
> The Lamb his Father now surveys,
>   As on this Altar slain,
> Still bleeding and imploring Grace
>   For every Soul of Man.[35]

A number of other illustrations of the correspondence between the heavenly and earthly altars could be quoted from the next section, which deals with the actual sacrifice of ourselves which that section expounds. But one more verse may be quoted from a hymn[36] not placed in our current *Hymn-book* amongst Sacramental hymns, but indicated by an asterisk as suitable for Holy Communion. Its true significance is only seen in its original context:

> With solemn Faith we offer up,
>   And spread before thy glorious Eyes
> That only Ground of all our Hope,
>   That precious, bleeding Sacrifice,
> Which brings thy Grace on Sinners down,
> And perfects all our Souls in One.

[33] No. 119.   [34] No. 96.   [35] No. 126.
[36] No. 125 (*M.H.B.*, No. 723).

And perhaps more than anything else this sense of correspondence is emphasized by the words:

> We need not now go up to Heaven
> To bring the long-sought Saviour down,
> Thou art to All already given:
> Thou dost ev'n Now thy Banquet crown.[37]

It is quite clear that these hymns, if they are taken out of their context, are tolerant of a Roman interpretation. But such an interpretation is really not reasonable when the symbolic character of the figures in them is kept in mind. It must never be forgotten that the symbols in Holy Communion are operative symbols: the sign itself, in some sense communicating the end that is signified. The real meaning of this symbolism is, that just as the Priest-Victim pleads the cause of the sinful man for whom He died in heaven, so on earth by means of the bread and wine, the tokens of His love, we plead the death of Christ. In a word, we do no more than say, by means of sacramental tokens:

> Nothing in my hand I bring,
> Simply to Thy Cross I cling.[38]

If, it may be argued, the earthly sacrifice means no more than that, what is the necessity for this elaborate symbolism? Is it not what every penitent sinner does, altogether apart from sacramental worship? To this the Wesleys' answer would undoubtedly have been and indeed was: 'Do as Jesus bids us do.'[39]

The distinction between a priest's offering of an expiatory or propitiatory sacrifice and the Eucharistic Oblation taught by Brevint and the Wesleys is made abundantly clear by the verses quoted above. The sacrifice on which God is asked to look is not our own but the one oblation for the sins of the whole world—His beloved Son's. Our sacrifices are only significant as they plead His. Wesley's hymns at the same time affirm the necessity of Eucharistic sacrifice though they firmly negate propitiatory sacrifices by any earthly priest.

But there is also a ground for such offerings which is quite apparent when the character of Eucharistic worship is examined. Such worship is always corporate, and however much individuals may make their individual plea, when they are

[37] No. 116.   [38] *M.H.B.*, No. 498.   [39] No. 118.

gathered together collectively they need some symbol to express not only their individual aspirations, but the total unified need of the whole Church. This is met by Our Lord's institution. The earthly symbol is the expression of the heavenly sacrifice. The broken bread and the poured-out wine, the tokens of the passion of Christ, plead that passion. When Brevint calls it a *kind* of sacrifice, he does not mean that it is no sacrifice, but that it is a sacrifice of a different kind from that of Calvary, but of similar meaning, and the whole content of it is what happens in heaven and is symbolized on earth. There is nothing so important for Christians as the centrality of the Cross. The Cross is central to all Eucharistic worship which is meaningless apart from its centrality. Even in the darkest ages, when the ceremonies were so elaborate as almost to obscure the meaning which they were intended to illustrate, it was quite impossible, and always has been impossible, to hide the fundamental facts of Christ's incarnation and atonement; and however twisted and obscured the celebration of Holy Communion was in the Middle Ages, it was impossible for any intelligent person to think of that broken bread and that poured-out wine without remembering Calvary. And even today, when in many Protestant Churches the Atonement is a subject of which nothing is ever heard, and the pulpit is often confined at its best to the preaching of Christian ethics, there never can be a Communion Service, whether simple or elaborate, which does not show forth the death of our Lord till He come. So long as a single Eucharist remains, the fundamental truth of the Gospel is declared. There are those who see in the hymns of Wesley, and the practice that they indicate, a needless repetition of what once was done. But they forget that what is emphasized is the eternal sacrifice of Christ 'ever new' and that the hope of the world hangs upon it. Calvary is not and cannot be repeated, but the pleading of His Sacrifice in Heaven, as recorded in the Epistle to the Hebrews, is re-presented on earth by means of the tokens, broken bread and wine poured out, which were ordained by Christ Himself.

I remember some years ago reading an article in *The Expositor* by the late Dr. P. T. Forsyth which had an abiding influence upon my thought. It is a long time since I read it, and my memory of it may not be accurate, but the figure that remains in my mind which he used was that of an oratorio: the Cross of Calvary was compared to the score of the oratorio and its first great performance. The Last Supper was regarded as a rehearsal, and every celebration of Holy Communion since was, according to that great Nonconformist divine, 'a performance', or, to use another term of his, a 'functioning' of the Cross. I would use slightly different terms in developing this beautiful and original analogy. The Lord's Supper seems to me to be more of an anticipation than a rehearsal of Calvary. What it was in the mind of Christ one can hardly say, but to the Disciples the words of Jesus must have been a puzzle, as He probably deliberately intended them to be, to give them matter for future thinking. When afterwards they took bread and blessed it, as Jews always did at their feasts—they could not but remember how solemnly Jesus had told them when they were doing what He did, particularly to remember Him. Then there came the crucifixion, the completion of the great atoning work of the Lord: as they experienced it, an inexplicable tragedy. But the days went on, and they realized that the very sufferings of Christ were a crown of glory and honour and were able to glory in that very Cross and death that had so shocked and hurt them. The words of Jesus at the Last Supper must have come continually to their minds. They were so significant, and their significance was so deep that the disciples naturally built up a special devotion in which the broken bread and the poured-out wine were the central features. Their Eucharistic liturgies formed themselves into a well-shaped service, and every time they called to mind the words of Jesus as they broke the bread and poured out the wine, they showed forth His death. And so it really happens time after time, as in all ages and in all places people call to memory by these tokens of His love His death for the sins of the world on Calvary, that each Eucharist in some sense is an actual performance of the eternal music of the Cross. And so by the formulation of Eucharistic worship they obeyed their Lord, as Charles Wesley sang:

And keep His kindest word[40]

—'did what Jesus bade them do', and thus reproduced, so far as they could, the music of Calvary, gave to their followers this

[40] No. 13; cf. No. 81.

example, even before the Scriptures had been collected, and thus, by corporate symbol, declared to each other and to the whole world the redeeming meaning of the Cross. It is encouraging and inspiring to realize today how, through the centuries, the same central truth has been told and how, not only with the little congregations that meet together at the Lord's Supper, but with the whole Church, with angels and archangels, and all the hosts of Heaven, we sing:

> Holy, Holy, Holy, Lord God of Hosts,
> Heaven and earth are full of Thy glory:
> Glory be to Thee, O Lord most High.

> O Lamb of God, that takest away the
> sins of the world, receive our prayer.

CHAPTER VII

# SACRIFICE OF THE CHURCH

I

WHILE THE sacrifice of Calvary can never be repeated, Brevint affirms that the Eucharist is 'a *kind* of sacrifice', a commemorative offering which mediates the benefits of the one true sacrifice of our Saviour; but, in addition, there is a real Eucharistic Sacrifice which we can offer, that of ourselves, our souls and bodies and goods, which, while 'needless and indeed superfluous to procure salvation, is necessary to our receiving it'. Unfortunately his excellent exposition of this theme is too long to quote in full. He argues (I condense in general terms) that the sacrifice we offer of ourselves, though subordinate to that of the Lamb of God, is supplementary to it—'cast on the main sacrifice', just as meal and drink-offerings were in the Old Dispensation: so our sacrifice is identified with Our Lord's in such a way that both are one sacrifice. This common oblation of our sacrifice and Our Lord's is founded on His identification of us with Himself. 'Christ never designed to offer himself for his People without his People'[1]—'Jesus Christ does nothing without his Church; insomuch that sometimes they are represented as only One Person.'[2] He is the Head of the body—His Church:

> As *Aaron* never came in before the Lord, without the whole People of *Israel*, represented both by the 12 Stones on his Breast, and by the two others on his Shoulders: so Jesus Christ does nothing without his Church; insomuch that sometimes they are represented as only One Person; Seeing Christ acts and suffers for his Body, in that Manner which becomes the Head, and the Church follows all the Motions and Sufferings of her Head, in such a Manner as is possible to its weak Members.[3]

The Church must therefore conform herself, as St. Paul teaches, to her Lord—she must be crucified with Christ. The offering

---
[1] Sect. VII, par. 6 (p. 189, *infra*).    [2] ibid., par. 2 (p. 188, *infra*).
[3] ibid.

of ourselves is a real offering, made one with Christ's, so as to be our common oblation with His.

As all the details and figures of Brevint are to be found in Wesley's hymns, it is less necessary to enumerate them here, but the hymns, notwithstanding, are no mechanical paraphrase of Brevint. The stress is in some ways different. The main purpose of Brevint is to show that the sacrifice of Christ and His Church are pre-figured in Hebrew ceremony and ritual and how they fulfil them. This is a subordinate feature of Wesley's teaching, whose main central theme is the sacrifice of Christ Himself. Nothing is so stressed, sometimes even with an iteration which mars the verses as poetry, as the blood of Christ—once,[4] at least, treated unfortunately with the Mithraic accentuation criticized in our previous chapter.[5] The hymns of the earlier part of this section (V), though of great theological value, are rather second-rate poetry; those of the latter part, which deal with individual consecration, which is relatively slightly treated by Brevint, rise to the sublimest heights of which Wesley was capable. They include what is perhaps the greatest hymn of personal consecration in our language.[6]

The order in which the hymns are set out rightly follows Brevint, but the different accent and the perpetual emphasis of the blood of Christ make them difficult to treat consecutively. The ideas in each hymn, while more or less described by the first line or couplet, are often more fully interpreted by ideas to be found in other hymns, but the main thoughts are in themselves striking and plain. The verses, generally considered in the earlier portion of the section, are rather to be called sacred poems than hymns, for though valuable as theology and devotion, they are little good for singing. I shall treat them with little regard to their numerical sequence, in the hope of giving some consecutive interpretation to their content, and shall often have to refer to single verses and lines rather than to whole poems. The later hymns of the section, genuine hymns of consecration, speak for themselves. Hence I will set down in propositional form several main principles to be deduced from these verses and illustrate them, making reference to Brevint only when Old Testament allusions (sometimes rather obscure) make this necessary.

[4] Hymn No. 122.   [5] p. 109, *supra*.   [6] No. 155.

1. *The dominant fact of all Eucharistic Sacrifice is the sacrifice of Christ once made, and all-sufficient for salvation.*

Wesley, like Brevint, emphasized the centrality of the one sacrifice once offered up, sufficient in itself for the salvation of the world. Its glory and power is decreased by no other sacrifice, though when our oblations are added to it, in a sense it is increased. The first hymn of this section strongly emphasizes this centrality. The thought is implicit in others, but in some quite explicit. Wesley's emphatic statement cannot be over-valued:

> All hail, Thou mighty to atone!
> To expiate Sin is thine alone,
>     Thou hast alone the Wine-press trod,
> Thou only hast for Sinners died,
> By one Oblation satisfied
>     Th' Inexorably righteous God:
>
> Should the whole Church in Flames arise,
> Offer'd as one burnt-Sacrifice
>     The Sinner's smallest Debt to pay,
> They could not, Lord, thine Honour share,
> With Thee the Father's Justice bear,
>     Or bear one single Sin away.[7]

2. *The identification of the Saviour and His Church.*

(a) Our Great High Priest's identification of His people with Himself.

(b) The identification by His people on earth with their Lord.

(c) The collectivity of the Church.

(a) At the base of our sacrifice of ourselves, and of any utility in it, is our identification with Christ, our conformity to Him. This is a point very emphatically made by Brevint in relation to our Saviour's High-Priestly work in heaven, 'Jesus Christ does nothing without His Church', which is one body with him. Several of Wesley's hymns teach the truth of this identity of Christ with His people. Two of them utilize Brevint's analogy of Aaron. Hymns in which Aaron's ephod and breast-plate are mentioned are unlikely to be sung today by people to

[7] No. 128.

whom the meaning of the word 'ephod' is only an antiquarian conundrum. The Old Testament use of it is not easy to determine, as it has different meanings in different places: sometimes it is an idol, sometimes a garment. But its early and basal meaning seems plain enough: it was a garment, a sort of vest, on which was fixed the breast-plate with its twelve stones representing the twelve tribes of Israel, probably with two shoulder straps which bore other hieratic gems. Thus, when Aaron went to the altar as priest, he was said to have brought Israel with him. So of Christ in Section IV of the sacrificial hymns we read:

> By thy Divine Oblation rais'd,
> And on our *Aaron's* Ephod plac'd
> We now with Thee in Heaven appear.[8]

and in Section V:

> See where our great High-Priest
> Before the Lord appears,
> And on his loving Breast
> The Tribes of *Israel* bears,
> Never without his People seen,
> The Head of all believing Men![9]

This hymn, theologically, is very important, because it describes with great felicity the corporate character of the Church, of which later we give further illustrations by showing that what makes it corporate—that is, a body—is its head, apart from which it would only be a corpse. It is so important that I shall quote the two other verses:

> With Him the Corner Stone
> The living Stones conjoin,
> Christ and His Church are One,
> One Body and one Vine,
> For us He uses all his Powers,
> And all He has, or is, is Ours.

> The Motions of our Head
> The Members all pursue,
> By his good Spirit led,
> To act, and suffer too
> Whate'er he did on Earth sustain,
> 'Till glorious all like Him we reign.

[8] No. 117.   [9] No. 129.

The third verse utilizes an expression of Brevint's 'the Motions of the Head';[10] and the second explains his reference to the body and further illustrates it by the Vine and the living Temple. Wesley brings out with great force and beauty the oneness of Christ with His people—always a living oneness; when, for instance, stones in a temple are described as *living* stones.

So we see how Christ Himself acknowledges identity with His people, a fact which is beautifully illustrated in the Epistle to the Hebrews, Chapters 2, 4, and 10: He is made like his brethren; He never forgets them; even when He is invisible behind the veil, He is touched with the feeling of their infirmities; He is in communication with them, when He stands in the presence of God, where, as their Intercessor and Forerunner, He is always one with them. The figures of St. Paul's Epistles and the Gospel of St. John make it clear that the unity is organic, living, the oneness of Head and Body, of Vine and Branches.

(*b*) But what is of great importance to notice is that this identification of His own with Christ is one which calls for recognition and action on earth. The Branch can be cut off from the Vine. How is union to be achieved from the earthly side? Wesley argues that it arises from an elevated human wish to share in the sufferings of so great a Saviour. To know the fellowship of His suffering is to make oneself a real companion of the Crucified. The Disciples lost a great opportunity at Calvary, but we must make that opportunity ours:

> O what a Time for offering up
>    Their Souls upon thy Sacrifice!
> Who would not with thy Burthen stoop
> And bow the Head when Jesus dies![11]

> Shall we let our God groan
>    And suffer alone,
>    Or to *Calvary* fly,
> And nobly resolve with our Master to die![12]

> Jesu, did they crucify
>    Thee by highest Heaven ador'd?
> Let us also go and die
>    With our dearest dying Lord![13]

[10] Sect. VII, par. 2 (p. 188, *infra*).    [11] No. 141.
[12] No. 142.    [13] No. 154.

> Would the Saviour of Mankind
>   Without his People die?
> No, to Him we all are join'd
>   As more than Standers by.[14]

So on earth, as in heaven, not merely through Christ's identification of us with Himself, but as the result of our love for Him, we will be sharers with our dying God and crucified below.

(c) The union of Christ with us indicates the oneness of the whole Church of Christ. We are not a mere collection of individuals, but a collective body; one temple, one body, one vine. The fellowship of the Christian community finds many illustrations in Wesley's hymns. It is a commonplace of the love and devotion of the early Methodists and its stress in these sacramental hymns is not unique. A very characteristic description of the collectivity of the Church in what is really the final hymn of the book is reminiscent of such familiar hymns as 'All praise to our Redeeming Lord'.[15] The hymn reads:

> How happy are thy Servants, Lord,
>   Who thus remember Thee!
> What Tongue can tell our sweet Accord,
>   Our perfect Harmony!
>
> Who thy Mysterious Supper share,
>   Here at thy Table fed,
> Many, and yet but One we are,
>   One undivided Bread.
>
> One with the Living Bread Divine,
>   Which now by Faith we eat,
> Our Hearts, and Minds, and Spirits join,
>   And all in Jesus meet.[16]

Now it is on account of the unity of the body of Christ with the Head, and thus of its members, that Brevint bases the claim that the offering made is a common oblation of the Lord and His people. The one offering is the conjoined offering of two; ours added to Christ's, as a supplementary sacrifice. The point in Brevint is that the supplementary offerings of the Old Testament—meal and drink offerings—are cast upon the primary sacrifice of the lamb, thus typifying the sacrifice of Christ and consumed in a common fire. This illustration is not without limitations to be considered later, but here the implication to

---

[14] No. 131.   [15] *M.H.B.*, No. 745.   [16] No. 165.

be emphasized is, our oblation is that of ourselves rather than of any other thing that we may give; and is joined to that of Christ Himself. For all oblations there must be priests. An earthly Priest-Victim is suggested, by the heavenly Priest-Victim. If we offer ourselves, we are both priest and victim, so Wesley sings:

> Ye Royal Priests of Jesus, rise,
> And join the Daily Sacrifice,
> Join all Believers in His Name
> To offer up the Spotless Lamb.
>
> . . . .
>
> Whate'er we cast on Him alone
> Is with His great Oblation one,
> His Sacrifice doth Ours sustain,
> And Favour and Acceptance gain.
>
> On Him, who all our Burthens bears,
> We cast our Praises and our Prayers,
> Ourselves we offer up to God,
> Implung'd in His atoning Blood.[17]

Now, while the main emphasis of this hymn lies on offerings of prayers and praise, which are relatively mean offerings, yet the words,

> Ourselves we offer up to God,[18]

stress the main thought of Brevint of an oblation of our persons, cast on the sacrifice of Christ, which makes them one with His —'The altar sanctifies the gift'[19]—and which brings out the primary meaning of a familiar hymn often sung, which today is separated from the Eucharistic hymns, and generalized by its current use. Addressing God the Father, we sing:

> Up to Thee our Souls we raise,
> Up to Thee our Bodies yield.
>
> Thou our Sacrifice receive,
> Acceptable thro' thy Son,
> While to Thee alone we live,
> While we die to Thee alone.[20]

---

[17] No. 137.  
[18] ibid.  
[19] Sect. VII, par. 9 (p. 190, *infra*).  
[20] No. 139 (*M.H.B.*, No. 566).

## II

I cannot find in Wesley and Brevint a definite expression of their main thought that the gift to God as a sacrifice supplementary to that of Christ is an offering of the Body of Christ, since the Church herself is that Body. This teaching, implicit in the writing both of Brevint and Wesley, should be made explicit in ours. Let us therefore express plainly, deferring the ethical problem which it raises for later consideration, what is the logical inference (to be drawn from the metaphors of Brevint and Wesley) which demonstrates the superlative importance of the Eucharistic Sacrifice. The inference is nothing less than that the Church collectively offering herself to God in the Eucharist is actually offering to God the Body of Christ—for the Church is His Body.

If the Church of Christ be the Body of Christ, it is obvious that when she offers herself to God it is the Body of Christ which is being offered. The Church is a community of 'royal priests'—a priestly nation—the Body which Christ uses here and now and has always used on earth as the instrument of His sacrificial work, not by repetition of the historical sacrifice of Calvary which was sufficient for the sins of the whole world but by a re-presentation of it. In some sense the Body of Christ composed of His own people, and identified with Him, continues the work on earth of the Priest-Victim which is perpetually going on in Heaven. We are to be crucified with Christ. The sacrifice of Christ, as Brevint teaches and Wesley sings, is 'ever new'. By means of the witness of His people it is proclaimed as the world's one hope. We are His earthly human body and not only symbolically by the Eucharistic offering, but *really* by daily sacrifice the oblation of the Church in the daily life of the world continually to be offered.

The Church can only make her sacrifice availing when, identified with Christ's, her sacrifice is His. It is one sacrifice with His because it is based on His, added to it and united with it. The Church can do nothing apart from Christ and out of union with Him. In reality, apart from Christ she would only be a decapitated corpse, not a body. When not only in ideal but in practice she is one with Christ, she shares alike His suffering and His glory. Such a realization and implementation of the oneness of the Church with Christ would be indeed a manifestation of the sons of God for which the whole creation waits.

This Eucharistic sacrifice which the Church offers is twofold: first, symbolical—by the tokens of the Passion which she offers, she pictures and makes the heavenly sacrifice the same plea on earth that the Lamb of God who takes away the sins of the world, as Priest-Victim, makes in heaven; secondly—when she offers herself by complete consecration to the will of God, she offers the Body of Christ because she herself is the Body of Christ. The symbolic offering is the outward sacrifice of the altar—the bread and wine, which are operative tokens of the Body of Christ; but the real offering is that of the actual human beings who compose the Church, the true Body of Christ. While this seems to be a legitimate inference from Brevint and Wesley—indeed a necessary inference when all the facts are taken into account—I ask whether sufficient significance has yet been given by scholars to the equation, so obvious in the First Epistle to the Corinthians,[21] of the bread and the Church, both called the Body of Christ. Jesus says of the bread: 'This is my body', but Paul also says that the Church is Christ's body. What distinction is there between the two bodies, one of which is sometimes called mystical, and the other sacramental? Would not the difficult metaphysical questions which have been so often canvassed to the hurt of Christ's 'little ones' be shelved if we realized that what is true of one body is true of the other? So that if one body be transubstantiated, then the other body is transubstantiated. And if one is not transubstantiated, then the other is not transubstantiated.

We are His body, hence our sacrifice of ourselves is a sacrifice of His body. He was crucified as an individual 1,900 years ago on Calvary, and today lives to plead our cause in heaven. But we are His human, earthly body, branches of the Vine, members of the Body of which He is the Head, combined together as an army to carry on His work in the world. Can we fail to be filled with amazement and fear and with penitent awe when we realize what it means to be crucified with Him, to know the fellowship of His sufferings, to fill up what is lacking of them? Dare we employ such words? Perhaps more depends on whether we will for the world's sake than we know, and our

[21] Chapter 11.

comfort is that He prayed not for the world but for those God had given Him out of the world, that they might be one and holy. But shall He ever see of the travail of His soul and be satisfied?

Stress must be laid on the twofold offering of the Church because the Body of Christ offered is not merely a sacred symbol but the living sacrifice of men and women. The sacrifice on the altar is stripped of its moral meaning apart from its spiritual counterpart. This was clear enough in the 'Offertory' of the early Church—behind the consecrated elements stood the consecrated men and women. As Wesley puts it:

> Saviour, to Thee our Lives we give,
> Our meanest sacrifice receive,
> And to thy own Oblation join.[22]

The loss of the 'Offertory' in the ancient sense of the term is perhaps the chief defect of Western modern Eucharistic devotion. A new emphasis, if not a new symbol or at least the renewal of the old one, is required. I discuss this more fully in the next chapter.[23] A realization of the twofold nature of the Oblation gives a quality of reality difficult to conceive when the elements are separated in thought from the oblation of the people. As Wesley writes:

> To us Thou hast Redemption sent;
> And we again to Thee present
> The Blood that speaks our Sins forgiven.
>
> .   .   .   .   .
>
> The Cross on *Calvary* He bore,
> He suffer'd once to die no more,
>   But left a Sacred Pledge behind:
> See here!—It on thy Altar lies,
> Memorial of the Sacrifice
> He offer'd once for All Mankind.[24]

With the symbolical Bread and Wine our offering is conjoined, laid on His, accepted by Him to be one with His. Our new offering is identified with a sacrifice which is 'ever new'. The offering on the Altar is not only an historical memorial of what once happened but a counterpart of what is eternally taking place in Heaven; with which our oblation of ourselves is identified.

[22] No. 128.   [23] See p. 156, *infra*.   [24] No. 121.

III

While the twofold character of Eucharistic oblation properly observed will save the Eucharist from superstitions to which historically it has been too prone, it also creates an ethical problem which must be faced and is well stated in Wesley's question:

How can the two Oblations join?[25]

How can there be any true union between our sinless Lord and our sinful selves?

> Thy sacrifice with heavenly Powers
> Replete, All-holy, All-divine,
> Human and weak, and sinful Ours;
> How can the two Oblations join?[26]

Again

> O Thou holy Lamb Divine
> How canst Thou and Sinners join?[27]

> Still all-involv'd with God we are
> And offer'd with the Lamb.[28]

> Thy offering doth to Ours impart
> Its Righteousness and Saving Grace,
>
> . . . . .
>
> Our mean imperfect Sacrifice
> On Thine is as a Burthen thrown,
> Both in a Common Flame arise,
> And both in God's Account are One.[29]

Now there is a sense in which Eucharistic action necessarily is ideal rather than practical, though with enormously practical results, and nothing is more solemn and spiritually real than the Eucharistic offering: the realization and re-presentation of the eternal sacrifice solemnly pleaded by sinful men who are themselves, when genuinely consecrated, the Body of Christ; the resolution to carry on in themselves continually a sacrificial oblation of their own lives so that they may be our Lord's human Body, the Church, through which He still works amongst men. But such corporate Church action involves saintliness of character and men with horror discover they fail to achieve their ideal because the Church is composed of

[25] No. 147.   [26] ibid.   [27] No. 136.   [28] No. 134.   [29] No. 147.

K

sinners only. Yet we must not forget that Paul called the very unsatisfactory Christians of Corinth saints. The exhortations of Romans 6 are made to people to live decently, whom St. Paul says have already been justified by faith! Ethical instructions and exhortations are given to the very people who are described in the Epistle to the Ephesians as sitting in heavenly places, yet it can hardly be denied that the joining of sinful people to the holy Christ must necessarily hamper and hinder the work of our Lord rather than further it. That is the ethical problem expressed in the words we have already quoted:

> How can the two Oblations join?

This problem was evidently very present to Brevint's mind. He declares the whole divinity of St. Paul turns upon the conformity both of action and sufferings, and shows that this is the meaning of Jesus when He says: 'Follow me.' So we are obliged to conform, to follow Him 'as much as in (us) lies'. While it is perhaps implied in the rest of the section, he does not in this context emphasize the fact of our natural inability to follow Christ far. It must not be forgotten that the desperate struggles of Luther and the Wesleys to conform to Christ which drove them to despair were the very experiences which cast them on Christ and His sacrifice. We never can, as sinful men, make ourselves fit to be united with Christ in a common oblation.

Returning, however, to the Eucharistic sacrifice, Brevint gets the right proportion. While it is necessary for Christians to be crucified with Christ, conformed to Him, 'Sinners indeed under the Law', he writes,

did not die at the Altar, the Victim alone being burn'd and destroy'd. But because they laid their Hands on it when it was dying, and fell on their Faces to the Ground, when it fell bleeding to Death, they were reputed to *offer* up themselves as well as the Victim.[30]

So Isaac Watts sang:

> My faith would lay her hand
> On that meek head of Thine,
> While as a penitent I stand,
> And here confess my sin.[31]

[30] Sect. VII, par. 7 (p. 189, *infra*).   [31] *M.H.B.*, No. 234.

We are not crucified, says Brevint, in the same way as Christ. When men, in utter penitence and complete consecration, cast themselves on Christ, suffering in sympathy with the sacrificial expression of His dying love and resolving to give up their lives to God's service by sincere penitence and consecration to the will of God, their sacrifice is accepted before God as one and the same sacrifice with Christ. It is one because to do God's will is to share the life and death, to share the sacrifice of Him who says: 'Lord I come to do thy will.' Now this is illustrated by Wesley's hymns, which make the blood of the Lamb the dominating fact of all human devotion and the only means by which it can be effected. No union of a sinful man with the perfect Son of Man is possible by a man's own efforts, because at the end he remains sinful still. But he must strive to be what he can be—what by union with Christ in reality he is. Goethe's famous saying is particularly true of the Christian man: *Werde was du bist.*

Illustrations of Wesley's treatment of Brevint are to be found in a number of the hymns which should be carefully read.[32] Conformity with our Lord's sacrifice and emphasis of the underlying basic need of the sacrifice are related to the Eucharistic worship of the Church. Unfortunately in one hymn he stresses the metaphor of crucifixion beyond its meaning and talks of the offering of sins:

> Our sins are on Thine Altar laid.[33]

While a man may say in despair: 'What can I, a sinful man, offer: there is nothing but sin for me to give!'—he is talking rhetorically. The actual laying of our sins on the altar would be quite a foolish thing, for it is an insult to God to offer Him our sins. What does He want with them? All that He wants is that we should get rid of them. If they are to be offered to anyone, let them be offered to the devil to whom they belong. But, really, this personification of sin, or dealing with it as some ponderable thing, has behind it a conception which is without intelligible psychological meaning. What we can offer to God is our best, not our worst; worthless enough it may be, but it is all. Love says: All for all. And when we give what we have that is good, the altar sanctifies the gift, however trivial

---

[32] Nos. 131, 132, 133, 136, and 142.  [33] No. 135.

or polluted it is. But the altar cannot sanctify sin. What we have to offer is our persons, our affections, our goods, stained as they may be by sin, but capable, since we are created in God's image, of righteousness. Only His sacrifice can make ours effective. We remain sinners, but in Christ we have shelter from sin. The truth is, Brevint and these hymns show clearly the central Protestantism of true Eucharistic sacrifice, because they declare that there is no hope for man except in God's mercy, and that all our sacrifices are unavailing except through His. Our life in Christ can only be His life in us, which can only be ours by perfect trust in Him. The Moravian hymn in John Wesley's noble translation, little sung today, puts more forcibly than anything I know this central truth of the Reformation, which is the central truth of the Eucharistic Sacrifice:

> Jesus, thy blood and righteousness
> My beauty are, my glorious dress,
> Midst flaming worlds, in these arrayed,
> With joy shall I lift up my head.[34]

Or as Wesley puts it

> Thy Offering doth to Ours impart
> Its Righteousness and Saving Grace.[35]

There are sentences in one of Charles Wesley's hymns which come very near to the central truth not only in its Eucharistic significance, but its ethical application—the hymn:

> Come we that record
> The Death of our Lord,
> The Death let us bear,
> By Faithful Remembrance his Sacrifice share.
>
> . . . . .
>
> Poor Penitents we
> Expect not to see
> His Glory above,
> Till first we have drunk of the Cup of his Love:
>
> Till first we partake
> The Cross for His Sake,
> And thankfully own
> The Cup of his Love and his Sorrow are One.[36]

[34] M.H.B., No. 370. [35] No. 147. [36] No. 142.

What he says about the Cup, as he is thinking, I do not doubt, of the Chalice, is this: first we have drunk of the Cup of His love, and then we learn from bitter experience that 'the Cup of his Love and his Sorrow are One': now the Cup of the divine love is a cup of salvation. His 'blood and righteousness' are the salvation which makes it possible for us to share in His sufferings and His deeds. Was not Jesus thinking of it when He doubted the ability of John and James to drink the Cup, but told them that they should? It often proves a Cup of suffering. But it is more. The weakness of Charles Wesley's hymns in this section is his anxiety only to know the fellowship of Christ's sufferings, and so they end on a note of resignation, as if to suffer under the will of God was the one call God makes upon men. He seems too often to forget that doing the will is quite as important as suffering it. That cup of love which was given to him is a cup of challenge to action, not merely to passive submission and suffering, though that may be required. Charles Wesley really knew better, but I could have wished that he had concluded these poems with one of his stirring, martial hymns, with a verse where the very shield of faith turns into a flaming sword, although his coat of arms is 'a bleeding Lamb'; yet the verse is one of magnificent defiance of evil which the constraining love of Christ perpetually manifested in His heavenly sacrifice and celebrated by the Church on earthly altars should compel.

> What tho' a thousand hosts engage,
> A thousand worlds, my soul to shake?
> I have a shield shall quell their rage,
> And drive the alien armies back,
> Portray'd it bears a bleeding Lamb:
> I dare believe in Jesu's Name.[37]

## IV

### HYMNS OF PERSONAL CONSECRATION

The last dozen poems of this section are genuine devotional hymns, sometimes for the society collectively, and sometimes for single individuals. Several of them, though much more significant when used in their original contexts as Communion

[37] *M.H.B.*, 483.

hymns, have been generalized. Half of them are quite individual and personal in character, and were obviously intended for penitent persons to use in secret self-searching and consecration. While the character of most of the verses of this section is corporate, and intended for the use of a collective assembly, the very private character of such hymns as Nos. 143–6, and particularly No. 155, must be noted. Indeed, they might be collected and made, like other groups of hymns referred to earlier, into a manual of private devotion.

Complaint is often made that the Evangelical Revival was a selfish, individualistic kind of religion, altogether out of date in these days when social Christianity is so greatly stressed. The antithesis between social and personal Christianity, neither of which is really exclusive of the other, is nearly as absurd as that between Sacramentalism and Evangelism; both antitheses unfortunately mislead many people. The early Methodists were, from the beginning, a social fellowship in which nothing was more emphasized than the obligation of the individuals to each other, and to those who were outside. Indeed, it is easy to say that the social value of the Revival was really created by the individual consecration of the Methodist converts.

A collective devotion like the Eucharist, with its emphasis on the priesthood of all believers—that is to say, a devotion of the whole body of Christ as a totality—must not delude us with the notion that the model of the Church is a hive or a formicary, in which a mechanical co-operation is achieved by organization. While the Church as the body of Christ, implies the inter-relation of its members as members of Him and of each other, a careful reading of the first Epistle to the Corinthians, Chapters 12, 13, and 14, will show that the co-operative character of the Church was not created by governments and hierarchies, but by the Spirit of Christ, which is love. Hence it is that in the midst of his discourse about the Church, St. Paul introduced his great hymn of love, and his final advice to the Church is, if it is to keep unity and also to retain liberty for individuals, 'follow after love'. While the Church then, is a collective body, the individualism of its members is never denied but plainly asserted. This digression shows the necessity of individual as well as corporate devotion.

No finer hymns are to be found in the volume than those of personal devotion, which conclude its sacrificial sections. The collectivity of the Church depends for its value on the devotion of each unit of the corporation. The ultimate question in all matters of sacrifice and devotion is the personal question which a man has to ask himself about his own relations to Christ and His sacrifice. I question whether it is possible to find a finer instrument for personal examination than the great hymn, 'Father, Son, and Holy Ghost.'[38] Perhaps Frances Ridley Havergal's 'Take my life and let it be'[39] is more popular, but then it is obviously derived from Wesley's verse:

> Take my Soul and Body's Powers,
> Take my Mem'ry, Mind, and Will,
> All my Goods, and all my Hours,
> All I know, and all I feel,
> All I think, and speak, and do;
> Take my Heart—but make it new.[40]

V

Little needs to be written of the seven post-Communion hymns and the appended poem, except that they are of a character expressive of the wider content of the Eucharist. Two or three express thankfulness for the joy and uplifting experience of the devotion, but the others (Nos. 160–5) are a paraphrase or variants on liturgical statements, such as the *Preface* and the *Sanctus*. Hymn No. 162, for instance, is a glorious variation of both:

> Hosannah in the Highest
> To our exalted Saviour,
>   Who left behind
>   For all Mankind
> These Tokens of his Favour:
>
>     .   .   .
>
> Louder than gather'd Waters,
> Or bursting Peals of Thunder,
>   We lift our Voice
>   And speak our Joys,
> And shout our loving Wonder!
>
>     .   .   .

---

[38] No. 155 (*M.H.B.*, No. 574).   [39] *M.H.B.*, No. 400.   [40] No. 155.

> Angels in fixt Amazement
> Around our Altars hover,
> With eager Gaze
> Adore the Grace
> Of our eternal Lover.

Certain hymns in earlier sections were deferred for later consideration. Two of them—'Come all who truly bear'[41] and 'Let all who truly bear'[42] have been considered in another connexion.[43] One verse in Hymn No. 13, however, should be noted, because it defines exactly Wesley's views of the relation of the Methodist Society to the Church of England:

> Part of his Church below
> We thus our Right maintain,
> Our Living Membership we shew,
> And in the Fold remain;
> The Sheep of *Israel's* Fold,
> In *England's* Pastures fed,
> And Fellowship with All we hold
> Who hold it with our Head.

Hymn No. 30 is especially noteworthy. The mystical significance, both sacramental and sacrificial, is generally stated in this hymn, perhaps more completely than in any other:

> Obedient to thy gracious Word
> We break the Hallow'd Bread,
> Commemorate Thee, our Dying Lord,
> And trust on Thee to feed.

So we come to the Lord's Table, singing:

> Jesu, at whose Supreme Command
> We thus approach to God,

and pray for a realization of His presence:

> Before us in thy Vesture stand
> Thy Vesture dipt in Blood
> .    .    .
> Now, Saviour, now Thyself reveal.

And then we sing:

> The Tokens of thy Dying Love,
> O let us All receive,
> And feel the Quick'ning Spirit move,
> And *sensibly* believe.

---

[41] No. 13.  [42] No. 4.  [43] See pp. 43, 44, *supra*.

SACRIFICE OF THE CHURCH 143

> The Cup of Blessing blest by Thee,
>     Let it thy Blood impart;
> The Bread thy Mystic Body be,
>     And chear each languid Heart.
>
> The Grace which sure Salvation brings
>     Let us herewith receive;
> Satiate the Hungry with good Things,
>     The Hidden Manna give.
>
> The Living Bread sent down from Heaven
>     In us vouchsafe to be;
> Thy Flesh for All the World is given,
>     And All may live by Thee.

The final poem of the book was evidently added as an appendix. It expresses with great emphasis Charles Wesley's zeal for the Sacrament and the need of its restoration as a daily sacrifice. He challenges the Church with vehemence as to whether its coldness and indifference is not attributable to the neglect of the Table of Our Lord. Charles Wesley wrote the Sacramental Hymns, not in his days of quiet retirement, but in the heat of revival, in the midst of persecution, in the most exciting hours of his career. They are essentially revival hymns. They express the same spirit of enthusiasm and joy as such verses as:

> Happy, if with my latest breath
>     I might but gasp His name;
> Preach Him to all and cry in death:
>     Behold, behold the Lamb![44]

It was in those fervent days of the great Revival that he pondered most on the Sacrament and made the appeal of this extraordinary poem:

> Why is the faithful Seed decreas'd
>     The Life of God extinct and dead?
> The daily Sacrifice is ceas'd,
>     And Charity to Heaven is fled.
>
> Sad mutual Causes of Decay,
>     Slackness and Vice together move,
> Grown cold we cast the Means away,
>     And quench'd our latest Spark of Love.[45]

[44] *M.H.B.*, No. 92.    [45] No. 166.

And so the great Revivalist—not the criticized ritualist—says:

> O wouldst Thou to thy Church return!
>    For which the faithful Remnant sighs,
>    For which the drooping Nations mourn,
> Restore the daily Sacrifice.[46]

At this point it may be well to summarize the entire teaching of the book. The Lord's Supper, though primarily a memorial of the crucifixion of Jesus—of Christ crucified—is much more; by means of it the risen and ascended Christ is called to mind, the Victim-Priest in heaven, whose death is 'ever new' and always availing for sinful men. Though ascended to heaven, He is present in His Church, because the ascension does not localize Him. Heaven is just behind the Veil. The Elements, the tokens of His dying Love, are the organs which the ever-present Christ uses to feed and refresh His people. Not only is He really present at the Supper, but heaven comes with Him, and His people find in their joyful experience heaven on earth and taste of the fullness that is to be. Furthermore, the bread and wine are the offering on earth of the tokens of the eternal sacrifice in heaven and correspond with that sacrifice, echoing as it were below, the plea made to the Father by the Priest-Victim, the Lamb of God who is also the Shepherd of the Sheep, who ever liveth to make intercession for us.

But the symbolic offering of Christ is not the whole sacrifice of the Church, which is a real oblation of itself, that is, of the body of Christ, for His body are we. The sacrifice is corporate, made by the collective body of believers who are the priests of God, who altogether offer both symbolically and really the body of Christ to God. The collective body is not a machine of regulated parts, but a congregation of people, each with his own individuality, although in relation to the body, members of it, bound together not by organization and hierarchy, but by the spirit of love, which is the Spirit of Jesus.

One question remains: 'What light do the hymns throw on an outward sacrifice and outward priesthood?'

(1) Clearly, the outward sacrifice is the solemn oblation of the earthly tokens of the Passion of Christ, which re-present the

---

[46] No. 166.

Heavenly sacrifice, 'ever new': and echo on earthly altars the continual intercession of our great High Priest in Heaven.

(2) As to the individual outward priesthood, I can find in these hymns no information whatever. Charles Wesley, in a later hymn-book, described the 'ministry' of the Church of England as 'a sacred order', but not a verse or line in this book gives the slightest indication of his views on the office and character of individual priests. The words 'faithful line' in the eccentric Hymn No. 47 may have reference, I think, to the Aaronic priesthood, but the hymn, as my note shows,[47] in any case is not one from which deductions can be made about the Ministry.

It must not be forgotten, however, that it was *after* the publication of *Hymns on the Lord's Supper* that John Wesley asserted his and his brother's belief in the outward priesthood. They never repudiated this belief either in outward priesthood or outward sacrifice, though the hymns make it impossible to argue that they regarded their individual priesthood as in any way independent of the corporate priesthood of the Church— but the word 'outward' had some meaning: what was it? It may be confidently asserted that wherever in the hymns priestly oblation is assumed or expressed it is always the Church—the collective priesthood—'royal priests', which offers, not the individual. No hymn reads '*I* offer . . .', but all '*We* . . .'.

> . . . offer up,
> And spread before thy glorious Eyes
>
> .    .    .    .    .
>
> That precious, bleeding Sacrifice.[48]

This is important because the distinction made by means of singular and plural pronouns in Charles Wesley's hymns is an illuminating feature of them. The distinction is easy to trace between individual and corporate oblation in the Sacrificial hymns by attention to whether the pronouns are singular or plural. There is no exception to the rule that the pronouns are plural in all the hymns of Eucharistic oblation.

The Wesleys regarded the order of priesthood as different from that of an order of preachers. The preachers responded to a direct vocation from God, but the priests were selected by

---
[47] See pp. 209–10.   [48] No. 125.

the Church for the special priestly services which, while the functions of the whole Church, required particular persons as instruments of corporate worship. Such functions the Wesleys thought were committed to a solemnly separated order of men, but there is no tittle of evidence that they regarded their priestly acts as other than representative of the whole Church, always remembering that the Church was the community in which the *living* Christ dwelt and through which He worked.

I can find no evidence that the Wesleys regarded their priesthood as an office which qualified them to offer sacrifice for other people: they offered the sacrifice of the whole Church, or shall I say more precisely the Church offered her oblation through their instrumentality. They did not offer sacrifice, in any sense, for other men's salvation: there is not the slightest hint of propitiatory sacrifices.

I have little doubt, though the Wesleys do not explicitly define their opinion, that they accepted the Lutheran doctrine of the Priesthood of all believers, but they gave it applications which Luther did not and would not have given.[49] Their sacrifice was meant to be 'the image of the Heavenly Sacrifice' —and though a sacrifice of praise and thanksgiving, was more than that in Luther's sense of the term.

The difference between Wesley and his followers is not to be found (at least amongst those to whom sacrifice is a necessary feature of Holy Communion) in the content of the term 'priest' so much as in the method of making a priest. That the Wesleys believed in succession—Charles in episcopal and John in presbyteral—must, I think, be admitted. They do seem to have thought the office and grace to perform its duties were transmitted from one generation of priests to another, through the laying-on of hands, but even so the *Minutes of Conference* of 1747[50] must be remembered, in which Wesley affirms his view that the New Testament did not settle questions of Church order for all time, and that to claim that ministries in other Churches were invalid because of some irregularity from the Anglican point of view landed people into 'monstrous absurdities'.

Today most Methodists believe that the Church is under no restrictions whatever in the making of Ministers so long as she

[49] See pp. 153, 157, *infra*.    [50] See Addendum I, pp. 159ff., *infra*.

is really the body of the Living Christ—a view I personally share. What John Wesley, if separation had been forced upon him, would have done in England we do not know, but the general course of his action and some of his opinions might suggest that he would have done what his followers did. Most Methodists today are perhaps a little too sure that he would have imitated his disciples. I don't know—but do think it probable that he would have developed a presbyteral succession of the same pattern as that of the American Church.[51]

It is unwise to write too confidently on this topic, for the simple reason that the Wesleys gave no explicit definition of their beliefs, either as to content of the term 'outward priesthood' or as to the priesthood of all believers. The general inferences I have set down will, I think, prove inevadable to persons who consider carefully the claims of the Wesleys to outward priesthood, their refusal to allow unordained preachers to celebrate, together with the hymns which so plainly teach the corporate Sacrifice, symbolical and actual, of the Church.

[51] See pp. 159ff., *infra*.

CHAPTER VIII

# THE EUCHARIST AND MODERN METHODISM

THE DECLINE of Sacramentalism in modern Methodism seems very strange when the outstanding enthusiasm for the Lord's Supper in the eighteenth century is called to mind. How can the decline be explained? Without any attempt to give a detailed account, which would entail a wide survey and careful analysis from many points of view of the history of nineteenth-century Methodism, it is possible to set down a few facts which throw considerable light upon the subject.

The first fact is that Wesley, at his death, though he had framed a Constitution capable of preserving his Society, did not leave behind him satisfactory provision for the administration of Sacraments. On one question he remained adamant, he would not permit unordained men, however effective they were as preachers, to administer Sacraments. The Methodist people generally had received, and he hoped would receive, Sacraments in the parish churches. A very few ordained priests of the Church of England helped him to celebrate every Sunday when he was unable to do so himself in a few chapels in London, Bristol, etc. In some places, as for instance, Great Queen Street, London, clergymen were hired, perhaps in his lifetime and certainly after his death, for this purpose sometimes with most unedifying results. Only a very few preachers had received from Wesley's hands presbyteral ordination, but it was quite impossible that more than relatively few Methodists could communicate at their own chapels. Serious difficulties arose immediately after Wesley's death.

Certain Societies desired the Conference to permit their preachers to administer Sacraments, but the Trustees, who were often men of substance and influence, offered every opposition, and controversy developed which might have wrecked that Society. It was chiefly on the question of Sacraments that a Left Wing party split off and formed the Methodist New Connexion.

Discussions and delays and compromises took place at Conference, till in 1795 a scheme, called 'The Plan of Pacification', was adopted which gave qualified right, under certain circumstances, where there were strong local demands for administration, to the preachers to administer. The few ordinations which Wesley had given were made valueless, because the other unordained preachers demanded equality, and authorization was given to all preachers who had been received into full connexion under the above-named qualifications, to administer.

Many Methodists no doubt became increasingly detached from the Society because, like Wesley, they declined to leave the Established Church. When the preachers did administer there were many mixed feelings among the Societies as to their right to do so. Not only were there such defections as those mentioned, but in point of fact, the number of preachers was insufficient, as it always has been, to meet the needs of the Methodist people throughout the country on anything like the scale which the Wesleys advocated, and Communion became infrequent and hence suffered decline. If there had been no other reason than this, decline would have been inevitable, but other causes may be mentioned.

The fact of the gradual development of the Methodist Society into a separate denomination meant that the distinctive devotions of the Society were naturally greatly emphasized. Services such as class meetings, love feasts, and the like, in their heyday did much to meet the spiritual needs of the people which Holy Communion might normally have satisfied. Nor must it ever be forgotten that these distinctive Methodist devotions, when generally practised, were of a very helpful character, and did build up the spiritual life of the Society and its individual members.

Another fact was that what Wesley called the 'overgrown fear of Popery' was greatly quickened by the Oxford Movement and by the birth or rebirth of Anglo-Catholicism. The simple devotions of the Methodist, intelligible and helpful, were contrasted with the pomp and ceremonial of Anglican ritual, with the consequence that a suspicion of ceremonial developed, and everything of its nature, even the Eucharistic Liturgy, was regarded as lacking the simplicity of the Gospel. These obvious causes of the decline of Sacramentalism are several among many, but the subject is too wide and complex for a brief treatment. Yet, while the decline in Eucharistic worship is a regrettable fact, the contribution which Methodists have made to it should never be forgotten, nor what they can make. A distinct return to Sacramental worship is undoubtedly making progress in our own days. There have even been recent instances of corporate Communion of many hundreds of people as fervent as those of Wesley's days. For instance, in the concluding meetings in Huddersfield of the Order of Christian Witness, led by Dr. Donald Soper, 5,000 people communicated at six simultaneous celebrations.

*What then is their contribution?*

(*a*) Nothing can diminish the value of the Eucharistic witness of early Methodism. At a period when the Sacraments confessedly were generally, if not universally, neglected in the Church of England, the Methodists, through their happy Evangelical experience, observed them with the greatest fervour. No parallel can be found in Anglican history to the immense multitudes of Methodists which crowded the parish churches to celebrate Holy Communion. John Wesley made a declining devotion popular, revivified it with a cleansing stream of Evangelical life. He continually practised and counselled sacramental worship. His advocacy in association with that of his brother Charles, and their fellow Anglican priests, are facts of immeasurable importance, not only in the history of Methodism, but in that of the Church of England. The founders of the Oxford Movement nearly all sprang from devout Evangelical homes. Who can measure the influence of the Sacramental Revival of the eighteenth century on their thought?

(*b*) Methodists, unlike other Free Churchmen, have often been brought up on the Anglican *Book of Common Prayer*. In recent years Morning Prayer has been used relatively less than it was in early Methodist times, but it is still used in a good many churches, and the Anglican Communion Office very slightly altered, has always been that of the parent Church in England and of the Methodist Episcopal Church of America.

When some of the smaller Methodist churches, which only in rare cases had ever used a printed liturgy for their Communion Services, were united with the parent Church in 1932, it is perhaps worth mentioning that the Anglican liturgy became and continues to be the authorized Order of Holy Communion in Methodism. Indeed, several omissions made in past years have actually been restored; for instance: the Lord's Prayer and the second Post-Communion Collect have been reinstated in their original places.

It is true that an alternative form was drawn up for Methodists who were unfamiliar with liturgical language, but on the whole it has preserved the substance of the ancient liturgy, and even the form. Scriptural language has sometimes been substituted for Cranmer's; Psalm 51, for instance, takes the place of the Confession, and quotations from Scripture are substituted for the Absolution. An unfortunate alteration has been made in the Prayer of Humble Access, which does not improve Cranmer's prose. It is noteworthy that the Prayer of Oblation is placed before Communion in this Order, not indeed because the Committee was of Anglo-Catholic sympathies—the contrary is the fact—but apparently because, not being learned liturgists, they rightly followed their sound Methodist instinct and felt that the oblation of ourselves, souls, and bodies, was the proper addition to make to that of Christ, before they communicated. They seem to have entirely forgotten that the position of this prayer was one of the causes of bitter controversy in the House of Commons and other places on the Anglican revision of the *Prayer Book*, but they followed a true Methodist instinct.

(*c*) Unquestionably our greatest contribution is the *Hymns on the Lord's Supper: literae scriptae manent*. Here is the authoritative Methodist doctrine which was preached and sung probably for the first seventy years or more of Methodist history. Negatively, they repudiate mere memorialism; positively, they were sung by people who sought for Christ Himself and found Him at the Eucharist. The Elements were the instruments of present graces and of the hope of future glory, and above all, the declaration was made on earth in correspondence with that in heaven, that the one hope of mankind was Christ, risen and ascended, but always the Crucified. The tokens of His dying love were offered to God in correspondence with the silent pleading of those

> Five bleeding wounds he bears
> Receiv'd on Calvary;[1]

and in union with this sacrifice, our fathers made at the Holy Table the great oblation of themselves. Methodism has no other authoritative Sacramental doctrine.

(d) The value of these hymns for collective worship and as an expression of the corporate life of the Church was illustrated (i) by the mere singing of them, and (ii) by their substance.

(i) Everyone realizes the collective value of community singing. The introduction of hymns into Holy Communion was a novelty in the eighteenth century, however much it may have been a revival of ancient practice. They introduced a note often of ecstatic joy. When there were sometimes more than a thousand communicants, attention and reverence would have been difficult to sustain without some such device. Charles Wesley not only gave opportunity for expression to hearts full of thanksgiving—the true Eucharist—but also made the people realize that the service was not the performance of a separate priest on their behalf, but of the whole priestly community, the Body of Christ.

(ii) And then there was the doctrine which the substance of the hymns involved. The service was the thanksgiving of a Community, not merely of its individuals, but of a community. Whatever the views of the Wesleys were about their personal priesthood, they realized that they were the ministers of a corporate priesthood, and though they have left no exposition of the doctrine, they have left us a clue to the true meaning of priesthood and an indication of how we are to develop Eucharistic worship and sacrifice.

The priesthood of all believers was one of the chief doctrines of Luther, but his treatment of it was too negative. After all, a priest is a person who offers a sacrifice, and Luther's claim that this was just the sacrifice of praise and thanksgiving was not enough. Too often the term 'priesthood of believers' has

[1] *M.H.B.*, No. 368.

been used by Protestants as a mere defiant catchword. They have denied the priesthood of Catholic hierarchies and used their belief in the priesthood of believers as a mere rejoinder, just as the Quakers now say they believe everything is sacramental as a reason for rejecting particular Sacraments. But what is clear is, that it was the fact of priesthood and the fact of Sacraments that give to certain Protestants and Quakers a vocabulary for their rejoinder. Really, the doctrine has never been properly developed. What Luther actually said, Free Churchmen believe:

> Our priest or minister stands before the altar, having been publicly called to his priestly functions. He repeats publicly and distinctly Christ's words of the institution; he takes the bread and the wine, and distributes it according to Christ's words; and we all kneel beside him and round him, men and women, young and old, master and servant, mistress and maid, all holy priests together, sanctified by the blood of Christ. We are there in our priestly dignity. . . . We do not let the priest proclaim for himself the Ordinance of Christ; but he is the mouthpiece of us all, and we all say it with him in our hearts with true faith in the Lamb of God who feeds us with his body and blood.[2]

These words of Luther are true and important, but their emphasis is on the priesthood of *each* believer rather than on the corporate priesthood of the whole Church. His natural loathing of the priestly abuses of his time made Luther treat everything that savoured in the least of oblation as frivolous ritual or even worse. The hymns of Wesley enlarge, develop, and enrich the Lutheran conception of the priesthood of each believer. The Church really is not a fortuitous group of individuals, but a corporate priesthood, and it is as she offers the symbolic oblation of Christ's body and herself as the body of Christ that the real value of priesthood can be understood. This is where the Eucharistic tradition of Methodism, if properly developed, may open out new ways of corporate Communion, to the deepening value of Eucharistic worship. Never was a doctrine, full and rich and intelligible, of the priesthood of all believers more needed than today. Such a priesthood is the best answer to the contrary claims made in the new Anglo-Catholic manifesto that the priesthood is a separate body.

[2] Lindsay, *Reformation*, Vol. I, p. 444.

*The Apostolic Ministry.*[3]

The Wesleys, while never Medievalists and, indeed, always anti-Roman, were Catholics of the ante-Nicene Church. John Wesley was a careful student of the Apostolic Fathers, and though he repudiated (largely because he discovered that the 'Apostolic Constitutions' were not in all parts as early as he had thought) his early belief that the Apostolic Fathers were of co-ordinate authority with the writers of the New Testament, he always regarded them as only just sub-ordinate.

Much has been learned through modern research in recent years about the customs and beliefs of the Church of the first three Christian centuries. One cannot but wonder what Wesley would have thought if he had had the privilege of modern studies and had read such a book as, for instance, *The Shape of the Liturgy*, by Dom Gregory Dix. It could hardly have failed to have had an influence on his views, nor can it on ours, when we examine them in the light of the writings of Leitzmann, Frere, Dix, and many other liturgiologists and scholars. This research shows the importance of the corporate priesthood of the Early Church. The worshippers of those days referred to the Eucharist as an offering, and to themselves as offerers. The Holy Sacrifice, as Wesley himself named it, was never exclusively the work of a priest, but of a whole body of 'royal priests'—the Christian community.

No book could give a more convincing account of the priesthood of all believers than that of the Anglo-Catholic, Dom Gregory Dix. Indeed, it is difficult to think of any work to which Free Churchmen can appeal with more confidence for the confirmation of their views on this subject than *The Shape of the Liturgy*. And this is so notwithstanding the fact that their inferences sometimes will differ from those of the author. Liturgy, in the Early Church, according to Dom Gregory, was something *done*—not said or sung or seen—but *done*. It is interesting to note that a great Nonconformist theologian, Dr. T. P. Forsyth, also held and inculcated this opinion. Our use of the word 'liturgy' as descriptive of the prayers, written and used in Christian worship, is not its original use. The Greek word from which it is derived means 'active service', and it was used to describe the actions—the corporate actions—of the

[3] See Addendum II, p. 164, *infra*.

Church. The Liturgy was not the work of a priest who said a Mass for people to listen to, or, when said in a foreign language, showed them a wafer to gaze upon. It was something everybody did. Liturgy was service, not in a literary sense, but in an active sense. Every member of the congregation where the Eucharistic sacrifice was offered was not only a worshipper but an offerer. The layman, as Dom Gregory says, was not merely a registered citizen of the country, but one of an Order in the Church, confirmed for his participation in liturgical action, as a priest was ordained for his. Both of them offered the Holy Sacrament that they might do as Jesus bade them do.

*The Holy Church* offered the Eucharist as the re-calling before God and men of the offering of Christ. All that which *He* had done, once and for all, as the Priest and Proclaimer of the revelation of the kingship of God, the Church, which is the fulfilling of Him, enters into and fulfills. Christ and His Church are one, with one mission, one life, one prayer, one Gospel, one offering, one being, one Father. Such a conception left little room for regarding one order in the Church, whether bishop or presbyter, as in any executive sense the representative of Christ *to* the Church.[4]

Dom Gregory does not mean by this that the functions of a bishop or a deacon were not important; but he does mean that each layman had his own function, and that that was of vital importance. In support of which view I may, perhaps, quote St. Paul:

And the eye cannot say unto the hand, I have no need of thee: nor again the head to the feet, I have no need of you.[5]

While Dom Gregory Dix qualifies his interpretation by saying that the method of worship in one generation does not bind another—which is obviously true—he does sympathize with the view of corporate worship of the priesthood and the whole body of believers, and appears to think, I am sure rightly, that the absorption of priestly action by any man who does by himself all that the whole body is called to do, so that there is nothing left for them but solemnly to listen or to look, is really degeneration. Now this is the general Free Church view of the ideal Eucharist, apart from the implications of the word 'offering', though in losing these, Free Churchmen have lost much

[4] *The Shape of the Liturgy.*  [5] 1 Corinthians 12$^{21}$.

that is valuable. The fact of the priesthood of believers is, or ought to be, determinative of all Eucharistic worship. Indeed, it might be argued that Eucharistic worship, which is performed by a priest of an Order separated from the Church, is fundamentally defective; whatever may be said of the need of Apostolic orders for the priest the lack of which according to some Anglo-Catholics invalidates Free Church Sacraments. What really seems to make such worship most defective is anything that undermines its corporate character.

In the Church of today we have to recognize that the early corporate character of the Eucharist, as Dom Gregory himself teaches us, is very imperfectly expressed by modern Western Liturgies. Most modern Catholic apologists argue that the corporate character is not altogether lacking. Roman Catholics claim that the proof of the historic, corporate character of the Mass is to be found in the fact that at one point the priest turns round to the people and says, '*Orate frates*', which is a call to them to join in prayer. Other liturgists remind us that this corporate character is expressed by such words as, 'The Lord be with you', with the response, 'And with thy spirit'—words notably missing, by the way, in the Anglican Communion Liturgy. Others seem to be impressed by the fact that every now and then the people are permitted to say 'Amen'. That these may be *vestigia*—footprints—which have been left behind by the worshippers of other days need not be denied, but they are so vague or slight that it needs a liturgical geologist of great skill to discern their meaning.

What is needed for the restoration of the daily sacrifice for which Charles Wesley yearned is the revival of the service in which each man has his liturgy; each has his part. If the service is a sacrifice, it should be clearly the oblation which all men make through the priest, and not the oblation of a priest isolated from the people for the people. In the Eastern Church the oblation of the people is still expressed by offertory and procession. Offertory means much more than a money collection. Money-gifts have been substituted in some sense as an equivalent of the early gifts of the Church, but the meaning of the ancient offertory has almost been lost in Western Christianity. When their goods and gifts were brought by the people and placed on the altar, they were the definite offerings by the people, from which were taken the bread and wine to be consecrated and given back to the offerers for their spiritual quickening. The offering of gifts was the offering of themselves. Irenaeus said: 'The poor woman, the Church, casts in *all her life into the treasury of God.*' St. Augustine, as Dom Gregory reminds us, said to his people at their first Communion:

There *you* are, upon the table; there *you* are, in the Chalice. If you have received well: *you* are what you have received.⁶

Now the teaching of the sacrificial hymns of Wesley though they imply, as I have tried to show, what St. Augustine said, lacks a symbol in a symbolic service to fasten down the meaning of the oblation. The offertory itself was dismissed by Luther as 'stinking of oblation'. Anything in the nature of sacrifice was repulsive to him. It is very regrettable that in Reformed liturgies, on account of the medieval abuses of the idea of sacrifice, the ritual of corporate oblation should have been banished. In any liturgical reform it is a matter of the greatest importance that some symbolic expression of the offering to God of ourselves should find a place. As I have noted, the Methodist instinct in its alternative Communion Office did place the Prayer of oblation before Communion, but more is needed than this. Methodism at least, by its Eucharistic hymns, has contributed something to a revival of genuine sacrifice at Holy Communion which is needed for the realization of the Eucharist as the act of the whole priesthood. If in the Reformed Protestant Churches some symbol of the sacrificial character, not merely of the symbolic offering by the use of the tokens of dying love, but in the actual oblation of men and women of their goods and themselves in union with the sacrifice of Christ, could be found, much would be done to make Eucharistic worship the great symbol of human consecration which it ought to be.

One word ought to be spoken about the relation of Eucharistic worship to Evangelism. This has been excellently said by Dr. Harold Roberts, who gives me permission to quote from his *Message* to the recent Commando Campaigners:

In the Sacrament which the Universal Church regards as central, the message of the Campaign is summed up. We gather as a community

⁶ Quoted by Dix, *The Shape of the Liturgy.*

at the Holy Table to receive the gift of a new life. Through the corporate memory of the historic Church, the mighty acts of redeeming love in the Cross and Resurrection of Christ our Lord are re-enacted. Christ in the fullness of His holiness and love offers Himself to all who desire to receive Him. The sincerity of our desire to receive the gift which He brings is conditioned by our willingness to grow in the image of Christ and to be united with Him in the offering of obedience He made to the Father's Will. If we are prepared to offer and present ourselves, our souls and bodies (for our bodies cannot be withheld from His service), to be a reasonable, holy, and living sacrifice, He will unite us to Himself in the fellowship of His sufferings and the power of His Resurrection. Through our faith-union with Him, we shall be knit together in one Body with all the redeemed in heaven and on earth. We shall go forth into the world as the Body of Christ to be used by God not for our own purpose but for His.

ADDENDUM I

# THE AMERICAN ORDERS

I AM NOT concerned to defend the validity of the orders given to the American Methodist Church by John Wesley. It is quite evident that Anglicans, and for that matter, Presbyterians, from their respective points of view, have a right to call the orders Wesley gave through Dr. Coke to American preachers invalid. Even the English Methodists refused to acknowledge any difference in 'Order' between the few English preachers he ordained and the mass of preachers he left unordained at his death. I defend his orders on quite other grounds.

It is a delusion to assert that Wesley ever intended to give Dr. Coke Episcopal orders. On his theory, orders could only be given by those who had them, and his orders were Presbyteral. He delegated to Dr. Coke his own superintendency in America, quite aware, of course, that such a superintendency meant the exercise of Episcopal functions which in his opinion any Presbyter had a right to exercise if the 'circumstances' made such activity necessary. Even Anglo-Catholics admit that Episcopacy was a function before it was an Order.[1] A New Testament *episcopos* was, according to Wesley, a General Superintendent. The historical bishop, on the other hand, was of an order which later monopolized the Episcopal functions of the Presbyterate. To such an office Wesley did not appoint Coke, and indeed was very indignant when he and Asbury called themselves bishops. Wesley claimed to be a New Testament bishop, not merely because he was a presbyter of the Church of England, but on account of his large pastoral responsibility which demanded superintendency, and which was impossible for him to exercise in distant America; hence he delegated his responsibility to others. It is important to understand that Wesley, when he talked about a presbyter as a New Testament bishop, did not mean that anyone who was in priest's orders had a right to ordain anybody according to his

[1] *The Apostolic Ministry.*

own will or whim. He claimed his right to transmit his orders, first, because he had orders to transmit; second, because his position was such that his responsibility for thousands of souls in America made him, to all intents and purposes, a New Testament—a missionary—bishop. When justifying orders he gave he always wrote 'under the circumstances'. The vital thing to be noticed is not the validity of the orders he gave according to Catholic or even Presbyterian usage, but the fact that the necessities of the case made the creation of a ministry, when he was organizing the new Church in America, properly equipped to minister Sacraments an essential. Dr. Sparrow Simpson,[2] the Anglo-Catholic, in his very fair-minded effort to give an objective account of Wesley's churchmanship, says that his American ordinations can only be judged on the background of American conditions and the Erastian character of eighteenth-century British Anglicanism, and acknowledges that these conditions explain the orders, even if they do not justify them. My contention is that they not only explain them but they justify them; furthermore, in the actual conditions, Wesley would have been most reprehensible if he had failed to create a ministry in the newly organized Methodist Episcopal Church of America.[3]

Now, to come to a conclusion, as Dr. Sparrow Simpson acknowledges, we must regard carefully American conditions and the actions of the British Episcopate. While the principal causes of action, no doubt, are to be found in the post-Revolution America, the condition of earlier Colonial America must be taken into account. America was regarded as part of the diocese of London in Colonial times, and was under the ecclesiastical jurisdiction of its Bishop. When Americans sought orders, they had to journey to London to receive them. As the Colonial population increased, some English ecclesiastics were in favour of consecrating a bishop for America, but they never achieved their purpose, purely on account of British political policy. Evidence can be found in Dr. Wilberforce's book that many American clergy were undisciplined and even immoral. But the Anglican Church, by law established, was so fettered by its political obligations and so controlled by Erastian bishops

---

[2] *John Wesley and the Church of England*, p. 78.
[3] *The History of the American Church*.

that the question of the Church of America was treated purely from the standpoint of English political interests. Archbishop Herring, defending his inactivity in reference to the extension of the Episcopate in America, said:

> When the king commanded me to consider that field he would do it to the best of his judgement, and with a principal regard to the tranquillity of the king's government and not before.

Archbishop Herring perhaps would not have gone so far in his political loyalties as Watson, another eighteenth-century bishop, who actually

> professed readiness to turn Unitarian if the legislature of this country could be persuaded that the Unitarian form of worship was more conformable than the Trinitarian to the Word of God.

It will be noticed that I make this quotation from Anglo-Catholic sources.[4]

Behind the American Church situation stands grimly the State-fettered Church of England of the eighteenth century. The situation, no doubt, was worsened by the American Revolution. The State Church of what had become an enemy and foreign country obviously could not function in America, where political severance had taken place and relations to a politically governed Church were impossible. There were few ordained American clergy in America. A good many men, of whom a considerable number lost their lives *en route*, travelled to England in order to be ordained, but those who survived could not receive orders when they arrived there until an Act of Parliament could be passed to absolve them from their oath of allegiance. An Anglican bishop in that age obviously would never have been tolerated in the newly separated country. When at last a bishop for America was appointed, he received his orders according to Anglo-Catholic authorities, rather irregularly from the Scottish Episcopal Church, since no Anglican bishop would give them to him.

In the meantime, what was to be done? In America there were some thousands of Methodists, scattered in groups throughout the country. They were not unified. One of the things that gravely concerned Wesley himself was that they could not receive the Sacraments (though they were, broadly

[4] *The Apostolic Ministry*, p. 414.

speaking, Anglicans), which he regarded as essential to the life of the Church. His famous letter to Dr. Coke contains one sentence which is decisive on this point:

> Here [in England] there are bishops who have legal jurisdiction: in America there are none, neither any parish ministers. So that for some hundred miles together there is none either to baptize or to administer the Lord's supper. Here, therefore, my scruples are at an end.[5]

So desperate was the need of Episcopalians in America that members of the Church had become so impatient that they were actually thinking of administering the Sacraments apart from Episcopal ordination—so a High Churchman, Holden, tells us. Wesley did his best to provide for regular administration to his people. He approached Bishop Lowth of London to ordain one of his preachers to administer the Sacraments, but the bishop refused. What could be done? No man in England had so great a responsibility as John Wesley for the souls of Americans. Thousands had been converted to God through the ministrations of Methodist preachers, such as the great American Apostle, Asbury. The regular forms of churchmanship had, through war and revolution, broken down. Wesley, with his deep sense of Apostolic vocation and pastoral responsibility for the people who had been gathered together, could not condone the existence of a chaos which he thought might be reduced to order. His scattered sheep must be shepherded and organized in such a way as to preserve the great work for the future. During the war, notable Methodist Revivals had increased the numbers of his people. All normal administration of the English Church in America was impossible. Wesley was the only living Englishman who had sufficient power and influence to meet the situation, so he constituted the Methodist Episcopal Church, provided a ministry, did his best to preserve Anglican traditions by circulating a slightly abridged Anglican Liturgy, and by forming a regular presbyterate, ordained through his delegated superintendents. Surely, the last people to criticize Wesley are Anglicans, whose eighteenth-century Erastianism paralysed their churchmanship. Wesley was not only justified, but had he not acted who knows what disastrous results would have ensued?

[5] *Letters of John Wesley*, Vol. VII, p. 238 (To 'Our Brethren in America').

The historical judgement upon him might well have been that he was as small a man as his contemporary English bishops, to whom so far as they administered Church Law, he was always loyal. He exercised the inherent right—I will even dare to say obligation—of an Apostolic man, and with deep wisdom and splendid foresight, framed the organization which was the foundation of a Church which, more than any other, evangelized that great Continent, stimulated a nation, and sent forth influences, by Christian ministers, of incalculable value to the cause of God all over the world. Thank God, he was big enough to rise above trifling ritualisms and do prayerfully the work God had called him to do. His responsibilities were tremendous, his opportunities great. He faced both and did what no other man could have done—but he did it.

ADDENDUM II

# APOSTOLIC MINISTRY AND VALIDITY

THE able manifesto of the Anglo-Catholics, *The Apostolic Ministry*, is written by men, so the Bishop of Oxford in his introductory essay tells us, who,

if confronted with a choice between the doctrine which makes the Ministry wholly dependent on the Church, and one which endows it with independence from everything except its original divine commission, the latter is the one we must embrace.[1]

This conclusion is developed at length in the essays that follow. It must be mentioned, however, that the Bishop dislikes the dilemma—Church before Ministry, or Ministry before Church. The Anglo-Catholic party as represented in this book seems to differ in opinion in many matters from those of most Anglicans, past and present, of whom not all would claim, I think, that

Roman Catholics believe their orders are valid because they belong to the true Church, and Anglicans that they belong to the true Church because their orders are valid.[2]

In this matter all Protestants stand on the side of the Roman Catholic Church as against the Anglo-Catholic party or that section of the Anglo-Catholic party represented by this book. Free Churchmen, I think, would not object to the saying, which is quoted from the late Archbishop Temple by Bishop Kirk, that 'he held his authority neither from the Church nor apart from the Church, but from Christ in the Church'. Our interpretation of the words, 'Christ in the Church', involves the fact that the Living Christ is always and permanently active in His Church. He is not limited by any tradition, however venerable, but acts creatively today. It is very difficult for those of us who knew the great Archbishop to believe that he would have differed from this view. This emphasis, however, is important. When Free Churchmen think of Christ, they do not merely

[1] p. 30.
[2] It must not be assumed that these essays express the opinion of all Anglo-Catholics.

think of the historic Jesus, but of the living present Christ, able to act creatively today, unfettered by any ecclesiastical tradition, even if proved to be true, which in the case of Episcopal Succession it cannot be.

Free Churchmen believe that a Church without Christ living in its midst is not a body, but a corpse, and they are horrified by any suggestion or assumption that He cannot act creatively by different methods than those even of the Apostles in the first century. Their view of the activity of Christ in His Church would not be in the least altered if Apostolic Succession were completely demonstrated as an historic fact. Since they know that no such demonstration is possible, they are the more horrified and cannot but feel that some of the arguments that are used to support that opinion are merely fantastic. When one reads with genuine appreciation, and often with spiritual profit, the learned and edifying essays of *The Apostolic Ministry*, it is with regret that one has to write of the surprising conclusions of these essays as to the Apostolic Ministry, the words, *non sequitur*. It would be irrelevant to the subject of this book, not to say rather ridiculous, to criticize in a few paragraphs not the fact and practice of historic episcopacy, which many Free Churchmen might, for the sake of union, accept, but the singular—as some might think even sectarian—theory of such Anglo-Catholics as this book stands for. Even the Council of Trent was less dogmatic on episcopal succession than the Anglo-Catholic apologists.

The Bishop of London, who himself is not regarded as a startling example of extreme Protestantism, in his review of this book in the *Sunday Times*, 22nd January 1947, says:

In due course it [that is, the essential Ministry] became identified with the episcopate.

The Bishop asks: How? Free Churchmen ask: How?

It is in relation to these transferred rights of bishops [Dr. Wand writes], that the argument is weakest. The authors are so anxious to characterize the transmission of Order as the sole necessary function of the essential Ministry that they fail to be coherent in regard to the decisive step.

There, I think, the question may be left.

This book was written amongst other things to show that union with the Free Churches is impossible for Anglo-Catholics, even if the historic episcopate were accepted as a frame-work of a united Church, unless the Anglo-Catholic dogma of the Ministry as here set forth is accepted at the same time.

Dr. Kirk is undoubtedly right in demanding that not only formulas but their meanings be examined. Let it be said (I speak, of course, as an individual, but as an individual in as deep sympathy with the Church of England as any living Free Churchman) that we genuinely believe in the priesthood of all believers, and that all priestly service is merely a function of that fundamental priesthood. We do not believe that any priesthood can be independent of the Church; that, indeed, the very validity of a ministerial priesthood becomes challengeable in the degree in which it is differentiated from the whole priestly body. The claim that a Ministry is determined by tradition, however venerable, seems to suggest a lack of faith in the creative reality and power of Christ's perpetual presence with His people. We believe that it is the Church itself which is fundamental, and that it becomes visible always where two or three are met together in Christ's name; we certainly do not believe that it is necessary that a priest in apostolic orders should be one of the two or three. The priesthood in which we believe is corporate—the priesthood of a collective body. While there is a potential priestly gift in every Christian, the corporate offices of the Church obviously need individuals to exercise and express the priesthood of the Church. Many, perhaps most, Free Churchmen would agree with Dr. Kirk that claims sometimes deduced from the priesthood of all believers, that any man, on account of it, should be able to exercise at any time according to his own will the priestly functions of the whole corporation, are obviously mistaken. The inherent priesthood of all believers does not mean that each believer can, without the authority of the Church, enact the corporate functions of the Church.

### THE HOLY CATHOLIC CHURCH

What do Anglo-Catholics mean by the Holy Catholic Church? It is not unfair to conclude after having read *The Apostolic Ministry* that they mean that visible body of baptized Christians, or combination of bodies, whose ministers have been episcopally ordained by bishops to whose earliest predecessors the Apostles transmitted their commission from Christ with the grace and power attending it. What differentiates the Holy Catholic Church, they seem to claim, from other Christian communities is the Apostolic ministry, which in the last analysis is a vital constitutive element of the Church and, indeed, the instrument by which our Lord created it.

Sometimes Anglo-Catholics seem rather annoyed with the uses that Protestants make of terms like 'Holy Catholic Church', 'Apostolic Succession', and 'Real Presence'—because they claim these terms have a fixed historical meaning. But they fail to see that the terms as they use them beg the questions which we wish to discuss. Most of us quite genuinely believe in the Holy Catholic Church, Apostolic Succession, and the Real Presence of Christ in the Eucharist, but claim that the meaning given to these terms by Anglo-Catholics is wrong, and that no amount of tradition makes a wrong thing right. We express our belief in the Holy Catholic Church and our membership of it when we say:

We are the very members incorporate in the mystical body of thy Son, which is the blessed company of all faithful believers.

We believe that the Church is constituted not by hierarchies, but by the presence of Christ amongst His people, by His headship of the faithful who love and serve Him and each other in Him. We believe in the visibility of the Church; that it becomes visible in every congregation of Christian people where He is in the midst. Visibility of the body of believers as a whole we do not understand, and even doubt if the writers of *The Apostolic Ministry* have ever been clever enough to visualize the whole Church. In whatever sense the Universal Church is visible, it is clear that it cannot be visualized.

### CHURCH AND MINISTRY

Dr. Mackenzie, late Bishop of Brecon, in his contribution to *The Apostolic Ministry*, quotes with approval the words of Dr. P. T. Forsyth:

The local church was a community which was not self-contained, but which included, spiritually, all Christians everywhere. . . . The local church was but the outcrop there of the total continuous Church, one and everywhere. . . .

And again:

We must get rid of the notion that the great Church was composed by the coagulation of a certain number of single Churches, each of which was a Church in its own right. . . . What the Apostles planted was not churches, but stations of the Church.[3]

So Dr. Mackenzie says:

To see the Church universal in the little means of grace—that is insight indeed, and it is a thing to emulate.

The Congregational view of the Ministry as expressed by Dr. Forsyth and approved by Anglo-Catholics is also ours.[4] Methodists accept 'men who are, when they have tested and proved the claim, convinced that God has called them to preach, and these men become the Ministry'. But we do not agree with some Free Churchmen that the fact of the prophetic vocation of the minister necessarily qualifies him for the administration of the Sacraments. Throughout the history of Methodism, at all events of the parent stem, no one has administered the Sacrament merely because he was a preacher, but only by the definite authorization of the Church through her official organs. That is to say, that, however strongly the prophetic calling of a minister is recognized, the Church itself is the priestly body whose corporate functions can only be performed by persons especially authorized for that purpose.

### APOSTOLIC SUCCESSION

We believe the whole Church of Christ is continuous with the Apostolic Church, and that this is the true Apostolic succession. The succession is always a living one, because the living links have never perished; hence the succession does not depend upon the appointment of an individual person to take the place of one who is dead. We believe, as Berdyaev has claimed, that the Churches carry the hierarchies, and not the hierarchies the Churches.

[3] p. 475.   [4] *The Apostolic Ministry*, p. 476.

### REAL PRESENCE

Calvin's doctrine of the Real Presence was no subterfuge, no use of a venerable term in a non-natural sense. Personal presence he thought did not depend on corporeality. The real presence in which many Free Churchmen, including Methodists, believe is the presence of a personality, unseen but realized through His power and grace. They do not mean by this term 'influence' or 'aroma', but personality. If this is not real presence, what is it? We acknowledge that in the Eucharist this presence is especially realized by those who seek Christ in His own ordained ways and find Him to be with them, 'even unto the end of the world'.

### VALIDITY

The question of validity of orders from the Anglican or Catholic point of view is of little interest to Free Churchmen, who agree with the Bishop of Chichester that in union discussions it is a question that had much better be postponed. The Bishop of Oxford has shown that validity, after all, is not the same thing as reality or efficaciousness, and expresses esteem of the 'non-episcopal Ministry for its zeal, sanctity, its disinterestedness, and its power of edifying'. And as if this were not sufficient, he adds on another page that these Ministries

> have been blessed and owned of the Holy Spirit as effective means of grace, and *at times when the valid Ministry has been disloyal to its trust, they have nobly borne the burden of the fight.*

When he acknowledges this reality in the sense of efficaciousness and spirituality, validity seems to be a matter of very second-rate importance to the communities where Anglican validity obviously has no application.

Validity, if I understand the Bishop rightly, might be called the 'guinea stamp', but it is not meant by that to deny the words of Burns that 'a man's a man for a' that'. I think he would admit that validity does not create reality, and (here I am uncertain) does not necessarily guarantee it. Or if so, why should he speak of the important witness of non-episcopal ministries 'when valid Ministries betray their trusts'? The word simply implies, within the bounds of a particular institution, a correspondence with the laws which that institution by its competent authorities has laid down. Gold in the time of Burns was not current coin of our realm without the guinea stamp, but our guinea stamp does not make it current in other countries. Unfortunately, we have sometimes been compelled to conclude that the guinea stamp has caused a good deal of copper and nickel to become current instead of gold.

We think that the reality of the Ministry is the end that matters, and not any local or institutional validity, although of course there must be regulations in any human society which people observe unless anarchy is to prevail. In the Methodist Church, for instance, we have our own rules of valid ministry; if it be true that ordination by bishops in Apostolic succession is an essential constituent of a Church, Ministries of non-episcopal Churches obviously cannot be considered valid. Nor can the so-called Churches be regarded as Churches except as a matter of polite usage of words. But what does that matter? The difficulty in dealing with the Anglo-Catholic is that he claims that episcopal ordination makes Ministries valid in any part of the Catholic Church as defined above, but unfortunately we discover when we examine the opinions of the great majority of Western Catholics that they regard the Anglican Ministry as invalid.

So, in conclusion, however much we desire the union of Christianity—and the present writer desires nothing more devoutly—it is quite impossible upon the basis of claims by a party of Anglo-Catholics to the independence of the Ministry from the Church, a view which they hold in our opinion in singular if not eccentric isolation.

ADDENDUM III

# CONSTANT COMMUNION[1]

'IT IS THE duty of every person to receive the Lord's Supper as often as he can, because (a) it is a plain command of Christ. This appears from the text, "Do this in remembrance of Me": by which, as the Apostles were obliged to bless, break, and give the Bread to all that joined with them in these holy things; so were all Christians obliged to receive those signs of Christ's Body and Blood. This command was given by our Lord, when He was just laying down His life for our sakes, and are therefore His dying words.

'(b) The benefits of receiving the Holy Communion are (1) the forgiveness of our past sins, and (2) the present strengthening and refreshing of our souls. The grace of God given herein confirms to us the pardon of our sins, and enables us to leave them. Christ's Body and Blood is the food of our souls; it gives strength to perform our duty, and leads us on to perfection. Whosoever, therefore, goes from the Holy Table when all things are prepared, either does not understand his duty, or does not care for the dying command of his Saviour, the forgiveness of his sins, the strengthening of his soul, and the refreshing it with the hope of glory.

'With the first Christians the Christian Sacrifice was a constant part of the Lord's-day service. For several centuries they received the Blessed Sacrament every day, and their opinion of those who turned their back upon it may be gathered from the ancient canon, "If any believer join in the prayers of the faithful, and go away without receiving the Lord's Supper, let him be excommunicate, as bringing confusion into the Church of God."

'We have no right to reject God's commands, or to choose between them. Considering this, therefore, to be a command of God, he that does not communicate as often as he can has no piety; considering it as a mercy, he that does not communicate as often as he can has no wisdom.'

To the objection of some persons, that they cannot communicate often, because they cannot pretend to lead so holy a life as constantly communicating would oblige them to do, Wesley answers: 'This would be an argument against communicating at all; for if they

[1] The analysis of Wesley's Sermon on Constant Communion is extracted from W. E. Dutton's Introduction to the Anglo-Catholic edition of *Hymns on the Lord's Supper* of 1875.

cannot live up to the profession of those who communicate once a week, neither can they live up to the profession of those who communicate once a year. But if this be true, it would be better for them that they had never been born. To say this, is neither better nor worse than renouncing Christianity. It is in effect renouncing their baptism, wherein they solemnly promised to keep all God's commandments.'

The way in which Wesley answers another objection deserves notice. It is the very common one, 'I have communicated constantly so long, but I have not found the benefit I expected'. Here is the answer: 'This has been the case with many well-meaning persons, and therefore deserves to be particularly considered. And consider this first; whatever God commands us to do, we are to do, because He commands, whether we feel any benefit thereby or no. Now God commands, "Do this in remembrance of Me." This, therefore, we are to do, because He commands; whether we find present benefit thereby, or not. But undoubtedly we shall find benefit sooner or later, though perhaps insensibly. We shall be insensibly strengthened, made more fit for the service of God, and more constant in it.'[2]

[2] Sermons 106.

1 ARISE, my soul, arise,
    Shake off thy guilty fears;
  The bleeding Sacrifice
    In my behalf appears:
  Before the throne my Surety stands;
  My name is written on His hands.

2 He ever lives above,
    For me to intercede,
  His all redeeming love,
    His precious blood, to plead;
  His blood atoned for all our race,
  And sprinkles now the throne of grace.

3 Five bleeding wounds He bears,
    Received on Calvary;
  They pour effectual prayers,
    They strongly speak for me:
  Forgive him, O forgive! they cry,
  Nor let that ransomed sinner die!

4 The Father hears Him pray,
    His dear Anointed One;
  He cannot turn away
    The presence of His Son:
  His Spirit answers to the blood,
  And tells me I am born of God.

5 My God is reconciled,
    His pardoning voice I hear;
  He owns me for His child,
    I can no longer fear;
  With confidence I now draw nigh.
  And Father, Abba, Father! cry.

PART THREE

'THE CHRISTIAN SACRAMENT
AND SACRIFICE'

AND

HYMNS ON THE LORD'S SUPPER

# THE CHRISTIAN SACRAMENT AND SACRIFICE
*Extracted from Dr. Brevint*

SECTION I

*The Importance of Well Understanding the Nature of this Sacrament*

1. THE SACRAMENT ordained by Christ the night before He suffered, which St. *Paul* calls The Lord's Supper, is without doubt one of the greatest mysteries of godliness, and the most solemn feast of the Christian religion. At the holy Table the people meet to worship God, and God is present to meet and bless His people. Here we are in a special manner invited to offer up to God our souls, our bodies, and whatever we can *give:* and God offers to us the Body and Blood of His Son, and all the other blessings which we have need to *receive.* So that the holy Sacrament, like the ancient Passover, is a great mystery, consisting both of *Sacrament* and *Sacrifice;* that is, of the religious *service* which the people owe to God, and of the full *salvation* which God hath promised to His people.

2. How careful then should every Christian be to understand what so nearly concerns both his happiness and his duty! It was on this account that the devil, from the very beginning, has been so busy about this Sacrament, driving men either to make it a *false God,* or an *empty ceremony.* So much the more, let all who have either piety towards God, or any care of their own souls, so manage their devotions as to avoid superstition on the one hand, and profaneness on the other.

SECTION II

*Concerning the Sacrament, as it is a Memorial of the Sufferings and Death of Christ*

1. The Lord's Supper was chiefly ordained for a *Sacrament.* 1. To *represent* the sufferings of Christ which are *past,* whereof it is a *memorial.* 2. To *convey* the firstfruits of these sufferings, in *present graces,* whereof it is a means; and 3. to *assure* us of *glory to come,* whereof it is an infallible *pledge.*

2. As this *Sacrament* looks back, it is a *memorial* which our Lord hath left in His Church, of what He was pleased to suffer for her. For though these sufferings of His were both so dreadful and holy,

as to make the heavens mourn, the earth quake, and all men tremble: yet because the greatest things are apt to be forgotten when they are gone, therefore He was pleased at His last Supper to ordain this, as a holy *memorial* and *representation* of what He was then about to suffer. So that when Christian posterity (like the young *Israelites* who had not seen the killing of the first Passover) should come to ask after the meaning of the *bread broken*, the *wine poured* out, and the *partaking* of both: this holy Mystery might set forth both the *martyrdom* and the *sacrifice* of this crucified Saviour; giving up His *Flesh*, shedding His *Blood*, and pouring out His very *soul*, to atone for *their* sins.

3. Therefore, as at the Passover the late Jews could say, *This is the lamb, these are the herbs, our fathers did eat in Egypt;* because these latter feasts did so effectually represent the former: so at our Holy Communion, which sets before our eyes Christ *our Passover who is sacrificed for us;* our Saviour, says St. *Austin, doubted not to say, This is my Body, when He gave the disciples the figure of His Body:* especially because this Sacrament, duly received, makes the thing which it represents, as really present for our use as if it were newly done. *Eating this bread, and drinking this cup, ye do shew forth the Lord's death.*

4. And surely, it is no *common* regard we ought to have for these venerable representations, which God Himself has set up in, and for His Church. For these are far more than an ordinary figure. And all sorts of *signs* and *monuments* are more or less venerable, according to the things which they represent. And these, besides their ordinary use, bear as it were on their face the glorious character of their Divine appointment, and the express design that God hath to revive thereby, and to expose to all our senses, His sufferings, as if they were present *now*.

5. Ought not then one who looks on these ordinances, and considers the great and dreadful passages which they set before him, to say in his heart, I observe on this Altar somewhat very like the Sacrifice of my Saviour! For thus the *Bread of Life* was broken: thus the *Lamb of God* was slain, and His *Blood* shed. And when I look on the minister, who by special order from God distributes this bread and this wine, I conceive, that thus God Himself hath both given His Son to die, and gives us still the virtue of His death.

6. Ought he not also to reverence and adore, when he looks towards that good Hand, which has appointed for the use of the Church the *Memorial* of these great things? As the *Israelites* whenever they saw the *cloud* on the Temple, which God had hallowed to be the sign of His Presence, presently used to throw themselves on their faces, not to worship the cloud, but God: so whenever I see these better signs of the glorious mercies of God, I will not fail both to

remember my Lord who appointed them, and to worship Him whom they represent.

7. To complete this worship, let us exercise such a faith as may answer the great end of this Sacrament. The main intention of Christ herein was not the bare *remembrance* of His Passion; but over and above, to invite us to His Sacrifice, not as done and gone many years since, but as to grace and mercy, still lasting, still *new*, still the same as when it was first offered for us. The Sacrifice of Christ being appointed by the Father for a propitiation that should continue to all ages; and withal being everlasting by the privilege of its own *order*, which is *an unchangeable Priesthood;* and by His worth who offered it, that is, the Blessed *Son of God;* and by the power of *the Eternal Spirit*, through whom it was offered: it must in all respects stand eternal, the same yesterday, today, and for ever.

8. Here then *faith* must be as true a *subsistence* of those things past which we *believe*, as it is of the things yet to come which we *hope* for: by the help of which the believer, being prostrate at the Lord's Table, as at the very foot of His Cross, should with earnest sorrow confess and lament all his sins, which were the nails and spears that pierced his Saviour. We ourselves *have crucified that Just One. Men and brethren, what shall we do?* Let us fall amazed at that stroke of Divine justice, that could not be satisfied but by the death of God! *How dreadful is this place!* How deep and holy is this Mystery! What thanks should we pay for those inconceivable mercies of God the Father, who so gave up His only Son! and for the mercies of God the Son, who thus gave Himself up for us!

9. My Lord and my God, I behold in this Bread, made of corn that was cut down, beaten, ground, and bruised by men, all the heavy blows and plagues and pains which Thou didst suffer from Thy murderers. I behold in this Bread, dried up and baked with fire, the fiery wrath which Thou didst suffer from above! My God, my God, why hast Thou forsaken Him? The violence of wicked men first hath made Him a *Martyr;* then the fire of heaven hath made Him a *Burnt-Sacrifice;* and, lo, He has become to me the *Bread of Life!*

Let me go, then, to take and eat it. For though the instruments that bruised Him be broken, and the flames that burnt Him be put out, yet this *Bread* continues new. The spears and swords that slew, and the burnings that completed the Sacrifice, are many years since scattered and spent. But the sweet smell of the Offering still remains, the Blood is still warm, the Wounds still fresh, and *the Lamb* still *standing as slain*. Any other sacrifice by time may lose its strength: but Thou, O Eternal Victim, offered up to God through the Eternal Spirit, remainest always the same. And as Thy years shall not fail, so they shall never abate anything of Thy saving strength and mercy. O help me, that they abate nothing of my faith! Help me to grieve for my sins and Thy pains, as they did who saw Thee suffer. Let my heart burn to follow Thee now, when this Bread is broken at this Table, as the hearts of Thy disciples did when Thou didst break it in *Emmaus*. O Rock of *Israel*, Rock of Salvation, Rock struck and cleft for me, let those two streams of *Blood* and *Water*, which once gushed out of Thy side, bring down *pardon* and *holiness* into my soul. And let me thirst after them now, as if I stood upon the mountain whence sprung this *Water;* and near the *cleft* of that Rock, the wounds of my Lord, whence gushed this sacred *Blood*. All the distance of time and countries between *Adam* and me doth not keep his sin and punishment from reaching me, any more than if I had been born in his house. *Adam* descended from above, let Thy Blood reach as far, and come as freely to save and sanctify me as the blood of my first father did both to destroy and to defile me. Blessed Jesu, strengthen my faith, prepare my heart, and then bless Thine Ordinance. If I but *touch* as I ought *the hem of Thy garment*—the garment of Thy Passion—virtue will proceed out of Thee; it shall be done according to my faith, and my poor soul shall be made whole!

SECTION III

*Concerning the Sacrament as it is a Sign of Present Graces*

1. As to the *present graces* that attend the due use of this Sacrament, it is (1) a *figure* whereby God *represents;* (2) an *instrument* whereby He *conveys* them.

First, it is a *figure* or sign thereof. It is the ordinary way of God, when He either promises or bestows on men any considerable blessing, to confirm His *word* and His *gift* with the addition of some sign. So the *burning bush* was a *sign* to *Moses*, and the *cloud* that went with them to the *Israelites*. And in like manner hath Christ ordained outward visible signs of His inward and spiritual grace, to assure every one who believes that he shall be cleansed from his sins as certainly as he sees that *water*, and that he shall be fed with the grace of God as certainly as he feeds on the *bread* and *wine*.

2. And as *water* was fitly chosen for the outward sign in *Baptism*, because of the virtue it hath to cleanse and purify, so were bread and wine fitly chosen for the outward signs of what is represented in the Lord's Supper; *viz.*, first, the sufferings of Christ; and second, the blessings which we receive thereby. First: the sufferings of Christ. This bread and wine do not sustain me, till the one has been

cut down, ground, and baked with fire, and the other pressed and trodden under foot. Nor did the Son of God save me but by being bruised, and pressed, and consumed as it were by the fire of God's wrath. As the best corn is not bread while it stands in the field, so neither could Jesus, living, teaching, working miracles, be the Bread of Life: it must be Jesus suffering, Jesus crucified, Jesus dying. Nothing less than the Cross, than wounds and death, my Lord, my God, could of Thy dearest Son make my Saviour!

3. This Sacrament, secondly, represents the blessings which we receive by His Passion. Now, as without bread and wine, or something answerable thereto, the strongest bodies soon decay, so without the virtue of the Body and Blood of Christ the holiest souls must soon perish. And as bread and wine keep up our *natural life*, so doth our Lord Jesus, by a continual supply of strength and grace, represented by bread and wine, sustain that *spiritual life* which He hath procured by His Cross.

4. The first breath of spiritual life in our nostrils is the first purchase of Christ's Blood. But, alas! how soon would this first life vanish away, were it not followed and supported by a second? Therefore the Sacrifice of Christ procures also grace to renew and preserve the life He hath given. As the Blood which He shed satisfied the Divine Justice, and removed our punishment, so the water washes and cleanses the pardoned soul; and both these blessings are inseparable, even as the Blood and the Water were which flowed together out of His side.

5. There remains yet another life, which is an absolute redemption from death and our miseries. This, as to the right of it, is together with the other purchased by the same Sacrifice; but as to the possession, it is reserved for us in heaven till Christ become our full and final redemption. Now the giver of these lives is the preserver of them too; and to this end He sets up a table by His Altar, where He engages to feed our souls with the constant supply of His mercies as really as He feeds our bodies with this Bread and Wine. In the deliverance from *Egypt* here is a people saved by the sacrifice of the Passover; and lest they should die in the wilderness, there you see an angel leading them with his light, keeping them cool under the shadow of his cloud, and feeding them with manna. Jesus is the Truth foreshewed by these figures. He was the true Passover when He died upon the Cross, and He feeds from heaven, by continually pouring out His blessings, the souls He redeemed by pouring out His Blood.

6. Thus the Sacrament alone represents at once both what our Lord suffered, and what He still doth for us. What we take and eat is made of a substance cut, bruised, and put to the fire; that shows

my Saviour's Passion: and it was used thus that it might afford me food; that shows the benefit I receive from His Passion. In the Sacrament are represented both life and death; the life is mine, the death my Saviour's. O Blessed Jesus, my life comes out of Thy death, and the salvation which I hope for is purchased with all the pain and agonies which Thou didst suffer.

7. Author of my salvation, bestow on me these two blessings which this Sacrament shews together,—mercy, and strength to keep mercy. *Hosanna, O Son of* David, save and preserve! Save me, that I may not fall by the hand of the destroyer; and preserve me, that after this salvation I may not fall by my own hand: but set forward in me, notwithstanding all my sins, the work of Thy faithful mercies. Let me not increase my guilt by abusing what Thou givest. My Saviour, my Preserver, give me always what Thou givest once. Create in me a new heart; but keep what Thou createst, and increase more and more what Thou plantest. O Son of God, feed this tender branch, which without Thee cannot but wither; and strengthen Thou a bruised reed, which without Thee cannot but fall. Father of everlasting compassions, forsake not in the wilderness a feeble *Israelite* whom Thou hast brought a little way out of *Egypt;* and let not a poor soul whom Thou hast helped a while ever faint and fall from the right way. Thou art as able to perfect me with the blessings out of Thy throne as to redeem me by the Sacrifice on Thy Cross. O Thou who art the Truth of what Thou biddest me take, perform in me what Thou dost show. Give me eternal life by those Thy sufferings; for here is the *Body broken;* give also strength and nourishment for this life; for here is the *Bread of heaven.*

SECTION IV

*Concerning the Sacrament, as it is a Means of Grace*

1. Hitherto we have considered this holy Sacrament both as a *memorial* of the death of Christ, and a sign of those graces wherewith He sustains and nourishes believing souls. But this is not all; for both the end of the Holy Communion, the wants and desires of those who receive it, and the strength of other places of the Scripture, require that much more be contained therein than a bare *memorial* or *representation.* (1) The end of the Holy Communion, which is to make us partakers of Christ in another manner than when we only hear His word. (2) The wants and desires of those who receive it, who seek not a bare *representation* or *remembrance.* I want and seek my Saviour Himself, and I haste to this Sacrament for the same purpose

that SS. *Peter* and *John* hasted to His sepulchre—because I hope to find Him there. (3) The strength of other places of Scripture, which allow it a far greater virtue than that so representing only. *The cup of blessing, which we bless, is it not the Communion of the Blood of Christ?* A *means* of communicating the Blood there represented and remembered to every believing soul!

2. And that it doth convey grace and blessing to the true believer, is evident from its conveying a curse to the profane. *Whosoever eateth unworthily,* saith St. *Paul, eateth damnation to himself.* And how can we think that it is thus really hurtful when abused, but not really blissful in its right use; or that this Bread should be *effectual* to procure death, but not *effectual* to procure salvation? God forbid that the Body of Christ, who came to save, not destroy, should not shed as much of its *savour of life* to the devout soul, as it doth of its *savour of death* to the wicked and impenitent!

3. I come then to God's Altar, with a full persuasion that these words, *This is my Body*, promise me more than a *figure;* that this holy Banquet is not a bare *memorial* only, but may actually *convey* as many blessings to me, as it brings curses on the profane receiver. Indeed, in what manner this is done, I know not; it is enough for me to admire. *One thing I know* (as said the blind man of our Lord), *He laid clay upon mine eyes, and behold I see.* He hath blessed, and given me this Bread, and my soul receiveth comfort. I know that clay hath nothing in itself, which could have wrought such a miracle. And I know that this Bread hath nothing in itself, which can impart grace, holiness, and salvation. But I know also, that it is the ordinary way of God to produce His greatest works at the presence, thought not by the power, of the most useless instruments. At the very stroke of a rod He divided the sea. At the blowing some trumpets He threw down massive walls. At the washing in *Jordan* He cured *Naaman* of a plague that was naturally incurable. And when but a shadow went by, or some oil was dropped, or clothes were touched by those that were sick, presently *virtue went out*; not of rods, or trumpets, or shadows, or clothes—but of Himself.

4. It was the right hand of the Lord which of old time brought these mighty things to pass, either when the Red Sea opened a way for *Israel* to march, or when the rock poured out rivers to refresh them. And so now it is Christ Himself, with His Body and Blood, once offered to God upon the Cross, and ever since standing before Him as slain, who fills His Church with the perfumes of His Sacrifice, whence faithful communicants return home with the first-fruits of salvation. Bread and wine can contribute no more to it than the rod of *Moses* or the oil of the apostles. But yet since it pleaseth Christ to work thereby, O my God, whensoever Thou shalt bid me

*go and wash in* Jordan, I will go; and will no more doubt of being made clean from my sins, than if I had bathed in Thy Blood. And when thou sayest, *Go, take and eat this Bread* which I have blessed, I will doubt no more of being fed with the Bread of Life, than if I were eating Thy very Flesh.

5. This Victim having been offered up in the fulness of times, and in the midst of the world, which is Christ's great temple, and having been thence carried up to heaven, which is His sanctuary; from thence spreads salvation all around, as the burnt-offering did its smoke. And thus His Body and Blood have everywhere, but especially at this Sacrament, a true and real Presence. When He offered Himself upon earth, the vapour of His Atonement went up and darkened the very sun; and, by rending the great veil, it clearly showed He had made a way into heaven. And, since He is gone up, He sends down to earth the graces that spring continually both from His everlasting Sacrifice and from the continual intercession that attends it. So that we need not say, *Who will go up into heaven?* since, without either ascending or descending, this sacred Body of Jesus fills with atonement and blessing the remotest part of this temple.

6. Of these blessings Christ from above is pleased to bestow sometimes more, sometimes less, in the several ordinances of His Church, which, as the stars in heaven, differ from each other in glory. Fasting, prayer, hearing His word, are all good vessels to draw water from this well of salvation; but they are not all equal. The Holy Communion, when well used, exceeds as much in blessing as it exceeds in danger of a curse, when wickedly and irreverently taken.

7. This great and holy Mystery communicates to us the death of our Blessed Lord, both as *offering Himself to God*, and as giving Himself to man. As He *offered Himself to God*, it enters me into that mystical body for which He died, and which is dead with Christ: yea, it sets me on the very shoulders of that Eternal Priest, while He offers up Himself, and intercedes for His spiritual *Israel*. And by this means it conveys to me the *communion of His Sufferings*, which leads to a communion in all His graces and glories. *As He offers Himself to man*, the Holy Sacrament is, after the sacrifice for sin, the true sacrifice of peace-offerings, and the table purposely set to receive those mercies that are sent down from His Altar. *Take and eat; this is My Body, which was broken for you; and this is My Blood, which was shed for you.*

8. Here then I wait at the Lord's Table, which both *shews* me what an Apostle, who had heaven for his school, had the greatest mind to see and learn, and *offers* me the richest gift which a saint can receive on earth, the *Lord Jesus crucified*.

Amen, my Lord and my God! Give me all which Thou shewest,

and grant that I may faithfully keep all Thou givest. Bless Thine Ordinance, and make it an effectual means of Thy grace; then bless and sanctify my heart also. O my Father, here I offer up to Thee my soul; and Thou offerest to me Thy Son. What I offer is indeed an unclean habitation to receive the *Holy One of Israel*. Come in, nevertheless, Thou Eternal Priest; but cleanse my house at Thy coming. I am a poor, sinful, lost creature; but, such as I am, sinful and lost, I wait for Thy salvation. Come in, O Lord, with Thy salvation to a dying man, and make me whole; to a sinner bound hand and foot, and release me. Come as Thou didst to the publican. Oh, let this day salvation come to this house.

SECTION V

*Concerning the Sacrament, as it is a Pledge of Future Glory*

1. A pledge and an earnest differ in this, that an *earnest* may be allowed upon *account* for part of that payment which is promised, whereas *pledges* are taken back. Thus, for example, zeal, love, and those degrees of holiness which God bestows in the use of His Sacraments, will remain with us when we are in heaven, and there make part of our happiness. But the Sacraments themselves shall be taken back, and shall no more appear in heaven than did the cloudy pillar in *Canaan*. We shall have no need of these sacred *figures* of Christ when we see Him face to face, or of these *pledges* of that glory to be revealed when we shall actually possess it. But till this day the Holy Sacrament hath that third use, of being a *pledge* from the Lord that He will give us that glory.

2. Our Lord pointed at this when He said to His disciples, the Holy Cup being in His hands, that He would *drink no more of that fruit till He should drink it new in the kingdom of His Father*. In the purpose of God, His Church and heaven go both together, that being the way that leads to this, as the holy place to the holiest, both which are implied in what *Christ* calls the *kingdom of God*. Whosoever, therefore, are admitted to this *Dinner* of the Lamb, unless they be wanting to themselves, need not doubt of being admitted to the Marriage Supper of Him Who was dead, but *now liveth for evermore*.

3. Our Saviour hath given us by His death three kinds of life, and He promises to nourish us in every one of them by these tokens of bread and wine which He hath made His Sacrament. Two of these are already nourished hereby, but to the third we are not yet come. This is that eternal life for which we are as yet too vile vessels. We are now neither of age to enjoy our inheritance, nor able to bear the weight of eternal glory; and therefore it lies for us

in His hands. But we *know in Whom we have believed, and are persuaded He is able to keep that safe which we have committed unto Him against that day.* By faith we deposit or lay down this great treasure in the hands of God to keep; and God, by this Sacrament, assures us both that He will keep it safe and will restore it to us when we are meet for it.

4. This third use is the crown of the other two; and, indeed, they all aim at the same glory. The first is, to set out as new and fresh the holy sufferings which purchased our title to eternal happiness; the second is, both to represent and to convey to our souls all necessary graces to qualify us for it; and the third is, to assure us that when we are qualified for it, God will faithfully render to us the purchase. And these three make up the proper sense of those words, *Take, eat; this is My Body.* For the consecrated Bread doth not only represent His Body, and bring the virtue of it into our souls on earth, but as to our happiness in heaven, bought with that price, it is the most solemn instrument to assure our title to it.

5. Our Blessed Lord, being desirous before His death, as by a deed of His last will, to settle on His disciples both such a measure of grace in this life as might now make them holy, and after this life such a fulness of blessings as might make them eternally happy, He delivers into our hands, by way of instrument and conveyance, the blessed Sacrament of His Body and Blood, in the same manner as kings used to bestow dignities by the bestowing of a *staff* or a *sword,* and as the fathers bestow estates on their children by giving them some few *writings.*

6. The reason of all this is, the giver cannot put into his friend's hands houses and lands, because they are of an immoveable nature. And therefore this must be supplied by some forms or tokens by which his design may be sufficiently made known. Now Christ, and His estate, His happiness and His glory, His eternity and His heaven, are not things that may be moved more easily than the mountains on the earth; and therefore these can be no otherwise made over than great immoveable estates are. Wherefore, as the kingdom of *Israel* was once made over to *David,* with the oil that *Samuel* poured upon his head, so the Body and Blood of Jesus is *in full value,* and heaven with all its glory *in sure title,* made over to true Christians by that bread and wine which they receive in the Holy Communion, the minister of Christ having as much power from his Master for doing this as any prophet ever had for what he did.

7. O Lord Jesus, who hast ordained these Mysteries for a communion of Thy Body, a means of Thy grace, and a pledge of Thy glory, settle me hereby in the communion of Thy sufferings which they *shew forth;* feed me with that Living Bread which they *present,*

and sanctify me in body and spirit for that eternal happiness which they *promise*.

Eternal Priest, who art gone up on high to receive gifts for men, fill my heart, I beseech Thee, with blessings out of Thy holy seat, as now Thou fillest my mouth with the holy things of Thy Church. O that in the strength of this Meat I may walk my forty days, till I come to that holy mountain where, without the help of any bread or outward sign, I shall see my God face to face! Blessed Spirit, help me to drink so worthily of this fruit of the vine that I may drink it new in the kingdom of my Father!

SECTION VI

*Concerning the Sacrament, as it is a Sacrifice. And First, of the Commemorative Sacrifice*

1. There never was on earth a true religion without some kind of sacrifices. And the heathens who cast this slander on the Christian Church, did it for no better reason than this, because they saw neither altars set up, nor beasts slain or burnt among them. Even as they accused the Jews of adoring nothing but clouds, because they had no gods of stone or silver. Whereas in truth, as what was stone or silver could not be a god; so neither could the bare slaughter of beasts be a real sacrifice. None of these sacrifices could ever take away sin, but in dependence on that of Jesus Christ. And no sacrifice under the law could represent our service to God so fully as it is done under the gospel. The Holy Communion alone brings together these two great ends, atonement of sins, and acceptable duty to God, of which all the sacrifices of old were no more than weak shadows. As for the atonement of sin, 'tis sure the Sacrifice of Christ alone was sufficient for it. And that this great Sacrifice, being both of an infinite value, to satisfy the most severe justice, and of an infinite virtue, to produce all its effects at once, need never more be repeated. This perhaps was the want of faith in *Moses* (Numbers $20^{12}$); to strike a second time, and without order, that mysterious rock, which to strike once had been enough. For this second blow could only proceed from a faithless mistrust, as if the first, which alone was enjoined, could not suffice. But it were a much greater offence against the Blood of Christ, to question its infinite worth. The offering of it, therefore, must needs be one only; and the repeating thereof utterly superfluous.

2. Nevertheless this Sacrifice, which by a *real* oblation was not

to be offered more than once, is, by a devout and thankful commemoration, to be offered up every day. This is what the Apostle calls, *To set forth the death of the Lord;* To set it forth as well before the eyes of God His Father, as before the eyes of men: And what St. Austin *explained* when he said, The holy Flesh of Jesus was offered in three manners, by *prefiguring sacrifices* under the law before His coming into the world, in *real deed* upon His Cross, and by a *commemorative Sacrament* after He ascended into Heaven. All comes to this, (1) That the *Sacrifice* in itself can never be repeated; (2) That nevertheless, this Sacrament, by our remembrance, becomes a kind of *Sacrifice,* whereby we present before God the Father that precious Oblation of His Son once offered. And thus do we every day offer unto God the meritorious sufferings of our Lord, as the only sure ground whereon God may give, and we obtain, the blessings we pray for. Now there is no ordinance or mystery that is so blessed an instrument to reach this everlasting Sacrifice, and to set it solemnly forth before the eyes of God, as the Holy Communion is. *To men* it is a *sacred Table* where God's minister is ordered to represent from God his Master the Passion of His dear Son, as still fresh, and still powerful for their eternal salvation. And *to* God it is an *Altar* whereon men mystically present to Him the same Sacrifice as still bleeding and suing for mercy. And because it is the High Priest Himself, the true anointed of the Lord, who hath set up both this Table and the Altar, for the communication of His Body and Blood to men, and for the representation of both to God; it cannot be doubted but that the one is most profitable to the penitent sinner, and the other most acceptable to His gracious Father.

3. The people of *Israel,* in worshipping, ever turned their eyes and their hearts toward that sacrifice, the blood whereof the highpriest was to carry into the sanctuary. So let us ever turn our eyes and our hearts toward Jesus our eternal High Priest, who is gone up into the true sanctuary, and doth there continually present both His own Body and Blood before God, and, as *Aaron* did, all the true *Israel* of God in a *memorial.* In the meantime, we beneath in the Church present to God His Body and Blood in a *memorial,* that under the shadow of His Cross, and figure of His Sacrifice, we may present ourselves in very deed before Him.

4. O Lord, who seest nothing in me that is truly mine, but sinful dust and ashes, look upon the Sacrifice of Thy dear Son, once offered for my sins. Turn Thine eyes, O merciful Father, to the satisfaction and intercession of my Lord, who now sits at Thy right hand; to the Seals of Thy Covenant which lie before Thee upon this Table; and to all the wants, weaknesses, and distresses which Thou seest in my heart. O Father, glorify Thy Son; O Son of God, bless

Thou Thine Ordinance, and send with it the influences of that Spirit whom Thou hast promised to all flesh; that, by the help of these mercies, the world, the Church, and our souls may glorify Thee now and ever.

SECTION VII

*Concerning the Sacrifice of Ourselves*

1. Too many who are called Christians live as if under the Gospel there were no sacrifice but that of Christ on the Cross. And indeed there is no other that can atone for our sins or satisfy the justice of God. Though the whole Church should offer up herself as a burnt sacrifice to God, yet could she contribute no more towards bearing away the wrath to come, than those who stood near Christ when He gave up the ghost, did toward the darkening of the sun or the shaking of the earth. But what is not necessary to this Sacrifice which alone redeemed mankind, is absolutely necessary to our having a share in that redemption. So that though the sacrifice of ourselves cannot *procure* salvation, yet it is altogether needful to our *receiving* it.

2. As *Aaron* never came in before the Lord without the whole people of *Israel*, represented both by the twelve stones on his breast and by the two others on his shoulder; so Jesus Christ does nothing without His Church, insomuch that sometimes they are represented as only one person; seeing Christ acts and suffers for His Body in that manner which becomes the Head, and the Church follows all the motions and sufferings of her Head, in such a manner as is possible to its weak members.

3. The whole divinity of St. *Paul* turns upon this *conformity* both of actions and sufferings; and that of St. *John* likewise, upon this same *communion* or fellowship. The truth is, our Lord had neither birth, nor death, nor resurrection on earth, but such as we are to *conform* to; as He had neither ascension, nor everlasting life, nor glory in heaven, but such as we may have in *common* with Him.

4. This *conformity* to Christ, which is the grand principle of the whole Christian religion, relates first to our duty about His *sufferings*, and then to our happiness about His *exaltation*, presupposing His *sufferings*. And both make up a full comment on our Lord's frequent command to His disciples to *follow Him.* For without doubt we shall follow Him into heaven, if we will follow Him on earth; and shall have *communion* with Him in glory, if we have *conformity* with Him here in His *sufferings*.

5. These expressions, to *follow*, to have *conformity*, and to have *communion*, oblige us all to follow Him as much as in us lies, through all the parts of His life, and every function of His office. We must be born with Him, die on His Cross, be buried in His grave, suffer in His tribulations. *Christ* and Christians must be continually together: *Where I am*, saith He, *there shall My servant be*. But of all these duties, the most necessary is the bearing of His Cross, and dying with Him in *Sacrifice*.

6. Christ never designed to offer Himself for His people, without His people, no more than the high-priests of old. He presented Himself to God in this great temple, the world, at the head of whole mankind. He came as a voluntary Victim to the Altar, being attended on by His *Israel*, who, as it were, with their hands, laid all their sins upon His head. Therefore, as it was necessary that they who fought for atonement should wait upon the sacrifice, so it is, that whoever seeks eternal salvation should wait at that Altar, the Cross, whereon this eternal Priest and Sacrifice was pleased to offer up Himself.

7. The sinners indeed under the law did not die at the altar, the victim alone being burned and destroyed. But because they laid their hands on it when it was dying, and fell on their faces to the ground when it fell bleeding to death, they were reputed to *offer* up themselves as well as the victim. So Christians are not crucified in the same manner as Christ was; yet because they cast themselves upon His Cross and sufferings as the only means of atonement for their sins, and salvation for their souls; because of the grief they suffer to think of the Son of God thus dying, dying only for their sake, which is as a sword both to pierce their hearts and pierce and crucify their sins; and because their whole body of sin being thus crucified, there remains no life in them, but what is offered up to God's service. On all these grounds, the Saviour thus offering Himself, and the saved so united to Him by faith, so partaking of His sufferings, and so given up to His will, are accounted before God one and the same Sacrifice.

8. But be it observed, that in order to their being so accounted, they are to crucify their sinful members as really as Christ Himself had His sinless Body crucified; so that each may say, *I am crucified to the world, and the world crucified to me*. And thus Jesus Christ and His whole Church do together make up that complete Sacrifice which was foreshewn by that of old, whereof the kidney and fat were burnt upon the altar; but the flesh, the skin, feet, and dung—emblems of sin—were thrown and burnt without the camp. For Christ and His Church so join in one Offering, that He contributes all that can go up into heaven to appease and please God; and we contribute

nothing but sin, but what must be removed out of the way; yea, and so that it is needful further, in order to our being accounted one Sacrifice with Him, that not only our persons, but all our actions likewise, be wholly devoted to God. *I am crucified with Christ; now I live not*, saith the Christian, *but Christ liveth in me. And the life which I now live in the flesh, I live by faith in the Son of God.*

9. This act of the Church consecrating herself to God, and so joined to Christ, as to make but one Oblation with Him, is the Mystery which was once represented by the daily sacrifice; the first and chief part whereof was the lamb, which did foreshew the Lamb of God; the second was the *meat*—or rather *meal—and drink-offering*, made of flour, mingled with oil and wine; all which being thrown on the lamb continually, was accounted one and the same sacrifice. Now these, which were so thrown on the main sacrifice, signified properly these offerings which Christians must present to God of themselves, their goods and their praises. From this *meal* and *drink-offering* came the bread and wine to be used at the Lord's Supper. Now all we can offer on our own account is but such an oblation as this *meal* and *drink-offering* was, which cannot be presented alone, but only with the merits of Jesus Christ, and which cannot go to heaven but with the smoke of that Great Burnt Sacrifice. On the one side, neither our persons nor works can be presented to God, otherwise than as these additional offerings, which of themselves fall to the ground, unless the Great Sacrifice sustain them. And on the other side, this Great Sacrifice sustains and sanctifies only those things that are thrown into His fire, hallowed upon His Altar, and together with Him consecrated to God.

10. Now though we are called at all times to this *conformity* and *communion* in the sufferings of Christ, yet more especially when we approach this deadful Mystery let us take a peculiar care, that as both the principal and additional sacrifices went up towards heaven in the same flame, so Jesus Christ and all His members may jointly appear before God, that we may offer up our souls and bodies, at the same time, in the same place, and in the same Oblation. Let us take care to attend on this Sacrifice in such a manner (1) as may become faithful disciples, who are resolved to die for and with their Master; (2) as true members that cannot outlive their Head; and (3) as penitent sinners, who cannot look for any share in the glory of their Saviour, unless they really enter into the communion of that Sacrifice and those sufferings which their Master, their Head, and their Saviour has passed through, and which they are engaged to by this very Sacrament.

11. To this effect, the faithful worshipper, presenting that soul and body, which God hath given him, at the Altar, may say,—

*Lo, I come!* if this soul and body may be useful to anything, *to do Thy will*, O God. And if it please Thee to use the power that Thou hast over dust and ashes, over weak flesh and blood, over a brittle vessel of clay, over the work of Thine own hands; lo, here they are, to suffer also Thy good pleasure. If Thou please to visit me with either pain or dishonour, I will *humble myself* under it, and, through Thy grace, be *obedient unto death, even the death upon the Cross*. Whatsoever may befall me, either from neighbours or strangers, since it is Thou employest them, though they know it not (unless Thou help me to some lawful means of redressing the wrong), I will not *open my mouth before the Lord* who smiteth me, except only to sing the *Psalm* after I have eaten those bitter herbs which belong to this *Passover*, and to *bless the Lord*. Hereafter no man can take away anything from me, no life, no honour, no estate: since I am ready to lay them down, as soon as I perceive Thou requirest them at my hands. Nevertheless, *O Father, if Thou be willing, remove this cup from me; but if not, Thy will be done.* Whatever sufferings hereafter may trouble my flesh, or whatever agonies may trouble my spirit, *O Father, into Thy hand will I commend* my life, and all that concerneth it. And if Thou be pleased, either that I live yet a while, or not, I will with my Saviour *bow down my head*: I will humble myself under Thy hand; I will give up all Thou art pleased to ask, until at last I *give up the ghost*.

12. O God and Father, bestow on me such a measure of that *Spirit, through* which Thy Son *offered Himself*, as may sanctify for ever the body of soul which I now offer: a spirit of contrition, that I may loathe those sins which delivered my God to death; and a spirit of holiness, that I may never be tempted to them again, any more than a crucified man can be tempted. O let this body never be untied from His Cross, to return afresh to folly and vanity. Arm and rod of the Lord, who didst revenge my sins on Thy own Son, correct and destroy them also in me. O my God, accept of a heart that sheds now before Thee its tears, as a poor victim does its blood; and that raises up unto Thee all its desires, as a burnt-offering does its flames. And since my sacrifice can neither be holy nor accepted, being alone, receive it, O Father, clothed with the righteousness of Thy Son, and made acceptable with that holy perfume which rises from off His Altar: and grant that He who sanctifies, and they who are sanctified, may partake of one Passion, and enjoy with Thee the same glory.

SECTION VIII

*Concerning the Sacrifice of our Goods*

It is an express command of God by *Moses*, that no worshipper should appear before the Lord empty. Nor is this repealed by Christ. Sincere Christians therefore, at the receiving of the Holy Communion, should, together with the actual *sacrifice* of themselves, bring the *freewill-offering* of their goods. Indeed, this as naturally follows the former, as the fruits and leaves follow the tree, and as what we *have* or. *can* do comes after what we *are*. Otherwise, our sacrifice were maimed, and would not suit with that of Christ, which was whole and entire. Therefore, as our bodies and souls are sacrifices attending the Sacrifice of Christ, so must all our goods attend the sacrifice of our persons. In a word, whensoever we offer ourselves, we offer, by the self-same act, all that we *have*, all that we *can* do, and therein engage for all, that it shall be dedicated to the glory of God, and that it shall be surrendered into His hands, and employed for such uses as He shall appoint.

2. It behoved *Israel* to go forth out of *Egypt* with all their cattle and goods, to offer them unto the Lord, that He might take either all, or such a part, as He would be pleased to choose. And so it behoves every sinner at his conversion to God, and whenever he approaches His Table, to consecrate all he has to Jesus Christ. From that very moment that we give up ourselves to Christ, who hath likewise given Himself for us, as all He possesses becomes ours, namely, His grace, His immortality, His glory, which He bestows upon us at the times He sees best for our salvation; so all we have becomes His, and He may take it after, in what time and manner He shall see best for His glory. All things are His, as He is sovereign Lord and God. But all that we have is His by a further title, because we have given them, with our own persons, by our own act and deed. So that all which we are, which we can give, even to the least vessel in our houses, is made holy in this one consecration, according to the words of the prophet, *In that day shall be upon the very bridles of the horses, Holiness unto the Lord; and every pot in* Jerusalem *and* Judah *shall be holy unto the Lord* (Zechariah 14[20, 21]).

3. This consecration, whereby the worshipper offers up himself and all his concerns to God, is first, as to our souls and bodies, an inexpressible blessing, raising us to the very nature, the holiness, and immortality of God. Secondly, as to the consecrated things, it is a miraculous privilege, which infinitely multiplies whatever is thus

parted with. It blesses the use of it, although it be but presented, as long as we can enjoy it: and exchanges it, when we can enjoy it no more, not as if water was turned into wine, or dirt into gold; but as if we conceive a glass of water turned into streams of everlasting comforts, small cottages of clay into royal palaces, or the dust of *Israel* into so many stars of heaven.

4. Now though our Lord, by that everlasting Sacrifice of Himself, offer ourselves and all that is ours, to be a continual sacrifice; yet because Christ offers Himself for us at the Holy Communion, in a peculiar manner; we also should then, in a more special manner, renew all our sacrifices. Then and there, at the Altar of God, it is right both to repeat all the vows and promises which for some hindrance or other we had not yet the convenience to fulfil; and to renew all those other performances which can never be fulfilled but with the end of our days.

5. But at the same time that the Christian believer does any good work, let him draw out of the good measure of his heart *fire* and *frankincense*, that is, such zeal and love as may raise good, *moral* works into religious sacrifices. Whenever he helps his neighbour, let him so reverently and fervently lift up his heart to God, as may become both that Majesty he adores, and the pious act which he intends. And then whenever he do it at his door, or in the way, or in the temple, it matters not; for the hour is long since come, that acts of religion are not confined either to *Jerusalem*, or *to this mountain*. Wheresoever thou hast the occasion of doing a holy work, there God makes *holy ground* for thee: only, in order to become a spiritual worshipper, the work must be done *in spirit and in truth*: with such a mind and thought, with such faith and love, as though thou wert laying thy *oblation* upon the altar, where thou knowest that Christ will both effectually find, and graciously accept it.

6. I dare appear before the Lord, with all my sins and my sorrows. It is just also that I should appear with these few blessings. *Having* received them of Thy hand, now do I offer them to Thee again. Forgive, I beseech Thee, my sins, deliver me from my sorrows, and accept of this my sacrifice: or rather look, in my behalf, on that only true Sacrifice, whereof here is the Sacrament; the Sacrifice of Thy well-beloved Son, proceeding from Thee, to die for me. O let Him come unto me now, as the only begotten of the Father, full of grace and truth!

# HYMNS ON THE LORD'S SUPPER

## I. *As it is a Memorial of the Sufferings and Death of Christ*

### 1

1 In that sad memorable night,
   When Jesus was for us betray'd,
   He left His death-recording rite,
   He took, and bless'd, and brake the bread,
   And gave His own their last bequest,
   And this His love's intent exprest:

2 Take, eat, this is My body, given
   To purchase life and peace for you,
   Pardon and holiness and heaven;
   Do this My dying love to show,
   Accept your precious legacy,
   And thus, My friends, remember Me.

3 He took into His hands the cup,
   To crown the sacramental feast,
   And full of kind concern look'd up,
   And gave what He to them had blest;
   And drink ye all of this, He said,
   In Solemn memory of the dead.

4 This is My blood which seals the new
   Eternal covenant of My grace,
   My blood so freely shed for you,
   For you and all the sinful race;
   My blood that speaks your sins forgiven,
   And justifies your claim to heaven.

5 The grace which I to all bequeath
   In this Divine memorial take,
   And, mindful of your Saviour's death,
   Do this, My followers, for My sake,
   Whose dying love hath left behind
   Eternal life for all mankind.

### 2

1 In this expressive bread I see
   The wheat by man cut down for me,
     And beat, and bruised, and ground:
   The heavy plagues, and pains, and blows,
   Which Jesus suffer'd from His foes,
     Are in this emblem found.

2 The bread dried up and burnt with fire
   Presents the Father's vengeful ire,
     Which my Redeemer bore:
   Into His bones the fire He sent,
   Till all the flaming darts were spent,
     And Justice ask'd no more.

3 Why hast Thou, Lord, forsook Thine own?
   Alas! what evil hath He done,
     The spotless Lamb of God?
   Cut off, not for Himself, but me,
   He bears my sins on yonder tree,
     And pays my debt in blood.

4 Seized by the rage of sinful man
   I see Him bound, and bruised, and slain;
     'Tis done, the Martyr dies!
   His life to ransom ours is given,
   And lo! the fiercest fire of heaven
     Consumes the Sacrifice.

5 He suffers both from man and God,
   He bears the universal load
     Of guilt and misery;
   He suffers to reverse our doom;
   And lo! my Lord is here become
     The Bread of Life to me.

### 3

1 Then let us go, and take, and eat
The heavenly, everlasting meat,
   For fainting souls prepared;
Fed with the living Bread Divine,
Discern we in the sacred sign
   The body of the Lord.

2 The instruments that bruised Him so
Were broke and scatter'd long ago,
   The flames extinguish'd were;
But Jesu's death is ever new,
He whom in ages past they slew
   Doth still as slain appear.

3 The' oblation sends as sweet a smell,
Even now it pleases God as well
   As when it first was made;
The blood doth now as freely flow,
As when His side received the blow
   That show'd Him newly dead.

4 Then let our faith adore the Lamb
To-day as yesterday the same,
   In Thy great offering join,
Partake the sacrificial food,
And eat Thy flesh and drink Thy blood,
   And live for ever Thine.

### 4

1    Let all who truly bear
   The bleeding Saviour's name,
Their faithful hearts with us prepare,
   And eat the Paschal Lamb.
   Our Passover was slain
   At *Salem's* hallow'd place,
Yet we who in our tents remain
   Shall gain His largest grace.

2    This eucharistic feast
   Our every want supplies,
And still we by His death are blest,
   And share His sacrifice:
   By faith His flesh we eat,
   Who here His passion show,
And God out of His holy seat
   Shall all His gifts bestow.

3    Who thus our faith employ,
   His sufferings to record,
Even now we mournfully enjoy
   Communion with our Lord,
   As though we every one
   Beneath His cross had stood,
And seen Him heave, and heard Him groan,
   And felt His gushing blood.

4    O God! 'tis finish'd now;
   The mortal pang is past!
By faith His head we see Him bow,
   And hear Him breathe His last.
   We too with Him are dead,
   And shall with Him arise;
The cross on which He bows His head
   Shall lift us to the skies.

### 5

1 O Thou eternal Victim, slain
A sacrifice for guilty man,
By the eternal Spirit made
An offering in the sinner's stead,
Our everlasting Priest art Thou,
And plead'st Thy death for sinners now.

2 Thy offering still continues new,
Thy vesture keeps its bloody hue,
Thou stand'st the ever-slaughter'd Lamb,
Thy priesthood still remains the same,
Thy years, O God, can never fail,
Thy goodness is unchangeable.

3 O that our faith may never move,
But stand unshaken as Thy love!
Sure evidence of things unseen,
Now let it pass the years between,
And view Thee bleeding on the tree,
My God, who dies for me, for me!

## 6

1 Ah, give me, Lord, my sins to mourn,
My sins which have Thy body torn;
Give me with broken heart to see
Thy last tremendous agony,
To weep o'er an expiring God,
And mix my sorrows with Thy blood.

2 O could I gain the mountain's height,
And look upon that piteous sight!
O that with *Salem's* daughters I
Might stand and see my Saviour die,
Smite on my breast, and inly mourn,
But never from Thy cross return!

## 7

1 Come, Holy Ghost, set to Thy seal,
Thine inward witness give,
To all our waiting souls reveal
The death by which we live.

2 Spectators of the pangs Divine
O that we now may be,
Discerning in the sacred sign
His passion on the tree!

3 Give us to hear the dreadful sound
Which told His mortal pain,
Tore up the graves, and shook the ground,
And rent the rocks in twain.

4 Repeat the Saviour's dying cry
In every heart, so loud
That every heart may now reply,
This was the Son of God!

## 8

1 Come, to the supper come,
Sinners, there still is room;
Every soul may be His guest,
Jesus gives the general word;
Share the monumental feast,
Eat the supper of your Lord.

2 In this authentic sign
Behold the stamp Divine:
Christ revives His sufferings here,
Still exposes them to view;
See the Crucified appear,
Now believe He died for you.

## 9

1 Come hither all, whose groveling taste
Inslaves your souls, and lays them waste;
Save your expense, and mend your cheer:
Here God Himself's prepared and dress'd,
Himself vouchsafes to be your feast,
In whom alone all dainties are.

2 Come hither all, whom tempting wine
Bows to your father *Belial's* shrine,
Sin all your boast, and sense your God:
Weep now for what you've drank amiss,
And lose your taste for sensual bliss
By drinking here your Saviour's blood.

3 Come hither all, whom searching pain,
Whom conscience's loud cries arraign,
Producing all your sins to view:
Taste; and dismiss your guilty fear,
O, taste and see that God is here
To heal your souls and sin subdue.

4 Come hither all, whom careless joy
Does with alluring force destroy,
While loose ye range beyond your bounds:
True joy is here, that passes quite
And all your transient mean delight
Drowns, as a flood the lower grounds.

5 Come hither all, whose idol-love,
   While fond the pleasing pain ye prove,
      Raises your foolish raptures high:
   True Love is here; whose dying breath
   Gave life to us; who tas⁺ed death,
      And, tasting once, no more can die.

6 Lord, I have now invited all,
   And instant still the guests shall call,
      Still shall I all invite to Thee:
   For, O my God, it seems but right
   In mine, Thy meanest servant's sight,
      That where All is, there all should be!¹

## 10

1 FATHER, Thy own in Christ receive,
   Who deeply for our follies grieve,
      And cast our sins away,
   Resolved to lead our lives anew,
   Thine only glory to pursue,
      And only Thee obey.

2 Faith in Thy pardoning love we have,
   Willing Thou art our souls to save,
      For Jesu's sake alone:
   Jesus Thy wrath hath pacified,
   Jesus, Thy Well-beloved, hath died
      For all mankind t' atone.

3 The death sustain'd for all mankind
   With humblest thanks we call to mind,
      With grateful joy approve;
   And every soul of man embrace,
   And love the dearly ransom'd race
      In the Redeemer's love.

4 Receive us then, Thou pardoning God;
   Partakers of His flesh and blood
      Grant that we now may be;
   The Spirit's attesting seal impart,
   And speak to every sinner's heart,
      The Saviour died for thee!

## 11

1  O GOD, that hear'st the prayer,
      Attend Thy people's cry,
   Who to Thy house repair
      And on Thy death rely,
   Thy death which now we call to mind,
   And trust our legacies to find.

2  Thou meetest them that joy
      In these Thy ways to go,
   And to Thy praise employ
      Their happy lives below,
   And still within Thy temple gate
   For all Thy promised mercies wait.

3  We wait t' obtain them now;
      We seek the Crucified,
   And at Thy altar bow,
      And long to feel applied
   The blood for our redemption given,
   And eat the Bread that came from heaven.

4  Come then, our dying Lord,
      To us Thy goodness show,
   In honour of Thy word
      The inward grace bestow,
   And magnify the sacred sign,
   And prove the ordinance Divine.

## 12

1 JESU, suffering Deity,
   Can we help remembering Thee?
   Thee, whose blood for us did flow,
   Thee, who diedst to save Thy foe?

2 Thee, Redeemer of mankind,
   Gladly now we call to mind,
   Thankfully Thy grace approve,
   Take the tokens of Thy love.

¹ This hymn is an adaptation of George Herbert's 'The Invitation'. The sentiments expressed are Herbert's. See *Poetical Works*, Vol. I, p. 111. (See also note on Hymn No. 160.)

3 This for Thy dear sake we do,
Here Thy bloody passion show,
Till Thou dost to judgment come,
Till Thy arms receive us home.

4 Then we walk in means no more;
There their sacred use is o'er,
There we see Thee face to face,
Saved eternally by grace.

## 13

1 COME, all who truly bear,
   The name of Christ your Lord,
His last mysterious supper share,
   And keep His kindest word:
Hereby your faith approve
In Jesus crucified,
In memory of My dying love
Do this, He said, and died.

2 The badge and token this,
   The sure confirming seal
That He is ours, and we are His,
   The servants of His will,
Hid dear peculiar ones,
The purchase of His blood;
His blood which once for all atones,
And brings us *now* to God.

3 Then let us still profess
   Our Master's honour'd name,
Stand forth His faithful witnesses,
   True followers of the Lamb:
In proof that such we are
His saying we receive,
And thus to all mankind declare
We *do* in Christ believe.

4 Part of His church below,
   We thus our right maintain,
Our living membership we show,
   And in the fold remain;
The sheep of *Israel's* fold
In *England's* pastures fed,
And fellowship with all we hold
Who hold it with our Head.

## 14

1 FATHER, hear the blood of Jesus
   Speaking in Thine ears above;
From Thy wrath and curse release us,
   Manifest Thy pardoning love;
O receive us to Thy favour,
   For His only sake receive,
Give us to our bleeding Saviour,
   Let us by Thy dying live.

2 'To Thy pardoning grace receive them,'
   Once He prayed upon the tree;
Still His blood cries out, 'Forgive them,
   All their sins were purged by Me.'
Still our Advocate in heaven
   Prays the prayer on earth begun,
'Father, show their sins forgiven,
   Father, glorify Thy Son!'

## 15

1 DYING Friend of sinners, hear us,
   Humbly at Thy cross who lie,
In Thine ordinance be near us,
   Now th' ungodly justify;
Let Thy bowels of compassion
   To Thy ransom'd creatures move,
Show us all Thy great salvation,
   God of truth, and God of love.

2 By Thy meritorious dying
   Save us from the death of sin,
By Thy precious blood's applying
   Make our inmost nature clean;
Give us worthily t' adore Thee,
   Thou our full Redeemer be;
Give us pardon, grace, and glory,
   Peace, and power, and heaven in Thee.

## 16

1. Come, Thou everlasting Spirit,
   Bring to every thankful mind
   All the Saviour's dying merit,
   All His sufferings for mankind;
   True Recorder of His passion,
   Now the living faith impart,
   Now reveal His great salvation,
   Preach His gospel to our heart.

2. Come, Thou Witness of His dying,
   Come, Remembrancer Divine,
   Let us feel Thy power applying
   Christ to every soul and mine;
   Let us groan Thine inward groaning,
   Look on Him we pierced and grieve,
   All receive the grace atoning,
   All the sprinkled blood receive.

## 17

1. Who is this that comes from far,
   Clad in garments dipp'd in blood?
   Strong triumphant Traveller,
   Is He man, or is He God?

2. I that speak in righteousness,
   Son of God and man I am,
   Mighty to redeem your race;
   Jesus is your Saviour's name.

3. Wherefore are Thy garments red,
   Dyed as in a crimson sea?
   They that in the wine-fat tread
   Are not stain'd so much as Thee.

4. I, the Father's favourite Son,
   Have the dreadful wine-press trod,
   Borne the vengeful wrath alone,
   All the fiercest wrath of God.

## 18

1. Lift your eyes of faith, and look
   On the signs He did ordain!
   Thus the Bread of Life was broke,
   Thus the Lamb of God was slain,
   Thus was shed on *Calvary*
   His last drop of blood for me!

2. See the slaughter'd Sacrifice,
   See the altar stain'd with blood!
   Crucified before our eyes
   Faith discerns the dying God,
   Dying that our souls might live,
   Gasping at His death, Forgive!

## 19

1. Forgive, the Saviour cries,
   They know not what they do;
   Forgive, my heart replies,
   And all my soul renew;
   I claim the kingdom in Thy right,
   Who now Thy sufferings share,
   And mount with Thee in *Sion's* height,
   And see Thy glory there.

## 20

1. Lamb of God, whose bleeding love
   We thus recall to mind,
   Send the answer from above,
   And let us mercy find;
   Think on us, who think on Thee,
   And every struggling soul release:
   O remember *Calvary*,
   And bid us go in peace.

2. By Thine agonizing pain
   And bloody sweat we pray,
   By Thy dying love to man,
   Take all our sins away;
   Burst our bonds, and set us free,
   From all iniquity release:
   O remember *Calvary*,
   And bid us go in peace.

3 Let Thy blood, by faith applied,
   The sinner's pardon seal,
  Speak us freely justified,
   And all our sickness heal:
  By Thy passion on the tree
  Let all our griefs and troubles cease;
   O remember *Calvary*,
   And bid us go in peace.

4 Never will we hence depart,
   Till Thou our wants relieve,
  Write forgiveness on our heart,
   And all Thine image give:
  Still our souls shall cry to Thee,
  Till perfected in holiness:
   O remember *Calvary*,
   And bid us go in peace.

21

1 GOD of unexampled grace,
   Redeemer of mankind,
  Matter of eternal praise
   We in Thy passion find:
  Still our choicest strains we bring,
  Still the joyful theme pursue,
  Thee the Friend of sinners sing,
   Whose love is ever new.

2 Endless scenes of wonder rise
   With that mysterious tree,
  Crucified before our eyes
   Where we our Maker see:
  Jesus, Lord, what hast Thou done?
  Publish we the death Divine,
  Stop, and gaze, and fall, and own
   Was never love like Thine!

3 Never love nor sorrow was
   Like that my Jesus show'd;
  See Him stretch'd on yonder cross,
   And crush'd beneath our load!
  Now discern the Deity,
  Now His heavenly birth declare;
  Faith cries out, 'Tis He, 'tis He,
   My God, that suffers there!

4 Jesus drinks the bitter cup,
   The wine-press treads alone,
  Tears the graves and mountains up
   By His expiring groan:
  Lo! the powers of heaven He shakes;
  Nature in convulsions lies,
  Earth's profoundest centre quakes,
   The great *Jehovah* dies!

5 Dies the glorious Cause of all,
   The true eternal *Pan*,
  Falls to raise us from our fall,
   To ransom sinful man:
  Well may *Sol* withdraw his light,
  With the Sufferer sympathise,
  Leave the world in sudden night,
   While his Creator dies.

6 Well may heaven be clothed with black,
   And solemn sackcloth wear,
  Jesu's agony partake,
   The hour of darkness share:
  Mourn th' astonied hosts above,
  Silence saddens all the skies,
  Kindler of seraphic love,
   The God of angels dies.

7 O, my God, He dies for me,
   I feel the mortal smart!
  See Him hanging on the tree—
   A sight that breaks my heart!
  O that all to Thee might turn!
  Sinners, ye may love Him too;
  Look on Him ye pierced, and mourn
   For One who bled for you.

8 Weep o'er your Desire and Hope
   With tears of humblest love;
  Sing, for Jesus is gone up,
   And reigns enthroned above!
  Lives our Head, to die no more;
  Power is all to Jesus given,
  Worshipp'd as He was before,
   The' immortal King of heaven.

9 Lord, we bless Thee for Thy grace
   And truth, which never fail,
Hastening to behold Thy face
   Without a dimming veil:
We shall see our heavenly King,
All Thy glorious love proclaim,
Help the angel choirs to sing
   Our dear triumphant Lamb.

### 22

1 PRINCE of Life, for sinners slain,
   Grant us fellowship with Thee;
Fain we would partake Thy pain,
   Share Thy mortal agony:
Give us now the dreadful power,
Now bring back Thy dying hour.

2 Place us near th' accursed wood
   Where Thou didst Thy life resign,
Near as once Thy mother stood;
   Partners of the pangs Divine,
Bid us feel her sacred smart,
Feel the sword that pierced her heart.

3 Surely now the prayer He hears;
   Faith presents the Crucified!
Lo! the wounded Lamb appears;
   Pierced His feet, His hands, His side,
Hangs our Hope on yonder tree,
Hangs, and bleeds to death for me!

### 23

1 HEARTS of stone, relent, relent,
   Break, by Jesu's cross subdued;
See His body mangled, rent,
   Cover'd with a gore of blood!
Sinful soul, what hast thou done?
Murder'd God's eternal Son!

2 Yes, our sins have done the deed,
   Drove the nails that fix Him here,
Crown'd with thorns His sacred head,
   Pierced Him with a soldier's spear,
Made His soul a sacrifice;
For a sinful world He dies.

3 Shall we let Him die in vain,
   Still to death pursue our God?
Open tear His wounds again,
   Trample on His precious blood?
No; with all our sins we part:
Saviour, take my broken heart!

### 24

1 EXPIRING in the sinner's place,
   Crush'd with the universal load,
He hangs!—adown His mournful face
   See trickling fast the tears and blood!
The blood that purges all our stains,
It starts in rivers from His veins.

2 A fountain gushes from His side,
   Open'd that all may enter in,
That all may feel the death applied,
   The death of God, the death of sin,
The death by which our foes are kill'd,
The death by which our souls are heal'd.

## 25

1 In an accepted time of love
  To Thee, O Jesus, we draw near;
  Wilt Thou not the veil remove,
  And meet Thy mournful followers here,
  Who humbly at Thy altar lie,
  And wait to find Thee passing by?

2 Thou bidd'st us call Thy death to mind;
  But Thou must give the solemn power:
  Come then, Thou Saviour of mankind,
  Bring back that last tremendous hour,
  And stand in all Thy wounds confest,
  And wrap us in Thy bloody vest.

3 With reverential faith we claim
  Our share in Thy great sacrifice:
  Come, O Thou all-atoning Lamb,
  Revive us by Thy dying cries,
  Apply to all Thy healing blood,
  And sprinkle *me, my Lord, my God.*

## 26

1 'Tis done! th' atoning work is done:
  Jesus, the world's Redeemer, dies!
  All nature feels th' important groan
  Loud echoing through the earth and skies;
  The earth doth to her centre quake,
  And heaven as hell's deep gloom is black!

2 The temple's veil is rent in twain,
  While Jesus meekly bows His head;
  The rocks resent His mortal pain,
  The yawning graves give up their dead;
  The bodies of the saints arise,
  Reviving as their Saviour dies.

3 And shall not we His death partake,
  In sympathetic anguish groan?
  O Saviour, let Thy passion shake
  Our earth, and rent our hearts of stone,
  To second life our souls restore,
  And wake us that we sleep no more.

## 27

1 ROCK of *Israel*, cleft for me,
  For us, for all mankind;
  See, Thy feeblest followers see,
  Who call Thy death to mind:
  *Sion* is the weary land;
  Us beneath Thy shade receive,
  Grant us in the cleft to stand,
  And by Thy death to live.

2 In this howling wilderness,
  On *Calvary's* steep top,
  Made a curse our souls to bless,
  Thou once wast lifted up;
  Stricken there by *Moses'* rod,
  Wounded with a deadly blow,
  Gushing streams of life o'erflow'd
  The thirsty world below.

3 Rivers of salvation still
   Along the desert roll,
Rivers to refresh and heal
   The fainting sin-sick soul;
Still the fountain of Thy blood
   Stands for sinners open'd wide;
Now, even now, my Lord and God,
   I wash me in Thy side.

4 Now, even now, we all plunge in,
   And drink the purple wave;
This the antidote of sin,
   'Tis this our souls shall save:
With the life of Jesus fed,
   Lo! from strength to strength we rise,
Follow'd by our Rock, and led
   To meet Him in the skies.

---

## II. *As it is a Sign and a Means of Grace*

### 28

1 AUTHOR of our salvation, Thee
   With lowly thankful hearts we praise,
Author of this great mystery,
   Figure and means of saving grace.

2 The sacred, true, effectual sign,
   Thy body and Thy blood it shows;
The glorious instrument Divine
   Thy mercy and Thy strength bestows.

3 We see the blood that seals our peace,
   Thy pardoning mercy we receive:
The bread doth visibly express
   The strength through which our spirits live.

4 Our spirits drink a fresh supply,
   And eat the bread so freely given,
Till borne on eagle's wings we fly,
   And banquet with our Lord in heaven.

### 29

1 O THOU who this mysterious bread
   Didst in *Emmaus* break,
Return, herewith our souls to feed,
   And to Thy followers speak.

2 Unseal the volume of Thy grace,
   Apply the gospel word,
Open our eyes to see Thy face,
   Our hearts to know the Lord.

3 Of Thee we commune still, and mourn
   Till Thou the veil remove;
Talk with us, and our hearts shall burn
   With flames of fervent love.

4 Enkindle now the heavenly zeal,
   And make Thy mercy known,
And give our pardon'd souls to feel
   That God and love are one.

### 30

1 JESU, at whose supreme command
   We thus approach to God,
Before us in Thy vesture stand,
   Thy vesture dipp'd in blood.

2 Obedient to Thy gracious word,
   We break the hallow'd bread,
Commemorate Thee, our dying Lord,
   And trust on Thee to feed.

3 Now, Saviour, now Thyself reveal,
   And make Thy nature known;
Affix the sacramental seal,
   And stamp us for Thine own.

4 The tokens of Thy dying love
   O let us all receive,
And feel the quickening Spirit move,
   And *sensibly* believe.

5 The cup of blessing, blest by Thee,
　Let it Thy blood impart;
　The bread Thy mystic body be,
　And cheer each languid heart.

6 The grace which sure salvation brings
　Let us herewith receive;
　Satiate the hungry with good things,
　The hidden manna give.

7 The living Bread sent down from heaven
　In us vouchsafe to be;
　Thy flesh for all the world is given,
　And all may live by Thee.

8 Now, Lord, on us Thy flesh bestow,
　And let us drink Thy blood,
　Till all our souls are fill'd below
　With all the life of God.

### 31

1 O ROCK of our salvation, see
　The souls that seek their rest in Thee;
　Beneath Thy cooling shadow hide,
　And keep us, Saviour, in Thy side;
　By water and by blood redeem,
　And wash us in the mingled stream.

2 The sin-atoning blood apply,
　And let the water sanctify,
　Pardon and holiness impart,
　Sprinkle and purify our heart,
　Wash out the last remains of sin,
　And make our inmost nature clean.

3 The double stream in pardons rolls,
　And brings Thy love into our souls;
　Who dare the truth Divine receive,
　And credence to Thy Witness give,
　We here Thy utmost power shall prove,
　Thy utmost power of perfect love.

### 32

1 JESU, to Thee for help we call,
　Plunged in the depth of *Adam's* fall,
　　Plagued with a carnal heart and mind;
　No distance or of time or place
　Secures us from the foul disgrace
　By him entail'd on all mankind.

Six thousand years are now past by;
Yet still, like him, we sin and die,
　As born within his house we were;
As each were that accursed *Cain*,
We feel the all-polluting stain,
　And groan our inbred sin to bear.

2 Thou God of sanctifying love,
　*Adam* descended from above,
　　The virtue of Thy blood impart;
　O let it reach to all below,
　As far extend, as freely flow,
　　To cleanse, as his t' infect our heart.

Ruin in him complete we have;
And canst not Thou as greatly save,
　And fully here our loss repair?
Thou canst, Thou wilt, we dare believe,
We here Thy nature shall retrieve,
　And all Thy heavenly image bear.

### 33

1 JESU, dear, redeeming Lord,
　Magnify Thy dying word;
　In Thy ordinance appear,
　Come, and meet Thy followers here.

2 In the rite Thou hast enjoin'd
　Let us now our Saviour find,
　Drink Thy blood for sinners shed,
　Taste Thee in the broken bread.

3 Thou our faithful hearts prepare,
    Thou Thy pardoning grace declare;
    Thou that hast for sinners died,
    Show Thyself the Crucified.

4 All the power of sin remove,
    Fill us with Thy perfect love,
    Stamp us with the stamp Divine,
    Seal our souls for ever Thine.

## 34

1 LORD of life, Thy followers see,
    Hungering, thirsting after Thee;
    At Thy sacred table feed,
    Nourish us with living bread.

2 Cheer us with immortal wine,
    Heavenly sustenance Divine;
    Grant us now a fresh supply,
    Now relieve us, or we die.

## 35

1 O THOU Paschal Lamb of God,
    Feed us with Thy flesh and blood;
    Life and strength Thy death supplies,
    Feast us on Thy sacrifice.

2 Quicken our dead souls again,
    Then our living souls sustain,
    Then in us Thy life keep up,
    Then confirm our faith and hope.

3 Still, O Lord, our strength repair,
    Till renew'd in love we are,
    Till Thy utmost grace we prove,
    All Thy life of perfect love.

## 36

1 AMAZING mystery of love!
    While posting to eternal pain,
    God saw His rebels from above,
    And stoop'd into a mortal man.

2 His mercy cast a pitying look;
    By love, unbounded love inclined,
    Our guilt and punishment He took,
    And died a Victim for mankind.

3 His blood procured our life and peace,
    And quench'd the wrath of hostile Heaven;
    Justice gave way to our release,
    And God hath all *my* sins forgiven.

4 Jesu, our pardon we receive,
    The purchase of that blood of Thine,
    And now begin by grace to live,
    And breathe the breath of love Divine.

## 37

1 BUT soon the tender life will die,
    Though bought by Thy atoning blood,
    Unless Thou grant a fresh supply,
    And wash us in the watery flood.

2 The blood removed our guilt in vain,
    If sin in us must always stay;
    But Thou shalt purge our inbred stain,
    And wash its relics all away.

3 The stream that from Thy wounded side
In blended blood and water flow'd
Shall cleanse whom first it justified,
And fill us with the life of God.

4 Proceeds from Thee the double grace;
Two effluxes, with life Divine
To quicken all the faithful race,
In one eternal current join.

5 Saviour, Thou didst not come from heaven,
By water or by blood alone;
Thou diedst that we might live forgiven,
And all be sanctified in One.

## 38

1 WORTHY the Lamb of endless praise,
Whose double life we here shall prove,
The pardoning and the hallowing grace,
The dawning and the perfect love.

2 We here shall gain our calling's prize,
The gift unspeakable receive,
And higher still in death arise,
And all the life of glory live.

3 To make our right and title sure,
Our dying Lord Himself hath given,
His sacrifice did all procure,
Pardon, and holiness, and heaven.

4 Our life of grace we here shall feel
Shed in our loving hearts abroad,
Till Christ our glorious life reveal,
Long hidden with Himself in God.

5 Come, great Redeemer of mankind,
We long Thy open face to see;
Appear, and all who seek shall find
Their bliss consummated in Thee.

6 Thy presence shall the cloud dispart,
Thy presence shall the life display;
Then, then our all in all Thou art,
Our fulness of eternal day!

## 39

1 SINNER, with awe draw near,
And find thy Saviour here,
In His ordinances still,
Touch His sacramental clothes;
Present in His power to heal,
Virtue from His body flows.

2 His body is the seat
Where all our blessings meet;
Full of unexhausted worth,
Still it makes the sinner whole,
Pours Divine effusions forth,
Life to every dying soul.

3 Pardon, and power, and peace,
And perfect righteousness
From that sacred Fountain springs;
Wash'd in His all-cleansing blood
Rise, ye worms, to priests and kings,
Rise in Christ, and reign with God.

## 40

1. Author of life Divine,
   Who hast a table spread,
   Furnish'd with mystic wine
   And everlasting bread,
   Preserve the life Thyself hast given,
   And feed and train us up for heaven.

2. Our needy souls sustain
   With fresh supplies of love,
   Till all Thy life we gain,
   And all Thy fulness prove,
   And, strengthen'd by Thy perfect grace,
   Behold without a veil Thy face.

## 41

1. Truth of the paschal sacrifice,
   Jesu, regard Thy people's cries,
   Nor let us in our sins remain:
   Surely Thou hear'st the prisoners groan;
   Come down to our relief, come down,
   And break the dire Accuser's chain.

2. Humble the proud oppressive king,
   Deliverance to Thine *Israel* bring,
   And while th' unsprinkled victims die,
   Thy death for us present to God,
   Write our protection in Thy blood,
   And bid the hellish fiend pass by.

## 42

1. Glory to Him who freely spent
   His blood, that we might live,
   And through this choicest instrument
   Doth all His blessings give.

2. Fasting He doth, and hearing bless,
   And prayer can much avail,
   Good vessels all to draw the grace
   Out of salvation's well.

3. But none, like this mysterious rite
   Which dying mercy gave,
   Can draw forth all His promised might
   And all His will to save.

4. This is the richest legacy
   Thou hast on man bestow'd:
   Here chiefly, Lord, we feed on Thee,
   And drink Thy precious blood.

5. Here all Thy blessings we receive,
   Here all Thy gifts are given,
   To those that would in Thee believe,
   Pardon, and grace, and heaven.

6. Thus may we still in Thee be blest,
   Till all from earth remove,
   And share with Thee the marriage feast,
   And drink the wine above.

## 43

1. Saviour, and can it be
   That Thou shouldst dwell with me?
   From Thy high and lofty throne,
   Throne of everlasting bliss,
   Will Thy majesty stoop down
   To so mean an house as this?

2. I am not worthy, Lord,
   So foul, so self-abhorr'd,
   Thee, my God, to entertain
   In this poor polluted heart:
   I am a frail sinful man,
   All my nature cries, Depart!

3. Yet come, Thou heavenly Guest,
   And purify my breast;
   Come, Thou great and glorious King,
   While before Thy cross I bow,
   With Thyself salvation bring,
   Cleanse the house by entering now.

## 44

1 Our Passover for us is slain,
The tokens of His death remain,
On these authentic signs imprest:
By Jesus out of *Egypt* led,
Still on the Paschal Lamb we feed,
And keep the sacramental feast.

2 That arm that smote the parting sea
Is still stretch'd out for us, for me;
The Angel-God is still our Guide,
And, lest we in the desert faint,
We find our spirits' every want
By constant miracle supplied.

3 Thy flesh for our support is given,
Thou art the Bread sent down from heaven,
That all mankind by Thee might live;
O that we evermore may prove
The manna of Thy quickening love,
And all Thy life of grace receive!

4 Nourish us to that awful day
When types and veils shall pass away,
And perfect grace in glory end;
Us for the marriage feast prepare,
Unfurl Thy banner in the air,
And bid Thy saints to heaven ascend.

## 45

1 Tremendous love to lost mankind!
Could none but Christ the ransom find?
Could none but Christ the pardon buy?
How great the sin of *Adam's* race!
How greater still the Saviour's grace,
When God doth for His creature die!

Not heaven so rich a grace can show
As this He did on worms bestow,
Those darlings of th' Incarnate God;
Less favour'd were the angel-powers;
Their crowns are cheaper far than ours,
Nor ever cost the Lamb His blood.

2 Our souls eternally to save,
More than ten thousand worlds He gave;
That we might know our sins forgiven,
That we might in Thy glory shine,
The purchase-price was blood Divine,
And bought th' *Aceldama* of heaven.

Jesu, we bless Thy saving name,
And trusting in Thy merits claim
Our rich inheritance above;
Thou shalt Thy ransom'd servants own,
And raise and seat us on Thy throne,
Dear objects of Thy dying love.

## 46

1 How richly is the table stored
Of Jesus, our redeeming Lord!
*Melchisedec* and *Aaron* join
To furnish out the feast Divine.

2 *Aaron* for us the blood hath shed,
*Melchisedec* bestows the bread,—
To nourish this, and that t' atone;
And both the priests in Christ are one.

3 Jesus appears to sacrifice
The flesh and blood Himself supplies;
Enter'd the veil, His death He pleads,
And blesses all our souls, and feeds.

4 'Tis here He meets the faithful line,[1]
Sustains us with His bread and wine;
We feel the double grace is given,
And gladly urge our way to heaven.

---

[1] 'The faithful line' may be a description of the Christian succession of priests which Wesley probably thought to be a continuation of the Levitical Aaronic priesthood. This is obviously the use of the expression in his hymn on Bishops, *Poetical Works*, Vol. II, pp. 341-3 (see *supra*, p. 85). See also Vol. V, p. 103. This is apparently a stereotyped phrase. Only a little later than 1745, Charles Wesley

(*Continuation of footnote on page 210.*)

## 47

1 JESU, Thy weakest servants bless,
Give what these hallow'd signs express,
And, what Thou givest, secure;
Pardon into my soul convey,
Strength in Thy pardoning love to stay,
And to the end endure.

2 Raise, and enable me to stand,
Save out of the destroyer's hand
This helpless soul of mine;
Vouchsafe me then Thy strengthening grace,
And with the arms of love embrace,
And keep me ever Thine.

## 48

1 SAVIOUR of my soul from sin,
Thou my kind Preserver be;
'Stablish what Thou dost begin,
Carry on Thy work in me,
All Thy faithful mercies show,
Hold, and never let me go.

2 Never let me lose my peace,
Forfeit what Thy goodness gave;
Give it still, and still increase,
Save me, and persist to save;
Seal the grant conferr'd before,
Give Thy blessing evermore.

## 49

1 SON OF GOD, Thy blessing grant,
Still supply my every want;
Tree of Life, Thine influence shed,
With Thy sap my spirit feed.

2 Tenderest branch, alas! am I,
Wither without Thee and die;
Weak as helpless infancy,
O confirm my soul in Thee.

3 Unsustain'd by Thee I fall,
Send the strength for which I call;
Weaker than a bruised reed,
Help I every moment need.

4 All my hopes on Thee depend,
Love me, save me to the end,
Give me the continuing grace,
Take the everlasting praise.

---

used the word 'Melchizedekean', and not very happily, as a nickname for the unordained preachers who wished to administer sacraments. The metaphors, however, of Melchizedek and Aaron seem to be used in the first three verses of this hymn in a sense not relevant to the question of succession, but to show that the *atoning* and *sustaining* values of both are combined in Jesus Christ our great High Priest, who sums up in Himself all the values of the priesthood both of Aaron and Melchizedek. As my friend, Dr. Ryder Smith, in a letter to me aptly says the meaning is that 'Christ first offered His own flesh and blood to God and then received them back from God to give to the worshippers in the bread and wine of the Sacrament'. But what does the meeting of Jesus the great High Priest with 'The faithful line' (verse 4, line 1) involve? 'The faithful line' with which he meets seems to be a priesthood. The problem is whether it can be identified with the outward successive priesthood or with the Church in its priestly character as expressed by the phrase, 'the priesthood of all believers'. I would like to think that the second is the right answer and as Dr. Ryder Smith says, the context would suggest that it is, but I cannot personally, nevertheless, accept this conclusion with any confidence because it seems to me highly unlikely that Charles Wesley would give this application to the idea of literal succession. If, as is possible, the phrase 'faithful line' is a deliberate differentiation from his usual expression 'Sacred line', it may be that the variation was made to exclude the priestly idea. In this case the words must be taken as a general description of the Church without any reference whatever to its priestly character. I think this an unlikely but possible explanation. I am puzzled and must leave others to solve the problem.

## 50

1 Father of everlasting love,
  Whose bowels of compassion move
  To all Thy gracious hands have made,
  See, in the howling desert see
  A soul from *Egypt* brought by Thee,
  And help me with Thy constant aid.

2 Ah, do not, Lord, Thine own forsake,
  Nor let my feeble soul look back,
  Or basely turn to sin again;
  No, never let me faint or tire,
  But travel on in strong desire,
  Till I my heavenly *Canaan* gain.

## 51

1 Thou very Paschal Lamb,
  Whose blood for us was shed,
  Through whom we out of *Egypt* came,—
  Thy ransom'd people lead.

2 Angel of gospel grace,
  Fulfil Thy character;
  To guard and feed the chosen race,
  In *Israel's* camp appear.

3 Throughout the desert way
  Conduct us by Thy light;
  Be Thou a cooling cloud by day,
  A cheering fire by night.

4 Our fainting souls sustain
  With blessings from above,
  And ever on Thy people rain
  The manna of Thy love.

## 52

1 O Thou who, hanging on the cross,
  Didst buy our pardon with Thy blood,
  Canst Thou not still maintain our cause,
  And fill us with the life of God,
  Bless with the blessings of Thy throne,
  And perfect all our souls in One?

2 Lo, on Thy bloody sacrifice
  For all our graces we depend;
  Supported by Thy cross arise,
  To finish'd holiness ascend,
  And gain on earth the mountain's height,
  And then salute our friends in light.

## 53

1 O God of truth and love,
  Let us Thy mercy prove;
  Bless Thine ordinance Divine,
  Let it now effectual be,
  Answer all its great design,
  All its gracious ends in me.

2 O might the sacred word
  Set forth our dying Lord,
  Point us to Thy sufferings past,
  Present grace and strength impart,
  Give our ravish'd souls a taste,
  Pledge of glory in our heart.

3 Come in Thy Spirit down,
  Thine institution crown;
  Lamb of God, as slain appear,
  Life of all believers Thou,
  Let us now perceive Thee near,
  Come, Thou Hope of glory, now.

## 54

1 Why did my dying Lord ordain
  This dear memorial of His love?
  Might we not all by faith obtain,
  By faith the mountain sin remove,
  Enjoy the sense of sins forgiven,
  And holiness, the taste of heaven?

2 It seem'd to my Redeemer good
  That faith should *here* His coming wait,
  Should here receive immortal food,
  Grow up in Him Divinely great,
  And, fill'd with holy violence, seize
  The glorious crown of righteousness.

3 Saviour, Thou didst the mystery give,
  That I Thy nature might partake;
  Thou bidd'st me outward signs receive,
  One with Thyself my soul to make;
  My body, soul, and spirit to join
  Inseparably one with Thine.

4 The prayer, the fast, the word conveys,
  When mix'd with faith, Thy life to me;
  In all the channels of Thy grace
  I still have fellowship with Thee:
  But chiefly here my soul is fed
  With fulness of immortal bread.

5 Communion closer far I feel,
  And deeper drink the' atoning blood;
  The joy is more unspeakable,
  And yields me larger draughts of God,
  Till nature faints beneath the power,
  And faith fill'd up can hold no more.

## 55

1 'Tis not a dead external sign
  Which here my hopes require,
  The living power of love Divine
  In Jesus I desire.

2 I want the dear Redeemer's grace,
  I seek the Crucified,
  The Man that suffer'd in my place,
  The God that groan'd and died.

3 Swift, as their rising Lord to find
  The two disciples ran,
  I seek the Saviour of mankind,
  Nor shall I seek in vain.

4 Come, all who long His face to see
  That did our burden bear,
  Hasten to *Calvary* with me,
  And we shall find Him there.

## 56

1 How dreadful is the mystery
  Which, instituted, Lord, by Thee,
  Or life or death conveys!
  Death to the impious and profane;
  Nor shall our faith in Thee be vain,
  Who here expect Thy grace.

2 Who eats unworthily this bread
  Pulls down Thy curses on his head,
  And eats his deadly bane;
  And shall not we who rightly eat
  Live by the salutary meat,
  And equal blessings gain?

3 Destruction if Thy body shed,
  And strike the soul of sinners dead
  Who dare the signs abuse,
  Surely the instrument Divine
  To all that are, or would be, Thine
  Shall saving health diffuse.

4 Saviour of life, and joy, and bliss,
  Pardon and power and perfect peace
  We shall herewith receive;
  The grace implied through faith is given,
  And we that eat the Bread of heaven
  The life of heaven shall live.

## 57

1 O THE depth of love Divine,
   Th' unfathomable grace!
Who shall say how bread and wine
   God into man conveys!
*How* the bread His flesh imparts,
   *How* the wine transmits His blood,
Fills His faithful people's hearts
   With all the life of God!

2 Let the wisest mortal show
   How we the grace receive,
Feeble elements bestow
   A power not theirs to give.
Who explains the wondrous way,
   How through these the virtue came?
These the virtue did convey,
   Yet still remain the same.

3 How can heavenly spirits rise,
   By earthly matter fed,
Drink herewith Divine supplies,
   And eat immortal bread?
Ask the Father's Wisdom *how*;
   Him that did the means ordain!
Angels round our altars bow
   To search it out in vain.

4 Sure and real is the grace,
   The manner be unknown;
Only meet us in Thy ways,
   And perfect us in one.
Let us taste the heavenly powers;
   Lord, we ask for nothing more:
Thine to bless, 'tis only ours
   To wonder and adore.

## 58

1 How long, Thou faithful God, shall I
Here in Thy ways forgotten lie?
When shall the means of healing be
The channels of Thy grace to me?

2 Sinners on every side step in,
And wash away their pain and sin;
But I, an helpless sin-sick soul,
Still lie expiring at the pool.

3 In vain I take the broken bread,
I cannot on Thy mercy feed;
In vain I drink the hallow'd wine,
I cannot taste the love Divine.

4 Angel and Son of God, come down,
Thy sacramental banquet crown,
Thy power into the means infuse,
And give them now their sacred use.

5 Thou seest me lying at the pool,
I would, Thou know'st I would be whole;
O let the troubled waters move,
And minister Thy healing love.

6 Break to me now the hallow'd bread,
And bid me on Thy body feed;
Give me the wine, Almighty God,
And let me drink Thy precious blood.

7 Surely if Thou the symbols bless,
The covenant blood shall seal my peace;
Thy flesh even now shall be my food,
And all my soul be fill'd with God.

## 59

1 GOD incomprehensible
   Shall man presume to know;
Fully search Him out, or tell
   His wondrous ways below?
Him in all His ways we find;
   *How* the means transmit the power—
Here He leaves our thoughts behind,
   And faith inquires no more.

2 How He did these creatures raise,
   And make this bread and wine
Organs to convey His grace
   To this poor soul of mine,
I cannot the way descry,
   Need not know the mystery;
Only this I know—that I
   Was blind, but now I see.

3 Now mine eyes are open'd wide,
    To see His pardoning love,
Here I view the God that died
    My ruin to remove;
Clay upon mine eyes He laid,
    (I at once my sight received,)
Bless'd, and bid me eat the bread,
    And lo! my soul believed.

## 60

1 COME to the feast, for Christ invites,
    And promises to feed;
'Tis here His closest love unites
    The members to their Head.

2 'Tis here He nourishes His own
    With living bread from heaven,
Or makes Himself to mourners known,
    And shows their sins forgiven.

3 Still in His instituted ways
    He bids us ask the power,
The pardoning or the hallowing grace,
    And wait th' appointed hour.

4 'Tis not for us to set our God
    A time His grace to give,
The benefit whene'er bestow'd
    We gladly should receive.

5 Who seek redemption through His love,
    His love shall them redeem;
He came self-emptied from above,
    That we might live through Him.

6 Expect we then the quickening word,
    Who at His altar bow;
But if it be Thy pleasure, Lord,
    O let us find Thee now.

## 61

1 THOU God of boundless power and grace,
    How wonderful are all Thy ways!
    How far above our loftiest thought!
In presence of the meanest things,
(While all from Thee the virtue springs,)
    Thy most stupendous works are wrought.

Struck by a stroke of *Moses'* rod,
The parting sea confess'd its God,
    And high in crystal bulwarks rose;
At *Moses'* beck it burst the chain,
Return'd to all its strength again,
    And swept to hell Thy church's foes.

2 Let but Thy ark the walls surround,
Let but the ram's-horn trumpet sound,
    The city boasts its height no more;
Its bulwarks are at once o'erthrown,
Its massy walls by air blown down,
    They fall before almighty power.

*Jordan* at Thy command shall heal
The sore disease incurable,
    And wash out all the leper's stains;
Or oil the medicine shall supply,
Or clothes, or shadows passing by,
    If so Thy sovereign will ordains.

3 Yet not from these the power proceeds,
Trumpets, or rods, or clothes, or shades
    Thy only arm the work hath done;
If instruments Thy wisdom choose,
Thy grace confers their saving use,
    Salvation is from God alone.

Thou in this sacramental bread
Dost now our hungry spirits feed,
    And cheer us with the hallow'd wine;
(Communion of Thy flesh and blood,)
We banquet on immortal food,
    And drink the streams of life Divine.

## 62

1 The heavenly ordinances shine,
And speak their origin Divine:
The stars diffuse their golden blaze,
And glitter to their Maker's praise;

2 They each, in different glory bright,
With stronger or with feebler light
Their influence on mortals shed,
And cheer us by their friendly aid.

3 The gospel ordinances here
As stars in Jesu's church appear;
His power they more or less declare,
But all His heavenly impress bear.

4 Around our lower orb they burn,
And cheer and bless us in their turn,
Transmit the light by Jesus given,
The faithful witnesses of heaven.

5 They steer the pilgrim's course aright,
And bounteous of their borrow'd light
Conduct throughout the desert way,
And lead us to eternal day.

6 But first of the celestial train,
Benignest to the sons of men,
The *sacramental glory* shines,
And answers all our God's designs.

7 The heavenly host it passes far,
Illustrious as the morning star,
The light of life Divine imparts,
While Jesus rises in our hearts.

8 With joy we feel its sacred power,
But neither stars nor means adore;
We take the blessing from above,
And praise the God of truth and love.

9 What He did for our use ordain
Shall still from age to age remain;
Whoe'er rejects the kind command,
The word of God shall ever stand.

10 Go, foolish worms, His word deny;
Go, tear those planets from the sky!
But while the sun and moon endure,
The ordinance on earth is sure.

## 63

1 O God, Thy word we claim,
Thou here record'st Thy name:
Visit us in pardoning grace,
Christ, the Crucified, appear,
Come in Thy appointed ways,
Come, and meet, and bless us here.

2 No local Deity
We worship, Lord, in Thee:
Free Thy grace and unconfined,
Yet it here doth freest move;
In the means Thy love enjoin'd
Look we for Thy richest love.

## 64

1 O the grace on man bestow'd!
Here my dearest Lord I see
Offering up His death to God,
Giving all His life to me;
God for Jesu's sake forgives,
Man by Jesu's Spirit lives.

2 Yes, Thy sacrament extends
All the blessings of Thy death
To the soul that here attends,
Longs to feel Thy quickening breath;
Surely we who wait shall prove
All Thy life of perfect love.

## 65

1 Blest be the Lord, for ever blest,
Who bought us with a price,
And bids His ransom'd servants feast
On His great sacrifice.

2 Thy blood was shed upon the cross,
To wash us white as snow;
Broken for us Thy body was,
To feed our souls below.

3 Now, on the sacred table laid,
   Thy flesh becomes our food,
   Thy life is to our souls convey'd
     In sacramental blood.

4 We eat the offering of our peace,
   The hidden manna prove,
   And only live t' adore and bless
     Thine all-sufficient love.

### 66

1 JESU, my Lord and God, bestow
   All which Thy sacrament doth show,
     And make the real sign
   A sure effectual means of grace,
   Then sanctify my heart, and bless,
     And make it all like Thine.

2 Great is Thy faithfulness and love,
   Thine ordinance can never prove
     Of none effect, and vain;
   Only do Thou my heart prepare
   To find Thy real presence there,
     And all Thy fulness gain.

### 67

1 FATHER, I offer Thee Thine own,
   This worthless soul, and Thou Thy Son
     Dost offer here to me:
   Wilt Thou so mean a gift receive,
   And will the holy Jesus live
     With loathsome leprosy?

2 Saint of the Lord, my soul is sin;
   Yet, O Eternal Priest, come in,
     And cleanse Thy mean abode;
   Convert into a sacred shrine,
   And count this abject soul of mine
     A temple meet for God.

### 68

1 JESU, Son of God, draw near,
   Hasten to my sepulchre;
   Help, where dead in sin I lie,
   Save, or I for ever die.

2 Let no savour of the grave
   Stop Thy power to help and save;
   Call me forth to life restored,
   Quicken'd by my dying Lord.

3 By Thine all-atoning blood
   Raise and bring me now to God,
   Now pronounce my sins forgiven,
   Loose, and let me go to heaven.

### 69

1 SINFUL, and blind, and poor,
   And lost without Thy grace,
   Thy mercy I implore,
   And wait to see Thy face;
   Begging I sit by the wayside,
   And long to know the Crucified.

2 Jesu, attend my cry,
   Thou Son of *David*, hear;
   If now Thou passest by,
   Stand still and call me near,
   The darkness from my heart remove,
   And show me now Thy pardoning love.

### 70

HAPPY the man to whom 'tis given
To eat the Bread of life in heaven:
This happiness in Christ we prove,
Who feed on His forgiving love.

## 71

1. Draw near, ye blood-besprinkled race,
   And take what God vouchsafes to give;
   The outward sign of inward grace,
   Ordain'd by Christ Himself, receive:
   The sign transmits the signified,
   The grace is by the means applied.

2. Sure pledges of His dying love,
   Receive the sacramental meat,
   And feel the virtue from above,
   The mystic flesh of Jesus eat,
   Drink with the wine His healing blood,
   And feast on th' Incarnate God.

3. Gross misconceit be far away!
   Through faith we on His body feed;
   Faith only doth the Spirit convey,
   And fills our souls with living bread,
   Th' effects of Jesu's death imparts,
   And pours His blood into our hearts.

## 72

1. Come, Holy Ghost, Thine influence shed,
   And realize[1] the sign;
   Thy life infuse into the bread,
   Thy power into the wine.

2. Effectual let the tokens prove,
   And made, by heavenly art,
   Fit channels to convey Thy love
   To every faithful heart.

## 73

1. Is not the cup of blessing, blest
   By us, the sacred means t' impart
   Our Saviour's blood, with power imprest
   And pardon to the faithful heart?

2. Is not the hallow'd broken bread
   A sure communicating sign,
   An instrument ordain'd to feed
   Our souls with mystic flesh Divine?

3. Th' effects of His atoning blood,
   His body offer'd on the tree,
   Are with the awful types bestow'd
   On me, the pardon'd rebel, *me*;

4. On all who at His word draw near,
   In faith the outward veil look through:
   Sinners, believe, and find Him here;
   Believe, and feel He died for you.

5. In memory of your dying God,
   The symbols faithfully receive,
   And eat the flesh and drink the blood
   Of Jesus, and for ever live.

## 74

1. This, this is He that came
   By water and by blood;
   Jesus is our atoning Lamb,
   Our sanctifying God.

2. See from His wounded side
   The mingled current flow!
   The water and the blood, applied,
   Shall wash us white as snow.

---

[1] The use of the word 'realize' is archaic. I suggest emendation of second line: 'And *real make* the sign.'

3   The water cannot cleanse
    Before the blood we feel,
To purge the guilt of all our sins,
    And our forgiveness seal.

4   But both in Jesus join,
    Who speaks our sins forgiven,
And gives the purity Divine
    That makes us meet for heaven.

## 75

1   FATHER, the grace we claim,
        The double grace, bestow'd
    On all who trust in Him that came
        By water and by blood.

2   Jesu, the blood apply,
        The righteousness bring in,
    Us by Thy dying justify,
        And wash out all our sin.

3   Spirit of faith, come down,
        Thy seal with power set to,
    The banquet by Thy presence crown,
        And prove the record true:

4   Pardon and grace impart;
        Come quickly from above,
    And witness now in every heart
        That God is perfect love.

## 76

1 SEARCHER of hearts, in ours appear,
  And make and keep them all sincere;
  Or draw us burden'd to Thy Son,
  Or make Him to His mourners known.

2 Thy promised grace vouchsafe to give,
  As each is able to receive;
  The blessed grief to all impart,
  Or joy, or purity of heart.

3 Our helpless unbelief remove,
  And melt us by Thy pardoning love;
  Work in us faith, or faith's increase,
  The dawning, or the perfect peace.

4 Give each to Thee as seemeth best,
  But meet us all at Thy own feast,
  Thy blessing in Thy means convey,
  Nor empty send one soul away.

## 77

1   How long, O Lord, shall we
        In vain lament for Thee?
    Come, and comfort them that mourn,
        Come, as in the ancient days,
    In Thine ordinance return,
        In Thine own appointed ways.

2   Come to Thy house again,
        Nor let us seek in vain;
    This the place of meeting be,
        To Thy weeping flock repair;
    Let us here Thy beauty see,
        Find Thee in the house of prayer.

3   Let us with solemn awe
        Nigh to Thine altar draw,
    Taste Thee in the broken bread,
        Drink Thee in the mystic wine;
    Now the gracious Spirit shed,
        Fill us now with love Divine.

4   Into our minds recall
        Thy death, endured for all:
    Come in this accepted day,
        Come, and all our souls restore,
    Come, and take our sins away,
        Come, and never leave us more.

## 78

1 LAMB OF GOD, for whom we languish,
      Make Thy grief Our relief,
      Ease us by Thine anguish.

2 O our agonizing Saviour,
      By Thy pain Let us gain
      God's eternal favour.

3 Suffer sin no more t' oppress us,
      Set us free, (All with me,)
      By Thy bonds release us.

4 Clear us by Thy condemnation;
      Slain for all, Let Thy fall
      Be our exaltation.

5 Thy deserts to us make over;
   Speak us whole, Every soul
   By Thy wounds recover.

6 Let us through Thy curse inherit
   Blessings' store, Love and power,
   Fulness of Thy Spirit;

7 The whole benefit of Thy passion,
   Present peace, Future bliss,
   All Thy great salvation.

8 Power to walk in all well-pleasing
   Bid us take, Come and make
   This th' accepted season.

9 In Thine own appointments bless us,
   Meet us here, Now appear,
   Our Almighty Jesus.

10 Let the ordinance be sealing,
   Enter now, Claim us Thou
   For Thy constant dwelling.

11 Fill the heart of each believer;
   We are Thine, Love Divine,
   Reign in us for ever.

### 79

1 JESU, regard the plaintive cry,
   The groaning of Thy prisoners here;
  Thy blood to every soul apply,
   The heart of every mourner cheer,
  The tokens of Thy passion show,
  And meet us in Thy ways below.

2 Th' atonement Thou for all hast made,
   O that we all might now receive!
  Assure us now the debt is paid,
   And Thou hast died that all may live,
  Thy death for all, for us reveal,
  And let Thy blood *my* pardon seal.

### 80

1 WITH pity, Lord, a sinner see,
   Weary of Thy ways and Thee;
   Forgive my fond despair
  A blessing in the means to find,
  My struggling to throw off the care,
   And cast them all behind.

2 Long have I groan'd Thy grace to gain,
   Suffer'd on, but all in vain:
   An age of mournful years
  I waited for Thy passing by,
  And lost my prayers, my sighs, and tears,
   And never found Thee nigh.

3 Thou wouldst not let me go away;
   Still Thou forcest me to stay.
   O might the secret power
  Which will not with its captive part
  Nail to the post of mercy's door
   My poor unstable heart.

4 The nails that fix'd Thee to the tree,
   Only they can fasten me:
   The death Thou didst endure
  For me let it effectual prove:
  Thy love alone my soul can cure,
   Thy dear expiring love.

5 Now in the means the grace impart,
   Whisper peace into my heart;
   Appear the Justifier
  Of all who to Thy wounds would fly,
  And let me have my one desire,
   And see Thy face, and die.

## 81

1 JESU, we thus obey
 Thy last and kindest word,
Here in Thine own appointed way
 We come to meet our Lord:
 The way Thou has enjoin'd
 Thou wilt therein appear;
We come with confidence to find
 Thy special presence here.

2 Our hearts we open wide,
 To make the Saviour room;
And lo! the Lamb, the Crucified,
 The sinner's Friend, is come!
 His presence makes the feast;
 And now our bosoms feel
The glory not to be exprest,
 The joy unspeakable.

3 With pure celestial bliss
 He doth our spirits cheer,
His house of banqueting is this,
 And He hath brought us here:
 He doth His servants feed
 With manna from above,
His banner over us is spread,
 His everlasting love.

4 He bids us drink and eat
 Imperishable food,
He gives His flesh to be our meat,
 And bids us drink His blood:
 Whate'er the' Almighty can
 To pardon'd sinners give,
The fulness of our God made man
 We here with Christ receive.

## 82

1 JESU, sinner's Friend, receive us,
 Feeble, famishing, and faint;
O Thou Bread of Life, relieve us
 Now, or now we die for want:
 Lest we faint, and die for ever,
 Thou our sinking spirits stay;
Give some token of Thy favour,
 Empty send us not away.

2 We have in the desert tarried
 Long, and nothing have to eat;
Comfort us, through wandering wearied,
 Feed our souls with living meat;
 Still with bowels of compassion
 See, Thy helpless people see;
Let us taste Thy great salvation,
 Let us feed by faith on Thee.

## 83

1 LORD, if now Thou passest by us,
 Stand and call us unto Thee,
Freely, fully justify us,
 Give us eyes Thy love to see,
 Love that brought Thee down from heaven,
 Made our God a man of grief;
Let it show our sins forgiven;
 Help, O help our unbelief.

2 Long we for Thy love have waited,
 Begging sat by the wayside;
Still we are not new-created,
 Are not wholly sanctified:
 Thou to some in great compassion
 Hast in part their sight restored,
Show us all Thy full salvation,
 Make the servants as their Lord.

## 84

1 CHRIST our Passover for us
 Is offer'd up and slain!
Let Him be remember'd thus
 By every soul of man:
We are bound above the rest
 His oblation to proclaim;
Keep we then the solemn feast,
 And banquet on the Lamb.

2 Purge we all our sin away,
 That old accursed leaven;
Sin in us no longer stay,
 In us, through Christ forgiven:
Let us all with hearts sincere
 Eat the new unleaven'd bread,
To our Lord with faith draw near,
 And on His promise feed.

3 Jesus, Master of the feast,
　　The feast itself Thou art,
　Now receive Thy meanest guest,
　　And comfort every heart:
　Give us living bread to eat,
　　Manna that from heaven comes down,
　Fill us with immortal meat,
　　And make Thy nature known.

4 In this barren wilderness
　　Thou hast a table spread,
　Furnish'd out with richest grace
　　Whate'er our souls can need;
　Still sustain us by Thy love,
　　Still Thy servants' strength repair,
　Till we reach the courts above,
　　And feast for ever there.

## 85[1]

1 O Thou, whom sinners love, whose care
　Does all our sickness heal,
Thee we approach, with heart sincere,
　Thy power we joy to feel.
To Thee our humblest thanks we pay,
To Thee our souls we bow;
Of hell erewhile the helpless prey,
　Heirs of Thy glory now.

2 As incense to Thy throne above
　O, let our prayers arise!
O, wing with flames of holy love
　Our living sacrifice!
Stir up Thy strength, O Lord of Might,
　Our willing breasts inspire:
Fill our whole souls with heavenly light,
　Melt with seraphic fire.

3 From Thy blest wounds our life we draw;
　Thy all-atoning blood
Daily we drink with trembling awe;
　Thy flesh our daily food.
Come, Lord, Thy sovereign aid impart,
Here make Thy likeness shine!
Stamp Thy whole image on our heart,
And all our souls be Thine!

## 86

1　And shall I let Him go?
　　If now I do not *feel*
　The streams of living water flow,
　　Shall I forsake the well?

2　Because He hides His face,
　　Shall I no longer stay,
　But leave the channels of His grace,
　　And cast the means away?

3　Get thee behind me, fiend,
　　On others try thy skill,
　Here let thy hellish whispers end,
　　To thee I say, *Be still!*

4　Jesus hath spoke the word,
　　His will my reason is;
　*Do this* in memory of thy Lord,
　　Jesus hath said, *Do this!*

5　He bids me eat the bread,
　　He bids me drink the wine;
　No other motive, Lord, I need,
　　No other word than Thine.

6　I cheerfully comply
　　With what my Lord doth say;
　Let others ask a reason why,
　　My glory is t' obey.

7　His will is good and just:
　　Shall I His will withstand?
　If Jesus bids me lick the dust,
　　I bow at His command.

8　Because He saith, *Do this,*
　　This I will always do;
　Till Jesus come in glorious bliss,
　　I *thus* His death will *show.*

[1] See *Poetical Works*, Vol. I, p. 185. The authorship of this hymn is unknown.

## 87

1 By the picture of Thy passion
    Still in pain I remain,
  Waiting for salvation.

2 Jesu, let Thy sufferings ease me;
    Saviour, Lord, Speak the word,
  By Thy death release me.

3 At Thy cross behold me lying,
    Make my soul Throughly whole
  By Thy blood's applying.

4 Hear me, Lord, my sins confessing;
    Now relieve; Saviour, give,
  Give me now Thy blessing.

5 Still my cruel sins oppress me,
    Tied and bound Till the sound
  Of Thy voice release me.

6 Call me out of condemnation,
    To my grave Come, and save,
  Save me by Thy passion.

7 To Thy foul and helpless creature
    Come, and cleanse All my sins;
  Come, and change my nature.

8 Save me now, and still deliver;
    Enter in, Cast out sin,
  Keep Thine house for ever.

## 88

1 Give us this day, all-bounteous Lord,
    Our sacramental bread,
  Who thus His sacrifice record
    That suffer'd in our stead.

2 Reveal in every soul Thy Son,
    And let us taste the grace
  Which brings assured salvation down
    To all who seek Thy face.

3 Who here commemorate His death,
    To us His life impart,
  The loving filial spirit breathe
    Into my waiting heart.

4 My earnest of eternal bliss
    Let my Redeemer be;
  And if even now He present is,
    Now let Him speak in me.

## 89

1 Ye faithful souls, who thus record
    The passion of that Lamb Divine,
  Is the memorial of your Lord
    An useless form, an empty sign?
  Or doth He here His life impart?
  What saith the witness in your heart?

2 Is it the dying Master's will
    That we should this persist to do?
  Then let Him here Himself reveal,
    The tokens of His presence show,
  Descend in blessings from above,
  And answer by the fire of love.

3 Who Thee remember in Thy ways,
    Come, Lord, and meet and bless us here;
  In confidence we ask the grace;
    Faithful and True, appear, appear,
  Let all perceive Thy blood applied,
  Let all discern the Crucified.

4 'Tis done; the Lord sets to His seal,
    The prayer is heard, the grace is given,
  With joy unspeakable we feel
    The Holy Ghost sent down from heaven;
  The altar streams with sacred blood,
  And all the temple flames with God!

## 90

1 Blest be the love, for ever blest;
   The bleeding love we thus record:
Jesus, we take the dear bequest,
   Obedient to Thy kindest word,
Thy word which stands divinely sure,
And shall from age to age endure.

2 In vain the subtle tempter tries
   Thy dying precept to repeal,
To hide the letter from our eyes,
   And break the testamental seal,
Refine the solid truth away,
And make us free—to disobey.

3 In vain he labours to persuade
   Thou didst not mean the word
     should bind;
The feast for Thy first followers made,
   For them and us and all mankind,
Mindful of Thee we still attend,
And this we do till time shall end.

4 Through vain pretence of clearer light,
   We do not, Lord, refuse to see,
Or weakly the commandment slight
   To show our Christian liberty,
Or seek rebelliously to prove
The pureness of our catholic love.

5 Our wandering brethren's hearts to gain,
   We will not let our Saviour go,
But in Thine ancient paths remain,
But thus persist Thy death to show,
Till strong with all Thy life we rise,
And met Thee coming in the skies!

## 91

1 All-loving, all-redeeming Lord,
   Thy wandering sheep with pity see
Who slight Thy dearest dying word,
And will not thus remember Thee:
To all who would perform Thy will
The glorious promised truth reveal.

2 Can we enjoy Thy richest love,
   Nor long that they the grace may share?
Thou from their eyes the scales remove,
Thou th' eternal word declare,
Thy Spirit with Thy word impart,
And speak the precept to their heart.

3 If chiefly here Thou mayst be found,
   If now, even now, we find Thee here,
O let their joys like ours abound,
   Invite them to the royal cheer,
Feed with imperishable food,
And fill their raptured souls with God.

4 Jesu, we will not let Thee go,
   But keep herein our fastest hold,
Till Thou to them Thy counsel show,
   And call and make us all one fold,
One hallow'd undivided bread,
One body knit to Thee our Head.

## 92

1 Ah, tell us no more
   The spirit and power
   Of Jesus our God
Is not to be found in this life-giving food!

2 Did Jesus ordain
   His supper in vain,
   And furnish a feast
For none but His earliest servants to taste?

3 Nay, but this is His will,
   (We know it and feel,)
   That *we* should partake
The banquet for all He so freely did make.

4 In rapturous bliss
   He bids us do this,
   The joy it imparts
Hath witness'd His gracious design in our hearts.

5 'Tis God we believe,
  Who cannot deceive,
  The witness of God
Is present, and speaks in the mystical blood.

6 Receiving the bread,
  On Jesus we feed:
  It doth not appear,
His manner of working; but Jesus is here!

7 With bread from above,
  With comfort and love
  Our spirit He fills,
And all His unspeakable goodness reveals.

8 O that all men would haste
  To the spiritual feast,
  At Jesus's word
*Do this*, and be fed with the love of our Lord!

9 True Light of mankind,
  Shine into their mind,
  And clearly reveal
Thy perfect and good and acceptable will.

10 Bring near the glad day
   When all shall obey
   Thy dying request,
And eat of Thy supper, and lean on Thy breast.

11 To all men impart
   One way and one heart,
   Thy people be shown
All righteous and spotless and perfect in One.

12 Then, then let us see
   Thy glory, and be
   Caught up in the air,
This heavenly supper in heaven to share.

## III. *The Sacrament a Pledge of Heaven*

### 93

1 COME, let us join with one accord
  Who share the supper of the Lord,
    Our Lord and Master's praise to sing;
  Nourish'd on earth with living bread,
  We now are at His table fed,
  But wait to see our heavenly King;
  To see the great Invisible
  Without a sacramental veil,
    With all His robes of glory on,
  In rapturous joy and love and praise
  Him to behold with open face,
    High on His everlasting throne!

2 The wine which doth His passion show,
  We soon with Him shall drink it new
    In yonder dazzling courts above;
  Admitted to the heavenly feast,
  We shall His choicest blessings taste,
    And banquet on His richest love.

We soon the midnight cry shall hear,
Arise, and meet the Bridegroom near,
  The marriage of the Lamb is come;
Attended by His heavenly friends,
The glorious King of saints descends
  To take His bride in triumph home.

3 Then let us still in hope rejoice,
  And listen for th' archangel's voice
    Loud echoing to the trump of God,
  Haste to the dreadful joyful day,
  When heaven and earth shall flee away,
    By all-devouring flames destroy'd:
  While we from out the burnings fly,
  With eagle's wings mount up on high,
    Where Jesus is on *Sion* seen;
  'Tis there He for our coming waits,
  And lo, the everlasting gates
    Lift up their heads to take us in!

4 By faith and hope already there,
　Even now the marriage-feast we share,
　　Even now we by the Lamb are fed;
　Our Lord's celestial joy we prove,
　Led by the Spirit of His love,
　　To springs of living comfort led:

94

1 O WHAT a soul-transporting feast
　　Doth this communion yield!
　Remembering here Thy passion past,
　　We with Thy love are fill'd.

2 Sure instrument of present grace
　　Thy sacrament we find,
　Yet higher blessings it displays,
　　And raptures still behind.

1 IN Jesus we live, In Jesus we rest,
　And thankful receive His dying bequest;
　The cup of salvation His mercy bestows,
　And all from His passion Our happiness flows.

2 With mystical wine He comforts us here,
　And gladly we join, Till Jesus appear,
　With hearty thanksgiving His death to record;
　The living, the living Should sing of their Lord.

1 HAPPY the souls to Jesus join'd,
　　And saved by grace alone;
　Walking in all Thy ways we find
　　Our heaven on earth begun.

2 The church triumphant in Thy love,
　　Their mighty joys we know;
　They sing the Lamb in hymns above,
　　And we in hymns below.

97

1 　　THEE, King of saints, we praise
　　　For this our living bread,
　　Nourish'd by Thy preserving grace,
　　　And at Thy table fed;

　Suffering and curse and death are o'er,
　And pain afflicts the soul no more
　　While harbour'd in the Saviour's breast;
　He quiets all our plaints and cries,
　And wipes the sorrow from our eyes,
　　And lulls us in His arms to rest!

3 It bears us now on eagle's wings,
　　If Thou the power impart,
　And Thee our glorious earnest brings
　　Into our faithful heart.

4 O let us still the earnest feel,
　　Th' unutterable peace,
　This loving Spirit be the seal
　　Of our eternal bliss!

95

3 He hallow'd the cup Which now we receive,
　The pledge of our hope With Jesus to live,
　(Where sorrow and sadness Shall never be found,)
　With glory and gladness Eternally crown'd.

4 The fruit of the wine (The joy it implies)
　Again we shall join To drink in the skies,
　Exult in His favour, Our triumph renew;
　And I, saith the Saviour, Will drink it with you.

96

3 Thee in Thy glorious realm they praise,
　　And bow before Thy throne;
　We in the kingdom of Thy grace,
　　The kingdoms are but one.

4 The holy to the holiest leads,
　　From hence our spirits rise,
　And he that in Thy statutes treads
　　Shall meet Thee in the skies.

　Who in these lower parts
　　Of Thy great kingdom feast,
　We feel the earnest in our hearts
　　Of our eternal rest.

2    Yet still an higher seat
       We in Thy kingdom claim,
       Who here begin by faith to eat
         The supper of the Lamb:
       That glorious heavenly prize
       We surely shall attain,
       And in the palace of the skies
         With Thee for ever reign.

## 98

1  WHERE shall this memorial end?
     Thither let our souls ascend,
     Live on earth to heaven restored,
     Wait the coming of our Lord.

2  Jesus terminates our hope,
     Jesus is our wishes' scope;
     End of this great mystery,
     Him we fain would die to see.

3  He whom we remember here,
     Christ shall in the clouds appear;
     Manifest to every eye,
     We shall soon behold Him nigh.

4  Faith ascends the mountain's height,
     Now enjoys the pompous sight,
     Antedates the final doom,
     Sees the Judge in glory come.

5  Lo, He comes triumphant down,
     Seated on His great white throne!
     Cherubs bear it on their wings,
     Shouting bear the King of kings.

6  Lo, His glorious banner spread
     Stains the skies with deepest red,
     Dyes the land, and fires the wood,
     Turns the ocean into blood.

7  Gather'd to the well-known sign,
     We our elder brethren join,
     Swiftly to our Lord fly up,
     Hail Him on the mountain-top;

8  Take our happy seats above,
     Banquet on His heavenly love,
     Lean on our Redeemer's breast,
     In His arms for ever rest.

## 99

1  WHITHER should our full souls aspire,
       At this transporting feast?
     They never can on earth be higher,
       Or more completely blest.

2  Our cup of blessing from above
       Delightfully runs o'er,
     Till from these bodies they remove
       Our souls can hold no more.

3  To heaven the mystic banquet leads;
       Let us to heaven ascend,
     And bear this joy upon our heads
       Till it in glory end.

4  Till all who truly join in this,
       The marriage supper share,
     Enter into their Master's bliss,
       And feast for ever there.

## 100

1  RETURNING to His throne above,
     The Friend of sinners cried,
    *Do this* in memory of My love:
     He spoke the word, and died.

2  He tasted death for every one:
     The Saviour of mankind
     Out of our sight to heaven is gone,
     But left His pledge behind.

3 His sacramental pledge we take,
   Nor will we let it go;
Till in the clouds our Lord comes back,
   We thus His death will show.

4 Come quickly, Lord, for whom we mourn,
   And comfort all that grieve;
Prepare the bride, and then return,
   And to Thyself receive.

5 Now to Thy glorious kingdom come;
   (Thou hast a token given;)
And while Thy arms receive us home,
   Recall Thy pledge in heaven.

### 101

1 How glorious is the life above,
   Which in this ordinance we *taste*;
That fulness of celestial love,
   That joy which shall for ever last!

2 That heavenly life in Christ conceal'd
   These earthen vessels could not bear,
The part which now we find reveal'd
   No tongue of angels can declare.

3 The light of life eternal darts
   Into our souls a dazzling ray,
A drop of heaven o'erflows our hearts,
   And deluges the house of clay.

4 Sure pledge of ecstasies unknown
   Shall this Divine communion be;
The ray shall rise into a sun,
   The drop shall swell into a sea.

### 102

1 O THE length, and breadth, and height,
   And depth of dying love!
Love that turns our faith to sight,
   And wafts to heaven above!
Pledge of our possession this,
   This which nature faints to bear;
Who shall then support the bliss,
   The joy, the rapture there!

2 Flesh and blood shall not receive
   The vast inheritance;
God we cannot see, and live
   The life of feeble sense;
In our weakest nonage here,
   Up into our Head we grow,
Saints before our Lord appear,
   And ripe for heaven below.

3 We His image shall regain,
   And to His stature rise,
Rise unto a perfect man,
   And then ascend the skies,
Find our happy mansions there,
   Strong to bear the joys above,
All the glorious weight to bear
   Of everlasting love.

### 103

1 TAKE, and eat, the Saviour saith,
   This My sacred body is!
Him we take and eat by faith,
   Feed upon that flesh of His,
All the benefits receive
   Which His passion did procure;
Pardon'd by His grace we live,
   Grace which makes salvation sure.

2 Title to eternal bliss
   Here His precious death we find,
This the pledge, the earnest this,
   Of the purchased joys behind:
Here He gives our souls a taste,
   Heaven into our heart He pours:
Still believe, and hold Him fast;
   God and Christ and all is ours!

## 104

1 RETURNING to His Father's throne,
  Hear all the interceding Son,
  And join in that eternal prayer:
  He prays that we with Him may reign,
  And He that did the kingdom gain
  For us, shall soon conduct us there.

2 'I will that those Thou giv'st to Me
  May all My heavenly glory see,
  But first be perfected in One.'
  Amen, Amen! our heart replies,
  Prepare, and take us to the skies;
  Thy prayer be heard, Thy will be done!

## 105

1 LIFT your eyes of faith, and see
  Saints and angels join'd in one,
  What a countless company
  Stands before yon dazzling throne!
  Each before his Saviour stands,
  All in milk-white robes array'd;
  Palms they carry in their hands,
  Crowns of glory on their head.

2 Saints begin the endless song,
  Cry aloud, in heavenly lays,
  Glory doth to God belong,
  God the glorious Saviour praise;
  All from Him salvation came,
  Him who reigns enthroned on high;
  Glory to the bleeding Lamb
  Let the morning stars reply.

3 Angel-powers the throne surround,
  Next the saints in glory they;
  Lull'd with the transporting sound,
  They their silent homage pay;
  Prostrate on their face before
  God and His Messiah fall,
  Then in hymns of praise adore,
  Shout the Lamb that died for all.

4 Be it so! they all reply;
  Him let all our orders praise,
  Him that did for sinners die,
  Saviour of the favour'd race:
  Render we our God His right,
  Glory, wisdom, thanks, and power,
  Honour, majesty, and might;
  Praise Him, praise Him evermore!

## 106

1 WHAT are these array'd in white,
  Brighter than the noon-day sun,
  Foremost of the sons of light,
  Nearest th' eternal throne?
  These are they that bore the cross,
  Nobly for their Master stood,
  Sufferers in His righteous cause,
  Followers of the dying God.

2 Out of great distress they came,
  Wash'd their robes by faith below
  In the blood of yonder Lamb,
  Blood that washes white as snow.
  Therefore are they next the throne,
  Serve their Maker day and night;
  God resides among His own,
  God doth in His saints delight.

3 More than conquerors at last,
  Here they find their trials o'er;
  They have all their sufferings past,
  Hunger now and thirst no more;
  No excessive heat they feel
  From the sun's directer ray,
  In a milder clime they dwell,
  Region of eternal day.

4 He that on the throne doth reign,
  Them the Lamb shall always feed,
  With the tree of life sustain,
  To the living fountains lead;
  He shall all their sorrows chase,
  All their wants at once remove,
  Wipe the tears from every face,
  Fill up every soul with love.

## 107

1. ALL hail, Thou suffering Son of God,
   Who didst these mysteries ordain,
   Communion of Thy flesh and blood,
   Some instrument Thy grace to gain,
   Type of the heavenly marriage feast,
   Pledge of our everlasting rest.

2. Jesu, Thine own with pity see,
   Our helpless unbelief remove,
   Empower us to remember Thee,
   Give us the faith that works by love,
   The faith which Thou hast given increase,
   And seal us up in glorious peace.

## 108

1. AH, give us, Saviour, to partake
   The sufferings which this emblem shows;
   Thy flesh our food immortal make,
   Thy blood which in this channel flows
   In all its benefits impart,
   And sanctify our sprinkled heart.

2. For all that joy which now we taste,
   Our happy hallow'd souls prepare;
   O let us hold the earnest fast,
   This pledge that we Thy heaven shall share,
   Shall drink it new with Thee above,
   The wine of Thy eternal love.

## 109

1. LORD, Thou know'st my simpleness,
   All my groans are heard by Thee;
   See me hungering after grace,
   Gasping at Thy table, see
   One who would in Thee believe,
   Would with joy the crumbs receive.

2. Look as when Thy closing eye
   Saw the thief beside Thy cross;
   Thou art now gone up on high,
   Undertake my desperate cause,
   In Thy heavenly kingdom Thou
   Be the Friend of sinners now.

3. Saviour, Prince, enthroned above,
   Send a peaceful answer down,
   Let the bowels[1] of Thy love
   Echo to a sinner's groan,
   One who feebly thinks of Thee;
   Thou for good remember me.

## 110

1. JESU, on Thee we feed
   Along the desert way,
   Thou art the living Bread
   Which doth our spirits stay,
   And all who in this banquet join
   Lean on the staff of life Divine.

2. While to Thy upper courts
   We take our joyful flight,
   Thy blessed cross supports
   Each feeble *Israelite*;
   Like hoary dying *Jacob*, we
   Lean on our Staff and worship Thee.

3. O may we still abide
   In Thee our pardoning God,
   Thy Spirit be our guide,
   Thy body be our food,
   Till Thou who hast the token given
   Shalt bear us on Thyself to heaven.

---

[1] An emendation of this beautiful hymn for singing is necessary. I suggest: 'Let the *music* of Thy love echo to a sinner's groan.' See p. 77, *supra*.

### 111

1 AND can we call to mind
  The Lamb for sinners slain,
  And not expect to find
  What He for us did gain,
What God to us in Him hath given,
Pardon and holiness and heaven?

2 We now forgiveness have,
  We feel His work begun,
  And He shall fully save
  And perfect us in one,
Shall soon in all His image drest
Receive us to the marriage feast.

3 This token of Thy love
  We thankfully receive,
  And hence with joy remove
  With Thee in heaven to live;
There, Lord, we shall Thy pledge restore,
And live to praise Thee evermore.

### 112

1 ETERNAL Spirit, gone up on high
  Blessings for mortals to receive,
  Send down those blessings from the sky,
  To us Thy gifts and graces give;
With holy things our mouths are fill'd,
O let our hearts with joy o'erflow;
Descend in pardoning love reveal'd,
And meet us in Thy courts below.

2 Thy sacrifice without the gate
  Once offer'd up we call to mind,
  And humbly at Thy altar wait
  Our interest in Thy death to find;
We thirst to drink Thy precious blood,
We languish in Thy wounds to rest,
And hunger for immortal food,
And long on all Thy love to feast.

3 O that we now Thy flesh may eat,
  Its virtues really receive;
  Empower'd by this immortal meat
  The life of holiness to live:
Partakers of Thy sacrifice,
O may we all Thy nature share,
Till to the holiest place we rise
And keep the feast for ever there.

### 113

1 GIVE us, O Lord, the children's bread,
  By ministerial angels fed,
    (The angels of Thy church below,)
  Nourish us with preserving grace
  Our forty years or forty days,
  And lead us through the vale of woe.

2 Strengthen'd by this immortal food,
  O let us reach the mount of God,
  And face to face our Saviour see;
  In songs of praise, and love, and joy,
  With all thy first-born sons employ
  A happy whole eternity.

### 114

1 SEE there the quickening Cause of all
  Who live the life of grace beneath!
  God caused on Him the sleep to fall,
  And lo, His eyes are closed in death!

2 He sleeps; and from His open side
  The mingled blood and water flow;
  They both give being to His bride,
  And wash His church as white as snow.

3 True principles of life Divine,
    Issues from these the second *Eve*,
    Mother of all the faithful line,
    Of all that by His passion live.

4 O what a miracle of love
    Hath He, our heavenly *Adam*, show'd!
    Jesus forsook His throne above,
    That we might all be born of God.

5 'Twas not a useless rib He lost,
    His heart's last drop of blood He gave;
    His life, His precious life it cost
    Our dearly ransom'd souls to save.

6 And will He not His purchase take,
    Who died to make us all His own,
    One spirit with Himself to make,
    Flesh of His flesh, bone of His bone?

7 He will, our hearts reply He will:
    He hath even here a token given,
    And bids us meet Him on the hill,
    And keep the marriage feast in heaven.

115

1 O GLORIOUS instrument Divine,
    Which blessings to our souls conveys,
    Brings with the hallow'd bread and wine
    His strengthening and refreshing grace,
    Presents His bleeding sacrifice,
    His all-reviving death applies!

2 Glory to God who reigns above,
    But suffer'd once for man below!
    With joy we celebrate His love,
    And thus His precious passion show,
    Till in the clouds our Lord we see,
    And shout with all His saints—'TIS HE!

---

## IV. *The Holy Eucharist as it implies a Sacrifice*

116

1 VICTIM DIVINE, Thy grace we claim
    While thus Thy precious death we show;
    Once offer'd up, a spotless Lamb,
    In Thy great temple here below,
    Thou didst for all mankind atone,
    And standest now before the throne.

2 Thou standest in the holiest place,
    As now for guilty sinners slain;
    Thy blood of sprinkling speaks, and prays,
    All-prevalent for helpless man;
    Thy blood is still our ransom found,
    And spreads salvation all around.

3 The smoke of Thy atonement here
    Darken'd the sun and rent the veil,
    Made the new way to heaven appear,
    And show'd the great Invisible;
    Well pleased in Thee our God look'd down,
    And call'd His rebels to a crown.

4 He still respects Thy sacrifice,
    Its savour sweet doth always please;
    The offering smokes through earth and skies,
    Diffusing life, and joy, and peace;
    To these Thy lower courts it comes,
    And fills them with divine perfumes.

5 We need not now go up to heaven,
   To bring the long-sought Saviour down;
Thou art to all already given,
   Thou dost even now Thy banquet crown:
To every faithful soul appear,
And show Thy real presence here!

### 117

1 THOU Lamb that sufferedst on the tree,
And in this dreadful mystery
Still offer'st up Thyself to God,
We cast us on Thy sacrifice,
Wrapp'd in the sacred smoke arise,
And cover'd with th' atoning blood.

Thy death presented in our stead
Enters us now among the dead,
Parts of Thy mystic body here,
By Thy Divine oblation raised,
And on our *Aaron's* ephod placed
We now with Thee in heaven appear.

2 Thy death exalts Thy ransom'd ones,
And sets 'midst the precious stones,
Closest Thy dear, Thy loving breast;
*Israel* as on Thy shoulders stands,
Our names are graven on the hands,
The heart of our Eternal Priest.

For us He ever intercedes,
His heaven-deserving passion pleads,
Presenting us before the throne;
We want no sacrifice beside,
By that great Offering sanctified,
One with our Head, for ever one.

### 118

1   LIVE, our Eternal Priest,
    By men and angels blest!
Jesus Christ the Crucified,
  He who did for us atone,
From the cross where once He died,
  Now He up to heaven is gone.

2   He ever lives, and prays
    For all the faithful race;
In the holiest place above
  Sinners' Advocate He stands,
Pleads for us His dying love,
  Shows for us His bleeding hands.

3   His body torn and rent
    He doth to God present,
In that dear memorial shows
  *Israel's* chosen tribes imprest;
All our names the Father knows,
  Reads them on our *Aaron's* breast.

4   He reads, while we beneath
    Present our Saviour's death,
Do as Jesus bids us do,
  Signify His flesh and blood,
Him in a memorial show,
  Offer up the Lamb to God.

5   From this thrice hallow'd shade
    Which Jesus' cross hath made,
Image of His sacrifice,
  Never, never will we move,
Till with all His saints we rise,
  Rise, and take our place above.

### 119

1 FATHER, God, who seest in me
   Only sin and misery,
See Thine own Anointed One,
   Look on Thy beloved Son.

2 Turn from me Thy glorious eyes
   To that bloody Sacrifice,
To the full atonement made,
   To the utmost ransom paid;

3 To the blood that speaks above,
  Calls for Thy forgiving love;
  To the tokens of His death
  Here exhibited beneath.

4 Hear His blood's prevailing cry,
  Let Thy bowels then reply,
  Then through Him the sinner see
  Then in Jesus look on me.

### 120

1 FATHER, see the Victim slain,
    Jesus Christ, the just, the good,
  Offer'd up for guilty man,
    Pouring out His precious blood;
  Him, and then the sinner see,
  Look through Jesu's wounds on me.

2 Me, the sinner most distrest,
    Most afflicted and forlorn,
  Stranger to a moment's rest,
    Rueing that I e'er was born,
  Pierced with sin's envenom'd dart,
  Dying of a broken heart.

3 Dying, whom Thy hands have made
    All Thy blessings to receive;
  Dying, whom Thy love hath stay'd,
    Whom Thy pity would have live;
  Dying at my Saviour's side,
  Dying, for whom Christ hath died.

4 Can it, Father, can it be?
    What doth Jesu's blood reply?
  If it doth not plead for me,
    Let my soul for ever die;
  But if mine through Him Thou art,
  Speak the pardon to my heart.

### 121

1 FATHER, behold Thy favourite Son,
    The glorious Partner of Thy throne,
    For ever placed at Thy right hand;
  O look on Thy Messiah's face,
  And seal the covenant of Thy grace
    To us who in Thy Jesus stand.

To us Thou hast redemption sent;
And we again to Thee present
  The blood that speaks our sins forgiven,
That sprinkles all the nations round;
And now Thou hear'st the solemn sound
  Loud echoing through the courts of heaven.

2 The cross on *Calvary* He bore,
  He suffer'd once to die no more,
    But left a sacred pledge behind:
  See here!—It on Thy altar lies,
  Memorial of the sacrifice
    He offer'd once for all mankind.

Father, the grand oblation see,
The death as present now with Thee
  As when He gasp'd on earth—*Forgive*:
Answer, and show the curse removed,
Accept us in the Well-beloved,
  And bid Thy world of rebels live.

### 122

1 FATHER, let the sinner go,
    The Lamb did once atone,
  Lo! we to Thy justice show
    The passion of Thy Son:
  Thus to Thee we set it forth;
    He the dying precept gave,
  He that hath sufficient worth
    A thousand worlds to save.

2 Can Thy justice aught reply
    To our prevailing plea?
  Jesus died Thy grace to buy
    For all mankind and me;
  Still before Thy righteous throne
    Stands the Lamb as newly slain:
  Canst Thou turn away Thy Son,
    Or let Him bleed in vain?

3 Still the wounds are open wide,
  The blood doth freely flow
  As when first His sacred side
  Received the deadly blow:
  Still, O God, the blood is warm,
  Cover'd with the blood we are;
  Find a part it doth not arm,
  And strike the sinner there!

### 123

1 O Thou whose offering on the tree
  The legal offerings all foreshow'd,
  Borrow'd their whole effects from Thee,
  And drew their virtue from Thy blood:
  The blood of goats and bullocks slain
  Could never for one sin atone:
  To purge the guilty offerer's stain
  Thine was the work, and *Thine* alone

2 Vain in themselves their duties were,
  Their services could never please,
  Till join'd with Thine, and made to share
  The merits of Thy righteousness;
  Forward they cast a faithful look
  On Thy approaching sacrifice,
  And thence their pleasing savour took,
  And rose accepted in the skies.

3 Those feeble types and shadows old
  Are all in Thee, the Truth, fulfill'd,
  And through this sacrament we hold
  The substance in our hearts reveal'd;
  By faith we see Thy sufferings past
  In this mysterious rite brought back,
  And on Thy grand oblation cast
  Its saving benefit partake.

4 Memorial of Thy sacrifice,
  This Eucharistic mystery
  The full atoning grace supplies,
  And sanctifies our gifts in Thee:
  Our persons and performance please,
  While God in Thee looks down from heaven,
  Our acceptable service sees,
  And whispers all our sins forgiven.

### 124

1 All hail, Redeemer of mankind!
  Thy life on *Calvary* resign'd
  Did fully once for all atone;
  Thy blood hath paid our utmost price,
  Thine all-sufficient sacrifice
  Remains eternally alone:

  Angels and men might strive in vain,
  They could not add the smallest grain
  T' augment Thy death's atoning power,
  The sacrifice is all complete,
  The death Thou never canst repeat,
  Once offer'd up to die no more.

2 Yet may we celebrate below,
  And daily thus Thine offering show
  Exposed before Thy Father's eyes;
  In this tremendous mystery
  Present Thee bleeding on a tree,
  Our everlasting Sacrifice;

  Father, behold Thy dying Son!
  Even now He lays our ransom down,
  Even now declares our sins forgiven;
  His flesh is rent, the living way
  Is open'd to eternal day,
  And lo, through Him we pass to heaven!

## 125

1 O God of our forefathers, hear,
   And make Thy faithful mercies known;
   To Thee through Jesus we draw near,
   Thy suffering, well-beloved Son,
   In whom Thy smiling face we see,
   In whom Thou art well pleased with *me*.

2 With solemn faith we offer up,
   And spread before Thy glorious eyes
   That only ground of all our hope,
   That precious bleeding Sacrifice,
   Which brings Thy grace on sinners down,
   And perfects all our souls in one.

3 Acceptance through His only name,
   Forgiveness in His blood we have;
   But more abundant life we claim
   Through Him who died our souls to save,
   To sanctify us by His blood,
   And fill with all the life of God.

4 Father, behold Thy dying Son,
   And hear His blood that speaks above;
   On us let all Thy grace be shown,
   Peace, righteousness, and joy, and love;
   Thy kingdom come to every heart,
   And all Thou hast, and all Thou art.

## 126

1 Father, to Him we turn our face
   Who did for all atone,
   And worship toward Thy holy place,
   And seek Thee in Thy Son.

2 Him the true ark and mercy-seat
   By faith we call to mind,
   Faith in the blood atoning yet
   For us and all mankind.

3 To Thee His passion we present,
   Who for our ransom dies;
   We reach by this great instrument
   Th' eternal sacrifice.

4 The Lamb as crucified afresh
   Is here held out to men,
   The tokens of His blood and flesh
   Are on this table seen.

5 The Lamb His Father now surveys,
   As on this altar slain,
   Still bleeding and imploring grace
   For every soul of man.

6 Father, for us, even us, He bleeds;
   The sacrifice receive;
   Forgive, for Jesus intercedes,
   He gasps in death—*Forgive!*

## 127

1 Did Thine ancient *Israel* go
   With solemn praise and prayer
   To Thy hallow'd courts below,
   To meet and serve Thee there?
   To Thy body, Lord, we flee;
   This the consecrated shrine,
   Temple of the Deity,
   The real house Divine.

2 Did they toward the altar turn
   Their hopes, their heart, and face,
   Whence the victim's blood was borne
   Into the holiest place?
   Toward the cross we still look up,
   Toward the Lamb for sinners given,
   Through Thine only death we hope
   To find our way to heaven.

## V. *Concerning the Sacrifice of our Persons*

### 128

1 ALL hail, Thou mighty to atone!
   To expiate sin is Thine alone,
     Thou hast alone the wine-press trod,
     Thou only hast for sinners died,
   By one oblation satisfied
     Th' inexorably righteous God.

   Should the whole church in flames arise,
   Offer'd as one burnt sacrifice,
     The sinner's smallest debt to pay,
     They could not, Lord, Thine honour share,
   With Thee the Father's justice bear,
     Or bear one single sin away.

2 Thyself our utmost price hast paid;
   Thou hast for all atonement made,
     For all the sins of all mankind:
   God doth in Thee redemption give:
   But how shall we the grace receive?
     But how shall we the blessing find?

   We only can *accept* the grace,
   And humbly our Redeemer praise,
     Who bought the glorious liberty;
   The life Thou didst for all procure
   We make, by our believing, sure
     To us who live and die to Thee.

3 While faith th' atoning blood applies,
   Ourselves a living sacrifice
     We freely offer up to God;
   And none but those His glory share,
   Who crucified with Jesus are,
     And follow where their Saviour trod.

   Saviour, to Thee our lives we give,
   Our meanest sacrifice receive,
     And to Thine own oblation join,
   Our suffering and triumphant Head,
   Through all Thy states Thy members lead,
     And seat us on the throne Divine.

### 129

1 SEE where our great High-Priest
    Before the Lord appears,
   And on His loving breast
    The tribes of *Israel* bears,
   Never without His people seen,
   The Head of all believing men!

2 With Him, the Corner-stone,
    The living stones conjoin;
   Christ and His church are one,
    One body and one vine;
   For us He uses all His powers,
   And all He has, or is, is ours.

3 The motions of our Head
    The members all pursue,
   By His good Spirit led
    To act, and suffer too
   Whate'er He did on earth sustain,
   Till glorious all like Him we reign.

### 130

1 JESU, we follow Thee,
    In all Thy footsteps tread,
   And pant for full conformity
    To our exalted Head;

   We would, we would partake
    Thy every state below,
   And suffer all things for Thy sake,
    And to Thy glory do.

2  We in Thy birth are born,
    Sustain Thy grief and loss,
Share in Thy want, and shame, and scorn,
    And die upon Thy cross.

Baptized into Thy death
    We sink into Thy grave,
Till Thou the quickening Spirit breathe,
    And to the utmost save.

3  Thou said'st, 'Where'er I am
    There shall My servant be';
Master, the welcome word we claim
    And die to live with Thee.

To us who share Thy pain,
    Thy joy shall soon be given,
And we shall in Thy glory reign,
    For Thou art now in heaven.

### 131

1  Would the Saviour of mankind
    Without His people die?
No, to Him we all are join'd
    As more than standers by.
Freely as the Victim came
    To the altar of His cross,
We attend the slaughter'd Lamb,
    And suffer for His cause.

2  Him even now by faith we see;
    Before our eyes He stands!
On the suffering Deity
    We lay our trembling hands,
Lay our sins upon His head,
    Wait on the dread Sacrifice,
Feel the lovely Victim bleed,
    And die while Jesus dies!

3  Sinners, see, He dies for all,
    And feel His mortal wound,
Prostrate on your faces fall,
    And kiss the hallow'd ground;
Hallow'd by the streaming blood,
    Blood whose virtue all may know,
Sharers with the dying God,
    And crucified below.

4  Sprinkled with the blood we lie,
    And bless its cleansing power;
Crying in the Spirit's cry,
    Our Saviour we adore!
Jesu, Lord, whose cross we bear,
    Let Thy death our sins destroy,
Make us who Thy sorrows share
    Partakers of Thy joy.

### 132

1  Let heaven and earth proclaim
    Our common Saviour's name,
Offer'd by Himself to God
    In His temple here beneath,
Him who shed for all His blood,
    Him for all who tasted death.

2  By faith even now we see
    The suffering Deity,
At the head of whole mankind;
    Lo! He comes for all to die,
Not a soul is left behind
    Whom He did not love and buy.

3  First-born of many sons,
    His blood for us atones,
Saves us from the mortal pain
    If we by His cross abide,
If we in the house remain
    Where our Elder Brother died.

## 133

1 O Thou who hast our sorrows took,
    Who all our sins didst singly bear,
  To Thy dear bloody cross we look,
    We cast us on Thy offering there,
  For pardon on Thy death rely,
  For grace and strength to reach the sky.

2 We look on Thee our dying Lamb,
    On Thee whom we have pierced, and mourn,
  Partakers of Thy grief and shame;
  Thy anguish hath our bosoms torn,
  For us Thou didst Thy life resign;
  Was ever love or grief like Thine?

3 O what a killing thought is this,
    A sword to pierce the faithful heart!
  Our sins have slain the Prince of Peace;
  Our sins which caused His mortal smart
  With Him we vow to crucify;
  Our sins which murder'd God shall die!

4 We nail th' old *Adam* to the tree,
    Till not one breath of life remain;
  But what we can present to Thee,
    (To Thee whose blood hath purged our stain,)
  Conjoin'd to Thy great sacrifice,
  Well-pleasing in Thy Father's eyes.

5 The saved and Saviour now agree,
    In closest fellowship combin'd;
  We grieve, and die, and live with Thee,
    To Thy great Father's will resign'd;
  And God doth all Thy members own
  One with Thyself, for ever one.

## 134

1 Jesu, we know that Thou hast died,
    And share the death we show:
  If the first-fruits be sanctified,
    The lump is holy too.

2 The sheaf was waved before the Lord,
    When Jesus bow'd His head,
  And we who thus His death record
    One with Himself are made.

3 The sheaf and harvest is but one
    Accepted sacrifice,
  And we who have Thy sufferings known
    Shall in Thy life arise.

4 Still all-involved in God we are,
    And offer'd with the Lamb,
  Till all in heaven with Christ appear
    Eternally the same.

## 135

1 Amazing love to mortals show'd!
    The sinless body of our God
      Was fasten'd to the tree.
  And shall our sinful members live?
  No, Lord, they shall not Thee survive,
      They all shall die with Thee.

2 The feet which did to evil run,
  The hands which violent acts have done,
    The greedy heart and eyes,
  Base weapons of iniquity,
  We offer up to death with Thee,
    A whole burnt sacrifice.

3 Our sins are on Thine altar laid,
  We do not for their being plead,
    Or circumscribe Thy power;
  Bound on Thy cross Thou seest them lie:
  Let all this cursed *Adam* die,
    Die, and revive no more.

4 Root out the seeds of pride and lust,
  That each may of Thy passion boast
    Which doth the freedom give:
  The world to me is crucified,
  And I who on His cross have died
    To God for ever live.

## 136

1 O Thou holy Lamb Divine,
How canst Thou and sinners join?
God of spotless purity,
How shall man concur with Thee;

2 Offer up one sacrifice
Acceptable to the skies?
What shall wretched sinners bring
Pleasing to the glorious King?

3 Only sin we call our own;
But Thou art the darling Son,
Thine it is our God t' appease,
Him Thou dost for ever please.

4 We on Thee alone depend,
With Thy sacrifice ascend,
Render what Thy grace hath given,
Lift our souls with Thee to heaven.

## 137

1 Ye royal priests of Jesus, rise,
And join the daily sacrifice;
Join all believers, in His name
To offer up the spotless Lamb.

2 Your meat and your drink offerings throw
On Him who suffer'd once below,
But ever lives with God above
To plead for us His dying love.

3 Whate'er we cast on Him alone
Is with His great oblation one;
His sacrifice doth ours sustain,
And favour and acceptance gain.

4 On Him, who all our burdens bears,
We cast our praises and our prayers,
Ourselves we offer up to God,
Implunged in His atoning blood.

5 Mean are our noblest offerings,
Poor feeble unsubstantial things;
But when to Him our souls we lift,
The altar sanctifies the gift.

6 Our persons and our deeds aspire
When cast into that hallow'd fire,
Our most imperfect efforts please
When join'd to Christ our righteousness.

7 Mix'd with the sacred smoke we rise,
The smoke of His burnt sacrifice;
By the Eternal Spirit driven
From earth, in Christ we mount to heaven.

## 138

1 All praise to the Lord, All praise is His due,
Today is His word Of promise found true;
We, we are the nations, Presented to God,
Well-pleasing oblations Through Jesus's blood.

2 Poor heathens from far To Jesus we came,
And offer'd we are To God through His name,
To God through the Spirit Ourselves do we give,
And saved by the merit Of Jesus we live.

## 139

1 God of all-redeeming grace,
By Thy pardoning love compell'd,
Up to Thee our souls we raise,
Up to Thee our bodies yield.

2 Thou our sacrifice receive,
Acceptable through Thy Son,
While to Thee alone we live,
While we die to Thee alone.

3 Just it is, and good, and right
  That we should be wholly Thine,
  In Thy only will delight,
  In Thy blessed service join.

4 O that every thought and word
  Might proclaim how good Thou art,
  HOLINESS UNTO THE LORD
  Still be written on our heart.

### 140

1 HE dies, as now for us He dies!
  That all-sufficient sacrifice
  Subsists, eternal as the Lamb,
  In every time and place the same;
  To all alike it co-extends,
  Its saving virtue never ends.

2 He lives for us to intercede,
  For us He doth this moment plead,
  And all who could not see Him die
  May now with faith's interior eye
  Behold Him stand as slaughter'd there,
  And feel the answer to His prayer.

3 While now for us the Saviour prays,
  Father, we humbly sue for grace;
  Poor helpless dying victims we,
  Laden with sin and misery,
  His infinite atonement plead,
  Ourselves presenting with our Head.

4 Assured we shall acceptance find,
  To Jesus in oblation join'd,
  Where'er the scatter'd members look
  To Him who all our sorrows took,
  The saving efflux we receive,
  And, quicken'd by His passion, live.

### 141

1 HAPPY the souls that follow'd Thee,
    Lamenting, to th' accursed wood;
  Happy, who underneath the tree
    Unmovable in sorrow stood.

2 When Nature felt the deadly blow
    By which Thy soul to God was driven,
  Which shook with sympathetic woe
    Temple, and graves, and earth, and heaven.

3 O what a time for offering up
    Their souls upon Thy sacrifice!
  Who would not with Thy burden stoop
    And bow the head when Jesus dies?

4 Not all the days before or since
    An hour so solemn could afford,
  For suffering with our bleeding Prince,
    For dying with our slaughter'd Lord.

5 Yet in this ordinance Divine
    We still the sacred load may bear;
  And now we in Thy offering join,
    Thy sacramental passion share.

6 We cast our sins into that fire
    Which did Thy sacrifice consume,
  And every base and vain desire
    To daily crucifixion doom.

7 Thou art with all Thy members here,
    In this tremendous mystery
  We jointly before God appear,
    To offer up ourselves with Thee.

8 True followers of our bleeding Lamb,
    Now on Thy daily cross we die,
  And, mingled in a common flame,
    Ascend triumphant to the sky.

### 142

1   COME we that record
      The death of our Lord,
      The death let us bear,
    By faithful remembrance His sacrifice share.

2   Shall we let our God groan
      And suffer alone?
      Or to *Calvary* fly,
    And nobly resolve with our Master to die?

3   His servants shall be
    With Him on the tree,
    Where Jesus was slain
    His crucified servants shall always
        remain.

4   By the cross we abide
    Where Jesus hath died,
    To all we are dead;
    The members can never outlive their
        own Head.

5   Poor penitents, we
    Expect not to see
    His glory above,
    Till first we have drank of the cup of
        His love;

6   Till first we partake
    The cross for His sake,
    And thankfully own
    The cup of His love and His sorrow
        are one.

7   Conform'd to His death
    If we suffer beneath,
    With Him we shall know
    The power of His first resurrection
        below.

8   If His death we receive,
    His life we shall live;
    If His cross we sustain,
    His joy and His crown we in heaven
        shall gain.

### 143

1   FATHER, behold I come to do
    Thy will, I come to suffer too
        Thy acceptable will;
    Do with me, Lord, as seems Thee good,
    Dispose of this weak flesh and blood,
        And all Thy mind fulfil.

2   Thy creature, in Thy hands I am.
    Frail dust and ashes is my name;
        The earthen vessel use,
    Mould as Thou wilt the passive clay,
    But let me all Thy will obey,
        And all Thy pleasure choose.

3   Welcome whate'er my God ordain!
    Afflict with poverty or pain
        This feeble flesh of mine,
    (But grant me strength to bear my
        load,)
    I will not murmur at Thy rod,
        Or for relief repine.

4   My spirit wound (but oh! be near)
    With what far more than death I fear,
        The darts of keenest shame;
    Fulfill'd with more than killing smart,
    And wounded in the tenderest part,
        I still adore Thy name.

5   Beneath Thy bruising hand I fall;
    Whate'er Thou send'st, I take it all,
        Reproach, or pain, or loss;
    I will not for deliverance pray,
    But humbly unto death obey,
        The death of Jesu's cross.

### 144

1   LET both *Jews* and *Gentiles* join,
    Friends and enemies combine,
    Vent their utmost rage on me,
    Still I look through all to Thee;

2   Humbly own it is the Lord!
    Let Him wake on me His sword:
    Lo, I bow me to Thy will;
    Thou Thy whole design fulfil.

3   Stricken by Thine anger's rod,
    Dumb I fall before my God;
    Or my dear Chastiser bless,
    Sing the paschal psalm of praise.

4   While the bitter herbs I eat,
    Him I for my foes intreat;
    Let me die, but oh! forgive,
    Let my pardon'd murderers live.

## 145

1 FATHER, into Thy hands alone
    I have my all restored,
My all, Thy property I own,
    The steward of the Lord.

2 Hereafter none can take away
    My life, or goods, or fame;
Ready at Thy demand to lay
    Them down I always am.

3 Confiding in Thy only love
    Through Him who died for me,
I wait Thy faithfulness to prove,
    And give back all to Thee.

4 Take when Thou wilt into Thy hands,
    And as Thou wilt require;
Resume by the *Sabean* bands,
    Or the devouring fire.

5 Determined all Thy will t' obey,
    Thy blessings I restore;
Give, Lord, or take Thy gifts away,
    I praise Thee evermore.

## 146

1 FATHER, if Thou willing be,
    Then my griefs awhile suspend,
Then remove the cup from me,
    Or Thy strengthening angel send;
Wouldst Thou have me suffer on?
Father, let Thy will be done.

2 Let my flesh be troubled still,
    Fill'd with pain or sore disease,
Let my wounded spirit feel
    Strong redoubled agonies;
Meekly I my will resign,
Thine be done, and only Thine.

3 Patient as my great High-Priest
    In His bitterness of pain,
Most abandon'd and distrest,
    Father, I the cross sustain;
All into Thy hands I give,
Let me die, or let me live.

4 Following where my Lord hath led,
    Thee I on the cross adore,
Humbly bow like Him my head,
    All Thy benefits restore,
Till my spirit I resign,
Breathed into the hands Divine.

## 147

1 JESU, to Thee in faith we look;
O that our services might rise
Perfumed and mingled with the smoke
Of Thy sweet-smelling sacrifice.

2 Thy sacrifice with heavenly powers
    Replete, all holy, all Divine;
Human and weak, and sinful ours:
    How can the two oblations join?

3 Thy offering doth to ours impart
    Its righteousness and saving grace,
While charged with all our sins Thou art,
    To death devoted in our place.

4 Our mean imperfect sacrifice
    On Thine is as a burden thrown;
Both in a common flame arise,
    And both in God's account are one.

## 148

1     FATHER of mercies, hear
        Through Thine atoning Son,
Who doth for us in heaven appear,
        And prays before Thy throne;

2     But that great sacrifice
        Which He for us doth plead,
Into our Saviour's death baptize,
        And make us like our Head.

3  Into the fellowship
    Of Jesu's sufferings take
  Us who desire with Him to sleep,
    That we with Him may wake:

4  Plant us into His death,
    That we His life may prove;
  Partakers of His cross beneath,
    And of His crown above.

### 149

1  Jesu, my strength and hope,
    My righteousness and power,
  My soul is lifted up
    Thy mercy to implore;
  My hands I still stretch out to Thee,
  My hands I fasten to the tree.

2  No more may they offend,
    But do Thy work below;
  Thou know'st I fain would spend
    My life Thy praise to show;
  Nor will Thy gracious love despise
  A sinner's meanest sacrifice.

3  Thy wounds have wounded me,
    Thy bloody cross subdued,
  I feel my misery
    And ever gasp for God;
  My prayers, and griefs, and groans I join,
  And mingle all my pangs with Thine.

4  Jesu, a soul receive,
    Upon Thine altar cast
  To die with Thee, and live
    When all my deaths are past;
  To live where grief can never rise,
  To reign with Thee above the skies.

### 150

1  Father, on us the Spirit bestow,
    Through which Thine everlasting Son
  Offer'd Himself for man below,
  That *we*, even *we*, before Thy throne
  Our souls and bodies may present,
  And pay Thee all Thy grace hath lent.

2  O let Thy Spirit sanctify
    Whate'er to Thee we now restore,
  And make us with Thy will comply;
    With all our mind, and soul, and power
  Obey Thee, as Thy saints above,
  In perfect innocence and love.

### 151

1  Come, Thou Spirit of contrition,
    Fill our souls with tender fears;
  Conscious of our lost condition,
    Melt us into gracious tears;
  Just and holy detestation
    Of our bosom sins impart,
  Sins that caused our Saviour's passion,
  Sins that stabb'd Him to the heart.

2  Fill our flesh with killing anguish,
    All our members crucify,
  Let th' offending nature languish
    Till on Jesu's cross it die;
  All our sins to death deliver,
    Let not one, not one survive;
  Then we live to God for ever,
    Then in heaven on earth we live.

### 152

1  Arm of the Lord, whose vengeance laid
  My sins upon my Saviour's head,
  In mercy now the sinner see,
  And oh! destroy them all in me.

2  Accept, all-gracious as Thou art,
  Accept a mournful sinner's heart,
  Who pour my tears before my God
  As a poor victim doth his blood.

3 My feeble soul would fain aspire;
    Its zeal, and thoughts, and whole desire
  Lift up to Thee, (through Jesu's name,)
    As a burnt sacrifice its flame.

4 And since it cannot please alone,
    Accept it, Father, through Thy Son;
  Supported by His sacrifice,
    O may it from His altar rise.

5 Clothed in His righteousness, receive,
    And bid me one with Jesus live;
  Join all He sanctifies in one,
    One cross, one glory, and one crown.

## 153

1 FATHER, Thy feeble children meet,
    And make Thy faithful mercies known;
  Give us through faith the flesh to eat,
    And drink the blood of Christ Thy Son;
  Honour Thine own mysterious ways,
    They sacramental presence show,
  And all the fulness of Thy grace,
    With Jesus, on our souls bestow.

2 Father, our sacrifice receive;
    Our souls and bodies we present,
  Our goods, and vows, and praises give,
    Whate'er Thy bounteous love hath lent.
  Thou canst not now our gift despise,
    Cast on that all-atoning Lamb,
  Mix'd with that bleeding Sacrifice,
    And offer'd up through Jesu's name.

## 154

1 JESU, did they crucify
    Thee, by highest heaven adored?
  Let us also go and die
    With our dearest dying Lord!

2 Lord, Thou seest our willing heart,
    Know'st its uppermost desire
  With our nature's life to part,
    Meekly on Thy cross t' expire.

3 Fain we would be all like Thee,
    Suffer with our Lord beneath:
  Grant us full conformity,
    Plunge us deep into Thy death.

4 Now inflict the mortal pain,
    Now exert Thy passion's power,
  Let the Man of Sin be slain;
    Die the flesh, to live no more.

## 155

1 FATHER, Son, and Holy Ghost,
    One in Three, and Three in One,
  As by the celestial host
    Let Thy will on earth be done;
  Praise by all to Thee be given,
  Glorious Lord of earth and heaven!

2 Vilest of the fallen race,
    Lo, I answer to Thy call;
  Meanest vessel of Thy grace,
    (Grace divinely free for all,)
  Lo, I come to do Thy will,
  All Thy counsel to fulfil.

3 If so poor a worm as I
    May to Thy great glory live,
  All my actions sanctify,
    All my words and thoughts receive;
  Claim me for Thy service, claim
  All I have and all I am.

4 Take my soul and body's powers,
    Take my memory, mind, and will,
  All my goods, and all my hours,
    All I know, and all I feel,
  All I think, and speak, and do;
  Take my heart—but make it new.

5 Now, O God, Thine own I am,
   Now I give Thee back Thy own,
Freedom, friends, and health, and fame
   Consecrate to Thee alone;
Thine I live, thrice happy I,
   Happier still, for Thine I die.

6 Father, Son, and Holy Ghost,
   One in Three, and Three in One,
As by the celestial host
   Let Thy will on earth be done;
Praise by all to Thee be given,
   Glorious Lord of earth and heaven.

## 156

1   ALL glory and praise
     To the Ancient of Days,
Who was born and was slain to redeem a lost race.

2   Salvation to God,
     Who carried our load,
And purchased our lives with the price of His blood.

3   And shall He not have
     The lives which He gave
Such an infinite ransom for ever to save?

4   Yes, Lord, we are Thine,
     And gladly resign
Our souls to be fill'd with the fulness Divine.

5   We yield Thee Thine own,
     We serve Thee alone,
Thy will upon earth as in heaven be done.

6   How, when it shall be
     We cannot foresee;
But oh! let us live, let us die unto Thee.

## 157

1 LET Him to whom we now belong
   His sovereign right assert,
And take up every thankful song,
   And every loving heart.

2 He justly claims us for His own
   Who bought us with a price:
The Christian lives to *Christ* alone,
   To *Christ* alone he dies.

3 Jesu, Thine own at last receive;
   Fulfil our heart's desire,
And let us to Thy glory live,
   And in Thy cause expire.

4 Our souls and bodies we resign,
   With joy we render Thee
Our all, no longer ours, but Thine
   Through all eternity!

---

## VI. *After the Sacrament*

### 158

1   ALL praise to God above,
     In whom we have believed,
The tokens of whose dying love
     We have even now received.
Have with His flesh been fed,
     And drank His precious blood:
His precious blood is drink indeed,
     His flesh immortal food.

2   O what a taste is this,
     Which now in *Christ* we know,
An earnest of our glorious bliss,
     Our heaven begun below!
When He the table spreads,
     How royal is the cheer!
With rapture we lift up our heads,
     And own that God is here.

3   He bids us taste His grace,
    The joys of angels prove,
  The stammerers' tongues are loosed to praise
      Our dear Redeemer's love.
      Salvation to our God
      That sits upon the throne;
  Salvation be alike bestow'd
      On His triumphant Son!

4   The Lamb for sinners slain,
    Who died to die no more,
  Let all the ransom'd sons of men
    With all His hosts adore:
  Let earth and heaven be join'd
    His glories to display,
  And hymn the Saviour of mankind
    In one eternal day.

## 159

1   ALL glory and praise To Jesus our Lord!
  His ransoming grace We gladly record,
  His bloody oblation And death on the tree
  Hath purchased salvation And heaven for me.

2   The Saviour hath died For *me* and for *you*,
  The blood is applied, The record is true;
  The Spirit bears witness And speaks in the blood,
  And gives us the fitness For living with God.

## 160[1]

1   WELCOME, delicious sacred cheer;
  Welcome, my God, my Saviour dear;
    O, with me, in me live and dwell!
  Thine earthly joy surpasses quite,
  The depths of Thy supreme delight
    Not angel tongues can taste or tell.

2   What streams of sweetness from the bowl
  Surprise and deluge all my soul,
    Sweetness that is, and makes Divine!
  Surely from God's right hand they flow,
  From thence derived to earth below
    To cheer us with immortal wine.

3   Soon as I taste the heavenly bread,
  What manna o'er my soul is shed,
    Manna that angels never knew!
  Victorious sweetness fills my heart,
  Such as my God delights to' impart,
    Mighty to save, and sin subdue.

4   I had forgot my heavenly birth,
  My soul degenerate clave to earth,
    In sense and sin's base pleasures drown'd:
  When God assumed humanity,
  And spilt His sacred blood for me,
    To find me groveling on the ground.

5   Soon as His love has raised me up,
  He mingles blessings in a cup,
    And sweetly meets my ravish'd taste;
  Joyous, I now throw off my load,
  I cast my sins and care on God,
    And Wine becomes a Wing at last.

6   Upborne on this, I mount, I fly;
  Regaining swift my native sky,—
    I wipe my streaming eyes and see
  Him, whom I seek, for whom I sue,
  My God, my Saviour there I view,
    Him, who has done so much for me!

7   O, let Thy wondrous mercy's praise
  Inspire and consecrate my lays,
    And take up all my lines and life;
  Thy praise my every breath employ:
  Be all my business, all my joy
    To strive in this, and love the strife!

[1] See note on Hymn 9. This hymn is part of Wesley's adaptation of George Herbert's poem, 'The Banquet'. The sentiments expressed are Herbert's; also published in *Poetical Works*, Vol. I, p. 113.

## 161[1]

1 LORD and God of heavenly powers,
Theirs—yet, O! benignly ours,
Glorious King, let earth proclaim,
Worms attempt to chant Thy name.

2 Thee to laud in songs Divine
Angels and archangels join;
We with them our voices raise,
Echoing Thy eternal praise:

3 'Holy, Holy, Holy Lord,
Live by heaven and earth adored!'
Full of Thee, they ever cry,
'Glory be to God most High!'

## 162

1 HOSANNAH in the highest
To our exalted Saviour,
Who left behind
For all mankind
These tokens of His favour:

His bleeding love and mercy,
His all-redeeming passion,
Who here displays
And gives the grace
Which brings us our salvation.

2 Louder than gather'd waters,
Or bursting peals of thunder,
We lift our voice
And speak our joys,
And shout our loving wonder.

Shout all our Elder Brethren,
While we record the story
Of Him that came,
And suffer'd shame
To carry us to glory.

3 Angels in fix'd amazement
Around our altars hover,
With eager gaze
Adore the grace
Or our eternal Lover;

Himself, and all His fulness,
Who gives to the believer;
And by this Bread
Whoe'er are fed
Shall live with God for ever.

## 163[2]

1 GLORY be to God on high,
God whose glory fills the sky:
Peace on earth to man forgiven,
Man the well-beloved of Heaven!

2 Sovereign Father, Heavenly King!
Thee we now presume to sing;
Glad Thine attributes confess,
Glorious all and numberless.

3 Hail! by all Thy works adored,
Hail! the everlasting Lord!
Thee with thankful hearts we prove
Lord of Power, and God of Love.

4 Christ our Lord and God we own,
Christ the Father's only Son!
Lamb of God for sinners slain,
Saviour of offending man!

5 Bow Thine ear, in mercy bow,
Hear, the World's Atonement Thou!
Jesu, in Thy name we pray,
Take, O, take our sins away.

6 Powerful Advocate with God,
Justify us by Thy blood!
Bow Thine ear, in mercy bow,
Hear, the World's Atonement Thou!

7 Hear; for Thou, O Christ, alone
With Thy glorious Sire art One!
One the Holy Ghost with Thee,
One supreme Eternal Three.

---

[1] Also published in *Poetical Works*, Vol. I, p. 114.
[2] ibid., p. 115.

## 164[1]

1 SONS of God, triumphant rise,
  Shout th' accomplish'd Sacrifice!
  Shout your sins in Christ forgiven,
  Sons of God, and heirs of heaven!

2 Ye that round our altars throng,
  Listening angels, join the song:
  Sing with us, ye heavenly powers,
  Pardon, grace, and glory ours!

3 Love's mysterious work is done!
  Greet we now th' accepted Son,
  Heal'd and quicken'd by His blood,
  Join'd to Christ, and one with God.

4 Christ, of all our hopes the seal;
  Peace Divine in Christ we feel,
  Pardon to our souls applied:
  Dead for all, for me He died!

5 Sin shall tyrannize no more,
  Purged its guilt, dissolved its power;
  Jesus makes our hearts His throne,
  There He lives, and reigns alone.

6 Grace our every thought controls,
  Heaven is open'd in our souls,
  Everlasting life is won,
  Glory is on earth begun.

7 Christ in us; in Him we see
  Fulness of the Deity.
  Beam of the Eternal Beam;
  Life Divine we taste in Him!

8 Him we only taste below;
  Mightier joys ordain'd to know,
  Him when fully ours we prove,
  Ours the heaven of perfect love!

## 165

1 How happy are Thy servants, Lord,
    Who thus remember Thee!
  What tongue can tell our sweet accord,
    Our perfect harmony?

2 Who Thy mysterious supper share,
    Here at Thy table fed,
  Many, and yet but one we are,
    One undivided bread.

3 One with the living Bread Divine
    Which now by faith we eat,
  Our hearts, and minds, and spirits join,
    And all in Jesus meet.

4 So dear the tie where souls agree
    In Jesu's dying love:
  Then only can it closer be,
    When all are join'd above.

## 166[2]

1 HAPPY the saints of former days,
    Who first continued in the word,
  A simple, lowly, loving race,
    True followers of their lamblike Lord.

2 In holy fellowship they lived,
    Nor would from the commandment move
  But every joyful day received
    The tokens of expiring Love.

3 Not then above their Master wise,
    They simply in His paths remain'd,
  And call'd to mind His sacrifice
    With steadfast faith and love unfeign'd.

4 From house to house they broke the bread
    Impregnated with life Divine,
  And drank the Spirit of their Head
    Transmitted in the sacred wine.

[1] Also published in *Poetical Works*, Vol. I, p. 170.

[2] Hymn 166 may be regarded as a poem appended to the hymn-book. It is interesting because of the use Anglo-Catholics made of its emphasis of the Daily Sacrifice in the controversies of 1870. There are several instances of Wesley's valuation of the Daily Sacrifice in these hymns, and John Wesley's Sermon No. 21 suggests the same conviction. The Wesleys did not give practical application to this aspiration.

5 With Jesu's constant presence blest,
 While duteous to His dying word,
They kept the Eucharistic feast,
 And supp'd in *Eden* with their Lord.

6 Throughout their spotless lives was seen
 The virtue of this heavenly food;
Superior to the sons of men,
 They soar'd aloft, and walk'd with God.

7 O what a flame of sacred love
 Was kindled by the altar's fire!
They lived on earth like those above,
 Glad rivals of the heavenly choir.

8 Strong in the strength herewith received,
 And mindful of the Crucified,
His confessors for Him they lived,
 For Him His faithful martyrs died.

9 Their souls from chains of flesh released,
 By torture from their bodies driven,
With violent faith the kingdom seized,
 And fought and forced their way to heaven.

10 Where is the pure primeval flame,
 Which in their faithful bosom glow'd?
Where are the followers of the Lamb,
 The dying witnesses for God?

11 Why is the faithful seed decreased,
 The life of God extinct and dead?
The daily sacrifice is ceased,
 And charity to heaven is fled.

12 Sad mutual causes of decay,
 Slackness and vice together move;
Grown cold, we cast the means away,
 And quench the latest spark of love.

13 The sacred signs Thou didst ordain,
 Our pleasant things, are all laid waste;
To men of lips and hearts profane,
 To dogs and swine and heathens cast.

14 Thine holy ordinance contemn'd
 Hath let the flood of evil in,
And those who by Thy name are named
 The sinners unbaptized out-sin.

15 But canst Thou not Thy work revive
 Once more in our degenerate years?
O, wouldst Thou with Thy rebels strive,
 And melt them into gracious tears"

16 O, wouldst Thou to Thy church return,
 For which the faithful remnant sighs,
For which the drooping nations mourn!
 Restore the daily sacrifice.

17 Return, and with Thy servants sit
 Lord of the sacramental feast;
And satiate us with heavenly meat,
 And make the *world* Thy happy guest.

18 Now let the spouse, reclined on Thee,
 Come up out of the wilderness,
From every spot and wrinkle free,
 And wash'd and perfected in grace.

19 Thou hear'st the pleading Spirit's groan,
 Thou know'st the groaning Spirit's will:
Come in Thy gracious kingdom down,
 And all Thy ransom'd servants seal.

20 Come quickly, Lord, the Spirit cries,
 The number of Thy saints complete;
Come quickly, Lord, the bride replies,
 And make us all for glory meet;

21 Erect Thy tabernacle here,
 The *New Jerusalem* send down,
Thyself amidst Thy saints appear,
 And seat us on Thy dazzling throne.

22 Begin the great millennial day;
 Now, Saviour, with a shout descend,
Thy standard in the heavens display,
 And bring the joy which ne'er shall end.

# INDEX

Aaron, 108, 118, 125, 127, 128
Abbey and Overton, 4
Abel's sacrifice, 112
Absolution, form of, 91
*Anamnesis*, 20, 104
Andrewes, Lancelot, Bishop, 82
Apostolic Fathers, 104
  Successors, 96, 168
'Arise, my Soul, Arise,' 117, 173
Article XXXI of Church of England, 81
Asbury, Bishop, 162
Atom bomb, 115
Atonement, 27, 28, 111
Augustine Saint, 157

Baptism:
  Administration of, 89
  *Re*-baptism of Dissenters, 89
  Roman doctrine, 89, 90
Barrett, T. H., 7, 90
Bett, Dr. Henry, 19, 53, 65
Bishops, Prayer for, 85
Body of Christ, 132
Bolzius, 89
Botticelli, 23
Brains Trust, 115
Brevint, Dr. Daniel:
  Biography, 14
  Emphasis on Sacrifice, 32, 33
  *Missale Romanum*, 14
  Sacrament and Sacrifice, 14
  Wesley's Extract of Brevint's book, 176
Buckle, *History of Civilization*, 114

Cain and Abel, 112
Calvin, 31, 59, 60
Children, religious Education of, 116ff.
Christian as to Epiphany, 9
Church and Ministry, 167
  Corporate, 132, 155
  visibility of, 167
Church of England:
  Eighteenth century, 150
  Neglect of Eucharist, 4, 150
Churches, Anglican and Free, 165
Churches, Free and Eucharist, 155
City Road Chapel, 8
Coke, Dr., 159, 162
*Common Prayer, Book of*, 150
Communion, crowded, 5, 150
Communion Office, 150, 151
  Methodist Alternative, 151
Community Singing, 152
Congregational View of Ministry, 168

Controversial hymns, 53
Cranmer, Archbishop, 81
Cross of Christ, its shocking character, 113
Crucifix, Protestant, 22

Daily Sacrifice, 144, 248
David, 4, 62
Dead, prayers for, 55
Dix, Dom Gregory, 51, 64, 81, 151, 154
Dodd, Dr. C. H., 63ff., 71
Dutton, W. E., 86, 171

Early Church, Corporate Communion, 154
  Methodist Preachers, 7
Eighteenth-century Anglican Erastianism, 161
Ephod, 28, 108, 118, 125, 127, 128
*Epiclesis*, 27, 50, 51
Episcopal succession, Wesley's rejection of, 84
Episcopus, New Testament, 159
Erastianism, 161
  Eighteenth-century, 162
Eschatology, realized, 68
Eucharist, centrality of, 7
  receptionist theory of, 41ff.
  and Evangelism, 157, 158
Evangelical Individualism, 140

Fletcher, Rev. John, 6, 17
Forsyth, Dr. P. T., 154, 122ff., 168
Frere, Bishop, 81, 82
Funeral hymns, 68

Georgia, 88
Gibbon, Edward, 66
Green, Richard, 8

Hall, Westley, 83, 100
Harnack, 165
Havergal, F. R., 141
Herbert, George, 12, 15, 90
Herring, Archbishop, 161
Hoads, Bishop, 53
Hocking, F., 86
Holden, H. W., 86, 162
Hymns:
  Authorship of, 11
  doctrinal character of, 11, 12
  Funeral, 68
Hymn-books for Church Festivals, Origin of, 18
Hymn-prayers, 26, 27, 40

# INDEX

Incantation, 51
Irenaeus, 157

Jackson, Thomas, 12, 92
Jones of Nayland, 30

Kempis, Thomas à, 86
King, Lord Chancellor, 84, 92
Kirk, Bishop of Oxford, 164ff.

Laski, Harold, 66
Leitzmann, Dr., 154
Liturgy, 184, 155
Lowth, Bishop, 162
Luther, Martin, 31, 56, 59, 136, 152, 156

Mackenzie, Bishop, 167–8
Means of Grace, Wesley's Sermon on, 9
Memorialism, 20–2
Methodism:
   Alternative Communion Office, 151
   contributing to, Eucharistic Worship 65
   Early Preachers, 7
   Individualism, 140
   London, Development of Sacramentalism, 150
   Myths, 87
   New Connexion, 148
   preachers and Charles Wesley, 96
   Primitive, 66
   Use of *Book of Common Prayer*, 150
Michal, 4
Middleton, Dr. Conyers, 38, 80
*Missale Romanum*, 14
Mithraism, 110, 126
*Mitre, The*, by Perronet, 98
Mixed Chalice, 9, 35ff., 55, 85
Moravian Quietism, 37, 54

Norton, Wesley's letter to, 96, 99

Oblations, 105, 118, 152, 154, 157
Octave, 8
Offertory, 134, 156
Osborn, Dr. George, 16
Outward Priesthood, 84, 144ff.
   Sacrifice, 84
Oxford Movement, 13, 82, 150

Perronet, Charles, 97
   Edward, 11, 97ff.
   Vincent, 97
Perugino, 25
Plan of Pacification, 149
Popery, 'Overgrown fear of', 149
*Popery Reconsidered*, 8
Prayer-hymns, 26, 27, 40
Prayers for the dead, 85

Preachers' Vocation, 145
Priesthood, Corporate, 152ff.
   Outward, 84, 144ff.
Priest-Victim, 103, 107, 121
Protestant character of Sacrificial hymns, 138
Crucifix, 22

Real Presence, 95, 169
Re-baptism of dissenters, 89
Revival, Sacramental, 3
Rigg, Dr. J. H., 87ff.
Roberts, Dr. Harold, 157
'Rock of Ages', 25, 38
Roman Mass, 82
Russell, Bertrand, 66
G. W. E., 21

Sacraments, defective, 155, 156
Sacrifice:
   Aesthetic reaction to, 109
   Brevint's emphasis on, 32, 33
   daily, 144, 248
   Eucharistic, Perronet's rejection of, 99
   of Cain and Abel, 112
   of Church, 132ff.
   outward, 84, 144ff.
   the unbloody, 106
Sacrifices, blood, 111
Saints, Communion of, 66, 75–6
San Clementi, Church of, 110
Scottish Episcopal Church, 161
Secker, Archbishop of, 4
Shaw, Bernard, 111ff.
Shock of the Cross, 113
Simeon, Charles, 8
Simon, Dr. J. S., 15, 90
Simpson, Sparrow, 87, 160
Sin, horror of, 115
Soper, Donald, 150
Stephenson, G. J., 91
Stillingfleet, 84
Stoddart, Jane, 4
Summary, Part One, 78
   of whole Book, 144

Taylor, Vincent, 82
*Taurabolium*, 110
Telford, John, 84, 85
Temple, Archbishop William, 164
Toplady, 38
Trade unionism, 66
Transubstantiation, 55, 93
Turenne, Vicomte de, 14
Tyerman, 10, 13, 87, 97, 100, 105

Ubiquity, Luther's doctrine of, 94–5, 102
Unbloody Sacrifice, 106
Urlin, R. D., 86

VALIDITY OF ORDERS, 169

WATERLAND, DEAN, 14, 82
Watson, Bishop, 161
Watts, Dr., 22
Wesley, Charles:
  and early Methodist preachers, 96
  anti-rational hymns, 42, 44, 54
  anti-Zwinglianism, 31
  arrangement of Sacramental hymns, 34
  controversial hymns, 42ff.
  Influence of Brevint on, 13, 30
  personal experience, 43, 47, 49
Wesley, John:
  a New Testament *Episcopos*, 159
  anti-Roman, 82
  anti-Zwinglianism, 31
  belief in outward priesthood and outward sacrifice, 84, 144
  Episcopal succession, rejection of, 96
  High Churchmanship, 3
  Joint responsibility for doctrine of eucharistic hymns, 11

Letter on Georgian failure, 89
  to Dr. Coke, 162
  to Dr. Middleton, 38, 85
  to Westley Hall, 84
Moravian Quietism, reaction from, 37, 54
Real Presence, 10, 59
relation to Perronet, Edward, 97ff.
Roman Catholics, 8
Sermons referred to:
  Korah, 96
  on daily bread (No. 21), 9
  on Means of Grace, 9
*Treatise on Christian Perfection*, 12
Wesley, Samuel junior, 83
  Susannah, 10
Whitefield, George, 8
Wilberforce, Samuel, Bishop, 160
  William, 66
World Wars, 114
Worship, mediate and immediate, 52

ZWINGLI, 31, 58, 59